D0196650

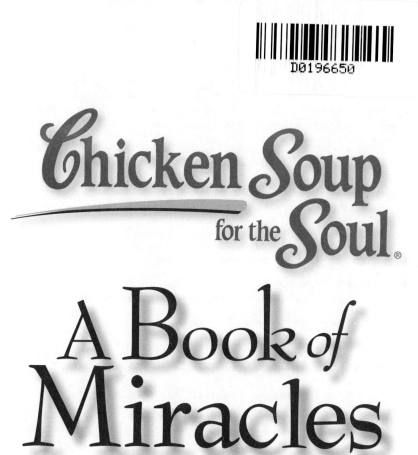

Chicken Soup for the Soul®

A Book of Miracles

CM

Chicken Soup for the Soul: A Book of Miracles
101 True Stories of Healing, Faith, Divine Intervention, and Answered Prayers
Jack Canfield, Mark Victor Hansen, LeAnn Thieman

Published by Chicken Soup for the Soul Publishing, LLC   www.chickensoup.com
Copyright © 2010 by Chicken Soup for the Soul Publishing, LLC. All Rights Reserved.
No part of this publication may be reproduced, stored in a retrieval system or transmit-
ted in any form or by any means, electronic, mechanical, photocopying, recording or
otherwise, without the written permission of the publisher.

CSS, Chicken Soup for the Soul, and its Logo and Marks are trademarks of
Chicken Soup for the Soul Publishing LLC.

Scripture taken from the HOLY BIBLE, NEW INTERNATIONAL VERSION®. NIV®.
Copyright© 1973, 1978, 1984 by International Bible Society. Used by permission of
Zondervan. All rights reserved.

The publisher gratefully acknowledges the many publishers and individuals who
granted Chicken Soup for the Soul permission to reprint the cited material.

Front cover photo courtesy of iStockphoto.com/duncan1890 (© Duncan Walker). Back cover
photo courtesy of PunchStock/Valueline. Interior photo courtesy of iStockphoto.com/suemack

Cover and Interior Design & Layout by Pneuma Books, LLC

For more info on Pneuma Books, visit www.pneumabooks.com

Distributed to the booktrade by Simon & Schuster. SAN: 200-2442

Publisher's Cataloging-in-Publication Data
(Prepared by The Donohue Group)

Chicken soup for the soul : a book of miracles : 101 true stories of healing, faith,
    divine intervention, and answered prayers / [compiled by] Jack Canfield, Mark
    Victor Hansen [and] LeAnn Thieman.

    p. ; cm.

    Summary: A collection of 101 true personal stories in which the contributors recount
miracles that have happened to them and attribute the miracles to God, Jesus, or other
Christian entities to whom they prayed. Stories are about instances of miraculous healing, answered prayers, divine intervention, faith, and divine appointments.

    ISBN: 978-1-935096-51-1

    1. Miracles--Literary collections. 2. Miracles--Anecdotes. 3. Prayer--Christianity-
-Literary collections. 4. Prayer--Christianity--Anecdotes. 5. Christians--Literary
collections. 6. Christians--Anecdotes. I. Canfield, Jack, 1944- II. Hansen, Mark Victor.
III. Thieman, LeAnn. IV. Title: Book of miracles

PN6071.M54 C45 2010

810.8/02/023173   2010930119

PRINTED IN THE UNITED STATES OF AMERICA
on acid∞free paper
18 17 16 15 14 13 12 11   05 06 07 08 09 10

Chicken Soup for the Soul

A Book of Miracles

101 True Stories of Healing, Faith,
Divine Intervention,
and Answered Prayers

Jack Canfield
Mark Victor Hansen
LeAnn Thieman

Chicken Soup for the Soul Publishing, LLC
Cos Cob, CT

www.chickensoup.com

Contents

❸

~Love from Beyond~

❹

~His Messenger~

❺

~His Saving Grace~

❻

~Answered Prayer~

❼

~Angels Among Us~

❽

~Everyday Miracles~

❾

~Divine Appointment~

Introduction

When my mother was on a spiritual retreat years ago, she posed this question to the pastor: "The Old Testament is filled with stories of miracles performed by God, and Jesus performed dozens more in the New Testament. So why doesn't God still do miracles today?"

The pastor answered, "He does them every day, but we ignore them, dismiss them or explain them away, with science or as a 'coincidence.'"

After reading nearly 3,000 stories submitted for *Chicken Soup for the Soul: A Book of Miracles*, I suggest there are no "coincidences." While some people recounted miraculous healings and even visions of angels and of God himself, others shared "everyday miracles" that others might have just "explained away."

I've learned that when we "explain away" miracles with science, chemistry, or coincidences, we fail to give credit where credit is due. God may be speaking to us, showing us, blessing us.

I think my grandma had it right. She said that the best proof of a miracle is in the planting of a seed and the beating of a heart.

Indeed, God performs miracles every day. As you read these stories, I hope you'll be alert to identify them in your life. The next time you see a timely rainbow, butterfly, penny or even a bird, give credit where credit is due.

Look to the heavens, smile and thank God for His miracles.

~LeAnn Thieman

A Book of Miracles

Signs from Above

Then the Lord said,
"If they do not believe you or pay attention to the first miraculous sign,
they may believe the second."

~Exodus 4:7-9

Yellow Butterfly

Why are you downcast, O my soul? Why so disturbed within me?
Put your hope in God, for I will yet praise him
~Psalm 42:5

As a young girl, my biggest dream was to be a mother. I always said I wanted four children—two boys and two girls. When I got older I was so blessed to have that dream come true. I loved those kids more than life itself. Many times I found myself standing in the doorway watching as they played outside and thinking just how blessed I was, and I was always amazed that all of them were mine.

Like most mothers, in the back of my mind there was the fear that something would happen to one of them. Sadly that horror came true.

It was in June when the knock on the door came.

When my husband came to tell me the news, he didn't have to say a word. I saw into his soul that night as I looked into his eyes. Our oldest son, fourteen-year-old Josh, was hit by a car and killed.

The years after that seemed to just run together as we struggled to learn how to live life without him.

A few years later, on a beautiful spring day, my daughter Chelsea and I were going fishing. It was our favorite hobby and we could never wait until the weather got warm enough to go again. The fresh smell of newly cut grass filled the air and the daffodils were in full bloom. Everything around us seemed to be coming back to life, including us, if only for a day.

We grabbed our buckets and fishing poles and climbed over the old fence and headed down the field toward the creek. I looked back at Chelsea, who was lagging behind slightly, and saw at least thirty white butterflies dancing all around her. It was a heavenly sight and I wondered if my Josh could communicate with us from where he was. So I called out to him several times, "Josh, if you are with us, please send us a yellow butterfly."

Then I stopped and waited as my daughter caught up with me and I told her, "If you see a yellow butterfly it means Josh is with us."

She said, "How do you know?"

"Because I asked him to send us one if he was here."

Then we both started calling out, "Josh, please send us a yellow butterfly so we'll know for sure that you are with us."

"God, please let Josh send us a yellow butterfly."

Then all of a sudden, out of nowhere a large yellow butterfly with rounded wings flew right in front of my face not three inches away! Our jaws dropped as our eyes met and when we turned back around it was gone just as quickly as it had appeared. We couldn't see it anywhere, but we didn't need to. We had the answer we needed. With a great sense of peace we started walking toward the creek again, saying, "Come on Josh, let's go fishing!"

~Deborah Derosier

"Are butterflies little reminders that there are angels among us?"

Reprinted by permission of
Jonny Hawkins ©2010.

Miracle on the Dance Floor

Trust in the Lord with all your heart
and lean not on your own understanding
~Proverbs 3:5

As a child, I dreamed of becoming an entertainer who could sing, dance, and act. Ironically, I was born crippled and contracted polio at age ten, so I was "dancing-challenged." I sang so far off key that people cringed. Gradually, my exuberant joy and enthusiasm for the arts were replaced by self-doubt and low self-esteem. Stifled childhood aspirations and prayers were packed up and put on a dusty shelf.

Half a century later, when multiple health problems and self-worth issues were remedied, my subdued creative caterpillar emerged and I even accepted a position to direct a drama program at our church.

As my fifty-second birthday approached, friends enticed me to join them at the annual Christian Artists' Seminar in the Rockies, where thousands of Christian artists assemble for competition, training, and nightly entertainment by top-notch celebrities.

My spirits soared. This was an opportunity to learn from experienced drama professionals. But there was one major obstacle... it was financially prohibitive.

I prayed, "Lord, if it is Your Will for me to learn more about the arts in church, I need financial assistance."

Within the week, I received unexpected checks that provided the total sum of all expenses!

I dropped to my knees in gratitude. "God, I am so overwhelmed with Your generosity. Since You've opened this door, what is Your plan?"

I wasn't prepared for the immediate response I perceived in my mind. "Dance for Me," and a louder echo in my heart, "Dance for Me in the competition."

I didn't get it. My limited dancing experiences were confined to the privacy of my own living room. The thought of dancing in public at my age and size was comical. "I do want to be obedient, Lord, but I don't get it."

Yet, soul-searching prayers inspired a dance routine and I was airborne to Colorado. Estes Park scenery was reminiscent of a picturesque travel brochure with sparkling lakes and fragrant pine trees. It seemed like paradise.

Monday morning, I reluctantly faced my dance competitors. Most were teenagers. Watching their warm-ups, I surmised that they were so accomplished they must have danced out of the womb. Dressed in their cute little leotards, they executed exquisite dance moves I didn't even know existed. Paradise was turning into a nightmare.

The four judges were professional dancers.

Three-minute constructive critiques were offered at the end of each competitor's routine. I felt out of my league as I waited for my turn, dressed in a makeshift costume recycled from old sheer beige curtains.

When my name was called, I timidly stepped forward, trying unsuccessfully to hide my half-century-old physique. "What am I doing here, Lord?" I screamed internally. "I really have to swallow my pride to dance for You in public."

My music started. I danced. The music ended.

As I waited vulnerably alone on the dance floor for the judges to confer, I felt doubtful and discouraged.

The head judge finally rose after what seemed like an eternity.

I braced myself for the evaluation. Her silence pounded in my ears. Eventually, she whispered, "Awesome."

Only a one-word critique? Was she at a loss because nothing would help this pathetic old lady? Weren't the judges going to at least acknowledge my courage or effort?

My face turned bright red with humiliation as I lowered my head and dejectedly slipped away from the dance floor.

Dance competitors were instructed to attend all dance classes offered during the week for eligibility in the competition. I was distressed. Both the dance and drama classes occurred at the same times. I wanted to do what God asked of me, but it was becoming very inconvenient.

With hot tears of discouragement, I decided it would be better to drop out of the dance competition instead of perpetuating this childish charade. Then I would be free to attend the drama training. I hoped God would understand that sometimes what He asks of us is too difficult and too sacrificial.

Again, a stronger persistent request filled my mind. "Dance for Me."

Struggling, I surrendered.

Participating in the required dance classes stretched not only my ability level but also my limbs into uncomfortable contortions. Muscles I hadn't heard from in years threatened to revolt completely.

Half conscious because of exhaustion, I slumped in my seat at Thursday evening's concert. Something I heard when the M.C. announced the competition finalists caused me to bolt upright… my name! Was it a mistake… or a miracle? It didn't matter. I could tell all who provided financial support, prayers and encouragement that their belief in me was not totally wasted.

In my room before the final competition on Friday, my heart overflowed with gratitude. "Thank you Lord for answered prayer. For the first time in my life, I feel like a dancer. Is there anything else I could do for You?"

An immediate response filled my being. "Dance for Me… without your wig."

Horror gripped my heart and I recoiled as if struck by a rattle-snake. "I'd feel naked without my wig, Lord. I couldn't possibly do that. Anything else! Please don't ask that of me!"

I had worn a wig for seventeen years. Tumor surgery and two heart attacks in 1980 caused my ample head of curly reddish hair to fall out in clumps. The sparse ash-gray straight hair that grew back was embarrassing. The thought of going anywhere without my "secu-rity blanket" was paralyzing.

Overwhelming turmoil consumed me because I didn't under-stand. Why would God continue to ask the impossible of me?

"Trust in the Lord with all your heart and lean not on your own understanding," flashed through my mind. I wanted to trust, to be obedient, but I was definitely wrestling.

Finally exhausted, I relented. I gave God the most difficult gifts I could… obedience, submission, and trust. I would return home transformed, a winner no matter what the outcome of the competi-tion. Slowly, I removed my wig and in "naked humility" headed to the final competition.

When the performances ended, I felt a great sense of relief and silently declared my commitment fulfilled. I had given everything I had to give. I was leaving the auditorium with my head up this time.

The head judge approached me. "Love your new hairdo, BJ. Great job today."

I smiled graciously.

"It is my privilege to tell you the judges have unanimously voted you the dance competition winner!"

In my numbness, all I could think was, "My cup runneth over. Thank you, God, for miracles."

"And, you are the Grand Prize winner of all the arts competitors. You'll dance center stage in the closing ceremonies tonight."

Tears gushed from my eyes. God had created a miracle to answer the prayers of a tone-deaf, crippled child. He rewarded my obedience and courage far beyond my wildest dreams.

That night, this liberated grandma with "au natural" gray pixie hairdo appeared in front of 600 contestants and 3,000 spectators to dance my testimony about rising above life's circumstances and limitations.

What an incredible mountaintop experience!

~BJ Jensen

What Is Your Feather?

What strength do I have, that I should still hope?
What prospects, that I should be patient?
~Job 6:11

I turned off the kitchen faucet and cocked my head toward the sound of the television. The subject of that afternoon's talk show was "What Is Your Feather?" and I could hear the roar of applause and the host's opening monologue from my father's kitchen where I was working. Since my mother's passing earlier that year, I had been coming to this house daily after my shift in the office to cook, clean, and just generally help out my elderly dad and disabled brother, only to repeat the same process in my own home later each evening. To say that I was tired was an understatement. So I decided to leave the kitchen and sit on the edge of the living room coffee table to watch the show, and rest, just for a moment.

The guest, a middle-aged woman whose husband had died after a brief battle with cancer, went on to describe an experience that she had several months after his death. She explained that as she was walking through one of her favorite places, a park where she and her husband had shared daily strolls, she became so consumed with grief that she begged to be shown a sign of her husband's love and an indication that he continued to watch over her. The guest recounted how, as she sat on a park bench with her head in her hands, she began to sob deeply. At that moment a perfect white feather floated down from the heavens and landed softly at her feet. She had received her sign and, amazed at her answered plea, she took the feather home, framed it, and kept it in her living room as a reminder of her husband's love for her.

"Oh, how sappy," I thought. "It was just a simple coincidence. Nothing more."

The guest went on to say that she had written to the talk show host about her husband's illness and decline, her journey with grief, and her amazing feather experience. He and his staff were so moved by her story that shortly thereafter a crew was sent, courtesy of the show, to redecorate her living room around the framed item. A videotape was shown of the beautiful renovations and the audience cheered wildly. Audience members were then asked to share their own "feather experiences" and a parade of stories began. Some participants spoke of poems, special notes, or photos all discovered post-mortem which represented a love passed, each item having its special place in their journey through grief and healing. The host then challenged all viewers to identify their own "feather" during the next commercial break.

Wearily, I rose from the spot where I sat and returned to the kitchen to continue my duties. In a moment of bitter exhaustion, I wondered why no one had yet been sent to my home to simply do a load of laundry or shop for some groceries. As I worked, I continued to consider the talk show host's challenge to define my own "feather."

My feather? I couldn't think of one. After nursing my mother through five years of what doctors called her final stages, I had no feather, just bad memories of late night phone calls followed by rushed visits to the hospital emergency room, endless hours spent waiting in doctors' offices, and incomprehensible medical explanations. And now, with all my added responsibilities to the remaining members of my family, I didn't even have a moment to myself to breathe.

My self-pity continued to grow as I recalled how dedicated my mother and I had been to each other. We truly enjoyed each other's company and had even been on several vacations together, just the two of us. We had been closer, I surmised, than most mothers and daughters I knew. Yet, when the time came for me to move on and live my own life, she had the good grace to let me go. Even after I married, though, we remained a strong part of each other's lives. We spoke on the phone daily and often met for lunch, hunched over our burgers and fries talking girl talk. Through the years, we continued to be each other's source of strength, she helping me to stay focused during a cancer scare in my late twenties and, me, helping her through her many years of illness. In those final years, she would always pat my hand before we would part. "Remember," she'd say, "no regrets when I'm gone. We had a wonderful time together here on earth."

During my drive home that evening I railed against the memories, good and bad. Didn't I, too, deserve a feather? Surely after all my mother and I had been through together, after all I had done for her, I also deserved a message of encouragement and a confirmation of love from beyond. I shook my head and tears spilled down my cheeks.

I arrived home and parked my car as I did each evening. Before exiting, I wiped my eyes and took a deep breath. Then I walked slowly down my front walkway with my head hung low. As I reached the top step I stopped, stunned. There lay one perfect white feather.

~Monica A. Andermann

Mustard Seed Angel

If you have faith as small as a mustard seed, you can say to this mountain,
"Move from here to there," and it will move.
Nothing will be impossible to you.
~Matthew 17:20

I never expected to be a young mother with a seriously ill child, much less at a world-renowned pediatric and research hospital. But then again, does any parent or child?

Like many other families there, we found immediate comfort with the caring staff and family accommodations, which even extended to lodging the child's healthy siblings. The hospital's mission? Discover cures and lengthen lives. Such miracles did happen there. However, other miracles were also occurring, often unseen by adult eyes, but thankfully claimed and witnessed through the eyes of children.

During one of our hospital stays, I wanted to have a heart-to-heart talk with another young mother in a similar situation. The well siblings were away playing in a nearby staff-supervised area while our sick children received treatments. I confided, "I could really use some time to talk without little ears to overhear."

It was such a release to share worries and encouragement with a kindred spirit. We soon found ourselves discussing mustard seed faith and what Jesus had said in scripture. "I tell you with certainty, if you have faith like the grain of mustard seed, you can say to this mountain, 'Move from here to there,' and it will move, and nothing will be impossible to you." Matthew 17:20 (ISV)

Suddenly, my new friend's response was interrupted mid-sentence by her healthy preschool son bursting through a swinging door from the adjacent community kitchen. He grinned from ear to ear and excitedly handed his mother a small jar. He was too young to read and we both could hardly believe the spice container labeled, "Mustard Seed."

"Matthew, where did you get this?" she asked.

"The big boy angel in the kitchen told me to give it to you."

We both stood motionless, temporarily frozen with mouths and eyes wide open in awe. My heart instantaneously warmed with indescribable joy.

Seconds later, Matthew led us to the empty room where he had seen the big boy angel, on a wall mural of handprints made by children once treated there. Chills rippled over us. Looking at all the painted handprints with each accompanying name, date, and diagnosis, we couldn't help but wonder. Could our mustard seed angel's handprints be somewhere on that wall?

Our gazes met the clock and we realized it was, unfortunately, all too soon, time for us to resume our schedules. We talked and walked to the elevator pondering the coincidences of the angel, mustard seeds, scripture reference from the book of Matthew and the angelic message given to her little boy, coincidentally named Matthew.

Overwhelmed, we glanced at one another saying, "Do you really think…?"

The empty elevator doors opened and we could hardly believe what awaited us as we stepped inside… little, white floating feathers filled the air all around us. They tickled smiles upon our surprised faces and touched our souls with promise.

Feathers from an angel? Heaven only knows.

All we did know for certain was that there was only one place for our elevator and hopes to go… "Up!"

~Patricia Morris as told to Lisa Dolensky

The Crucifix

You were shown these things so that you might know that the Lord is God;
besides him there is no other.
~Deuteronomy 4:35

For centuries, reports have surfaced across the globe about divine physical signs from heaven, things like weeping marble statues of the holy Madonna or visions of Christ in the clouds above, and even manifested appearances of Mother Mary or her Son during religious holidays. The events, when authenticated, are nothing less than a modern day miracle, and in fact, hundreds have claimed personal healings and extraordinary experiences when visiting the sites of these apparitions. As a Christian, and wanting to believe God was the mastermind behind these incredible actions and messages, I was still skeptical.

Growing up in a Christian family in Delaware, we attended church faithfully every Sunday. We professed our faith during each service with the Nicene Creed, and partook in Holy Communion most weekends. Inside our home there were numerous religious artifacts around, including portraits, crucifixes in several rooms, and a stunning sculpture of Christ that hung in my parents' bedroom, a gift from my father's grandmother.

My brother and I shared a small bedroom growing up as boys. The wooden knotty-pine walls gave the room the feeling of a warm lakeside cabin. For most of our pubescent years my brother and I slept in barracks-styled bunk beds. On the wall near the head of the top bunk, my bed, where I would often pray in the dark and seek the face of God after an adolescent nightmare, hung a gold-toned crucifix. Soldered to the brassy cross was the broken body of the suffering Savior, his head crowned with branches of tiny thorns, hanging in misery. It was a powerful piece, and could piously sculpt your spirit. The blessed icon had been a confirmation gift when I was twelve years old. After hanging the item with a single nail through a small metal loop, we simply and sadly forgot about it. Occasionally we'd remember to dust Jesus, but generally it was a forgotten fixture.

Years later, after I graduated college and obtained an entry-level job in banking, my parents said it was time to "get your stuff." I drove to their house on a brisk autumn evening and was greeted with numerous boxes of mementos, keepsakes, photo albums, yearbooks, old toys and junk. We spent time rummaging through the knick knacks, cherishing each memory. Suddenly I felt old, and heavy in spirit from the nostalgia. Then my brother emerged from the bedroom we once shared.

"Hey, did you want that cross hanging on the wall before you go? I'm pretty sure it was yours, not mine."

"Okay, yeah," I replied, remembering the item, and I followed him into the room.

I had grown in my faith over the years, and as a young man had come to trust and love Jesus Christ with all my heart. Recouping this forgotten treasure and adding it to my new home was at once a devoted quest.

I reached up and removed the crucifix from the wall, holding the tarnished metal figurine in my hands, gently and with great respect. The symbol of the cross had become the heart of my faith, and I turned most reverent anytime I viewed one. I felt the smoothness and the contrasting jaggedness of the crucifix across my palm and brooded over the agonizing pain and misery the Son of God suffered on my behalf. It made me shudder.

Then I noticed something else that made me shudder.

In the specific area where the crucifix had been hanging, there was a long, flowing stain on the pinewood. It was a dark black cherry color with a lacquered look. It glistened slightly as if wet and fresh. It resembled blood.

I touched the stain, which ran nearly to the flooring panel. It was part of the wood, and its prominence stood out suddenly as if under a spotlight. A speedy but thorough survey of the room showed no other panels even closely resembling this one. The bleeding stain was unique to this single panel of wood.

Puzzled, I replaced the crucifix on the wall, searching for a logical explanation. There had to be one. Perhaps, I reasoned, the screw that was used to hang the crucifix had somehow caused a fissure in the wood, which led ultimately to this meandering stain.

But the single tributary started exactly where Christ's nail-pierced hand laid against the cross beam, several inches away from the small screw hole.

The episode spooked me initially, but then my mood changed. I was overcome with emotion, looking down at the grief stricken face of my tortured Savior, then at the shed blood stained into the bedroom wall. I found myself rubbing my fingers deferentially across the stain as tears brimmed my eyes.

My brother confirmed, "It's a miracle." My parents agreed.

Years later, the stain remains, a permanent fixture on the panel of pine. I still have the crucifix in my home and on occasion have taken it over to my parents' house to again verify the miracle.

And now I am a believer. I believe He communicates with us in supernatural modes, through crying statues, or visions of Christ in the clouds above, and yes, even in simple crucifixes hung on a young boy's wall.

~David Michael Smith

Angel in the Snow

*See, I am sending an angel ahead of you to guard you along the way
and to bring you to the place I have prepared.*
~Exodus 23:20

I felt the vibration of my cell phone hiding in my pocket. I could barely hear through the screaming. "It's amazing and yet so mysterious! I don't know how it got there!"

"What got there, Kathy? What are you talking about?"

"The angel! There's a drawing of an angel in the snow outside Kelly's bedroom window! It's blowing a horn and has a flowing robe. It looks like a child drew it with a stick or something. It's smack in the middle of the big hill in our backyard. But how did it get there? There are no tracks around it!"

Later that afternoon, my minivan made its way up the familiar mountain to visit my friend. I explained to my two sons the reason for this trip. They were used to going with me to visit Kathy and her little girl Kelly, who had terminal brain cancer. She'd fought a tremendous battle and was now only days away from leaving the earth.

She'd had a miracle already. Her brain stem had ruptured, leaving her in a vegetative state. The doctors had proclaimed her clinically brain dead and took her off life support. A few hours later, she awoke and looked at her father and said, "Daddy, paint, hotdog."

Now Kelly was back home and the family was waiting. It had been two weeks since her big miracle and now her days were numbered. We all were praying.

The boys and I got out of our car into the freezing cold winds of February. Kathy met us and walked us out back. My sons had difficulty tromping in the deep snow. But soon they shouted, "Mommy, Mommy, I see the angel! There it is!"

My mouth hung open wide. In the middle of this massive snow-covered hill was a drawing of an enormous angel, seemingly drawn by a child. There was not a track or flaw in the snow around it.

Two weeks later, on Valentine's Day, with the setting sun and a brilliant red sky, little Kelly passed on. Likely, the heralding snow angel escorted her home.

~Marisa A. Snyder

7

The Little Lamb

He tends his flock like a shepherd; he gathers the lambs in his arms and
carries them close to his heart.
~Isaiah 40:11

"God, I really need You today," I whispered, grabbing a handful of sand and watching the grains flow from my closed fist. "Here I am, feeling like that little lost lamb again."

I loved this image of myself as a lamb being protected by the Good Shepherd. It helped me feel free to talk to God. As a single mother, I prayed for each of my four children and for the ability to take care of them. It was overwhelming keeping my family out of trouble, and at times I feared that I was failing miserably. Some days, like this, brought feelings of being alone and abandoned.

That morning, while reading the Bible I came across the verse, "He will feed His flock like shepherd; He will gather the lambs in His arm." (Isaiah 40:11) This scripture had a special meaning to me. It had been shown to me a few months earlier by a counselor, when I'd approached her for prayer because of a hard situation I was having with my daughter. The counselor, underlining the words with her finger, had emphasized the remaining text, "He will carry them in His bosom and will gently lead those with young." I took this as a promise from God that He was there to help me raise my children, providing the grace I needed. Although it was encouraging to be reminded of this again, my sadness lingered. I needed something more.

It was warm and sunny so on my way home from work I decided to go to the beach. I drove to State Beach, a stretch of shoreline over four miles long. Since it was September, off-season, the beach was deserted. I could choose anywhere along the road to stop. I arbitrarily picked a spot, parked my car, and trudged over the dune and down a path. As I sat on my towel, my gaze searched the untroubled sea and cloudless sky.

Picking up a seashell I started dragging it along the sand in a wide arc about me. "Father God," I murmured, recalling a verse from the psalms, "Your thoughts to me are precious and… they're more in number than the sand." I swallowed hard. "I need You."

As the shell in my hand dug into the sand, it struck something hard. I glimpsed a bit of white. Sweeping away the sand with my fingers, a little plastic figure emerged. I picked it up. When I realized what it was, a shock of surprise and joy hit me.

Had some child brought his toy farm animals to the beach last summer, leaving this behind? And if so, what were the odds that out of four miles of beach I picked this dune to walk down, and this spot on which to sit?

Or had a loving Creator planted it, a special gift, in the sand where I sat?

For in my hand was the figure of a lamb, a message from God to me.

~Donna Paulson

Reprinted by permission of
Steve Barr ©2010.

8

Bonnie's Miracle

The Lord will guide you always.
~Isaiah 58:11

Bonnie and Bob owned their own flower shop. Because of the economic conditions in the area, the availability of flowers at local grocery stores, shorter funeral viewings and Internet access, their floral business was not thriving as it had been three years earlier when they purchased it.

For about a year, my sister Bonnie and her husband Bob discussed what they should do. They debated selling. They talked about expanding into a gift shop or maybe a bookstore. But there just wasn't enough traffic or people around the area to support the business.

After reaching a point of despair one morning, Bonnie began sincerely praying and asking God for answers. Should they sell the business? Should they expand and put more money into it when it had little opportunity to survive? In desperation she prayed, "God, give me a sign telling us what You want us to do. Call me on the phone," she teased, "but show me what to do."

Soon the phone rang. A young woman was asking how much they wanted for the business. "My husband and I never take your road," she said, "but we were driving by yesterday and saw the 'For Sale' sign in the window."

Puzzled, Bonnie replied, "There isn't a sign in the window. My husband and I have been discussing whether or not we want to sell, but haven't reached a decision."

"But I saw the sign!" the young lady insisted. "My husband saw it too. It was blue and white in the large picture window facing the road."

Within two weeks, the young lady and her husband bought the flower shop.

~Kim D. Armstrong

Fishing for Rainbow Trout

We live in a rainbow of chaos.
~Paul Cézanne

O kay, so maybe it was a little irresponsible for my dad to embark on a fishing trip and leave his pregnant wife alone at home. My mother was seven months swollen with twins. Other, more rational couples might've promised to stay side-by-side, but we babies weren't due until August, and this fishing trip was a graduation present for my brother. Before the little girl duo was to come into the world, the two males of the family needed to bond in the manliest way they knew — fishing for rainbow trout.

So my dad bade goodbye to my very pregnant mother and set off for Oregon with my older brother. Perhaps Dad was oblivious to the foreshadowing of sudden rain and hot whistling winds, finding satisfaction in the masculine angst of raging seething rivers. Either way, it must have come as a shock to return to his lodge one evening and receive ten frantic messages left by my mother. It's hard to guess exactly what she babbled, for a hysterical woman in labor is not usually known for her eloquence, but my dad knew instantly he had to get home. He and my brother leapt into the car and rocketed down the road, racing off in less than five minutes for the fifteen-hour car ride to San Francisco.

Meanwhile, my mother felt her babies' impatience and rushed to her car. She was so enormous she couldn't even buckle her seatbelt and her stomach constantly set off the horn. Our neighbor had agreed to drive my mother to the hospital in case my dad was unavailable but Mom chose not to trouble her backup chauffeur and instead drove herself.

Meanwhile, my father and brother sped down the highway. Despite all efforts to surpass the speed limits as quietly and cautiously as possible, Dad was pulled over by a cop just as my mother teetered into the hospital. My parents' despair was mutual as Dad pleaded with an unsympathetic policeman and my mother hid in the elevator, embarrassed by her frazzled state.

At last, speeding ticket begrudgingly accepted, my dad was on the road again just as my mother leaned over and grasped the nurse's desk, mumbling, "I think something's wrong."

The nurse was a warm and no-nonsense woman. If her husband had asked to go on a fishing trip seven months into her pregnancy, she would have said, "You think some darn fish are more important than staying home and rubbing my feet? I don't have cravings for trout; I need chocolate ice cream!" The nurse told my mother to remove her pants and with one mighty sniff declared, "Honey, this ain't no false alarm. Your water broke!"

At the same time, massive rain clouds broke over Northern California, and a sudden downpour impaired my dad's speeding. This was enough to discourage anyone, for despite the near-slapstick calamity of our impromptu births, this premature labor was serious. There'd been another of us, my unknown brother, but our trio was reduced by a miscarriage before he even had a name.

As Dad's car flew through the rain, however, we decided we'd been patient long enough. My mother begged for painkillers. My father must have sensed her despair and agony. He sensed that he would never get to San Francisco in time for our births. Though the rain slowly let up, he knew he could never drive fast enough to make it… assuming we made it too. He was frightened and discouraged and tired. Just as his weary mind considered the worst possible scenario, he looked out the window and saw a glimmer on the horizon.

Across the sky stretched a double rainbow. Not one, but two radiant arcs, one on top of the other. My father stared long and hard at this double rainbow, two for his double dose of Gemini girls. He knew just by looking at that pair of rainbows that everything would be all right. This was a sign, and with hope restored he continued down the road, slowing his frantic speed to gaze at those rainbows a little longer.

He arrived at the hospital seven hours after we were born. Two months premature, I weighed three pounds, fifteen ounces; McKenzie was four pounds, three ounces. Though the double rainbow calmed my father, he was still terribly on edge until he saw us, our tiny wrinkled bodies warming under the orange glow of incubator lights. When Dad arrived, Mom awoke to hold us, and we smiled, brown eyes all around, except for my mother's glistening wet violet ones.

Dad's fishing trip had been cut short but he didn't mind. All he needed at that moment was the tenderness only two baby girls could give.

After that day, Dad never saw another double rainbow.

~Brittany Newell, age 16

Balloons of Hope

In your unfailing love you will lead the people you have redeemed.
In your strength you will guide them to your holy dwelling.
~Exodus 15:13

"Okay. One, two, three, let them go!" I shouted. Sue's three young children, Stephanie, Kristen and Billy, released the purple balloons covered with messages of love.

It was a cold March afternoon. A misty rain fell as we stood in Sue's driveway to mark the second anniversary of her passing. The dismal weather reflected how I felt in my heart, but I mustered up a smile for the children's sake. My twin sister Sue, just forty-one years old, had died suddenly, leaving behind her children and her husband Bill.

Just yesterday, while chatting with my friend, I mentioned Sue's upcoming anniversary. Mary, who knew firsthand the heartache of loss after the passing of her ten-year-old son John, offered me an idea.

"For John's birthday we write messages to him on balloons. Then we release them."

I headed for the store and bought three purple balloons, since purple was Sue's favorite color.

Now here I stood watching the balloons leave the little hands that held them so tightly. Privately, before liftoff, I read many of the messages. They tugged at my heart. *I miss you, Mommy. To my loving wife, all my love. We love you Aunt Suzy.* And the one I added, using her nickname: *I miss you Twinpop!*

Filled with anticipation, we watched as the balloons were released. Immediately, they drifted down onto the driveway. It was too cold. Realizing my mistake, I thought I should have waited for a nicer day. I prayed, "Please God help us!"

Suddenly, the wind kicked up. I held my breath as the balloons slowly lifted. Two floated up past the trees to the sky, but the third wedged itself between two branches. "Uh oh," Sue's youngest, Billy, exclaimed. "It's going to pop!" Sue's husband, Bill, and I looked at each other.

"Oh boy," he whispered. Again I prayed, "Please God don't let them pop!"

The kids began to cheer for the one lone purple balloon. Slowly, it began to creep out of its trap, bobbing along the prickly branches until it made its way to freedom. "Go! Go! Go!" the kids shouted. We let out a collective sigh as we watched the balloon finally edge its way around the trees, miraculously not popping. It then took off to catch up with the other two and sailed out of sight. "Thank you God," I offered silently. I looked around at all the smiles and I knew somewhere in heaven, Sue was smiling too.

A week later, my youngest, Caroline, was upstairs. She looked out her bedroom window, then called to me, "Mommy, there is a purple balloon out back. Is it the one we sent Aunt Suzy?"

I glanced out the kitchen window and spotted a purple balloon bouncing on the grass. I walked out the back door to take a closer look. As I approached, the balloon took off through my neighbor's yard, with me in my pajamas chasing after it. Finally, I grabbed the purple balloon. It looked identical to the ones we sent, minus the messages. Hmm. What a coincidence. I brought the balloon into our house. Caroline asked, "Mommy, did Aunt Suzy send you that balloon?"

"I wouldn't doubt it, Caroline," I answered with a smile.

That same spring my mom became very sick. After a series of mini strokes she was weak and confused and could no longer live alone. She soon developed dementia. I prayed daily as I placed Mom's name on several nursing home waiting lists. I knew they could care for her in a way I could not physically do.

Months passed and my mom continued to decline. It had been a frustrating afternoon of phone calls to nursing homes, agencies and family. After one particular phone call ended with an abrupt "no," tears filled my eyes. I was exhausted. Between dealing with the loss of my twin sister and now the concern I felt for my mom, I was overwhelmed emotionally, physically and spiritually. Wiping away my tears, I grabbed my coat and called to my kids, "I am going for a walk."

It had started to snow. As I walked, the snowflakes mingled with my tears. I talked to my sister and prayed to God. "Please God, help me! Sue, what am I going to do?" I thought about the past two years and wondered how much more I could handle. Where would I get the strength to continue?

As I turned the corner, I noticed the snow and wind beginning to pick up. But it was not all I noticed. On my neighbor's front lawn, one purple balloon gently bobbed up and down in the snow. I could not believe it. My heart lifted. The purple balloon again. I knew the days ahead would be tough but I was encouraged knowing I was not handling this alone.

On Christmas morning, my mom had a seizure and was admitted to the hospital. Ten days later, she was stabilized and scheduled for discharge. She was now blind in one eye and could no longer feed herself or walk. In addition, she was confused most of the time. Mom needed round-the-clock care. The hospital found a temporary placement for her fifteen miles away. After she was admitted, I gradually realized it was a terrible nursing home.

Once I found her asleep with her face lying in a full plate of food. She often looked disheveled, unclean and isolated. At first I thought, "Maybe they are just understaffed today. Or perhaps the staff is still getting her into a routine." But soon it became clear I had to get her out of that place.

I was filled with guilt; I could not physically care for her myself.

At this point I couldn't even lift her. I begged God, "Please find her another place. Sue, watch over her." Then I began my futile search for a new nursing home.

On my birthday, I drove over to see my mom. I thought back to happier days and all the celebrations my mom, Sue and I had shared on this special day. Turning into the parking lot, my joyful birthday memories were soon clouded with concern for Mom.

Saddened, I entered her room. There underneath her shabby metal-framed bed, was a purple balloon. I was stunned! "Mom, where did you get that purple balloon?" I asked in astonishment.

"I don't know," she answered. "Someone gave it to me this morning." I smiled.

A few weeks later, at work, my boss asked, "How are things with your mom?"

"Not good," I responded. "She is still on waiting lists for a better nursing home."

"My grandmother lived at Pembrooke for years. It was great!" a coworker chimed in.

I had never heard of Pembrooke, but I made a call. Miraculously a room was available.

My mom was being transferred by ambulance. I planned to be there when she arrived. Driving up the pike, I was so nervous. "Is this a nice place, Lord?" I kept watch for the new nursing home. But it was easy to spot.

Tied to the post just across from the Pembrooke sign was one lone purple balloon.

~Donna Teti

A Book of Miracles

The Healing Power of Prayer

O Lord my God, I called to you for help and you healed me.

~Psalm 30:1-3

Sarafina

See now that I myself am He! There is no god besides me.
I put to death and I bring to life, I have wounded and I will heal,
and no one can deliver out of my hand.
~Deuteronomy 32:38-40

I was twenty-two years old and a year away from getting my college degree. Although I didn't know exactly what I was supposed to do after graduation, I knew that it had something to do with missions. I didn't know where or how, but I knew my life would be spent in intentional ministry. With just a year left until "freedom," this was my taste of what life would be like after I took that last exam. So instead of working to save money or just relaxing that final summer between junior and senior year, I found myself in the small African country of Swaziland serving AIDS patients and hugging orphans.

It was a cold winter day in the southern hemisphere, and the sun was setting behind the mountains. My group had to be back before dark, so it was time to leave the hut we'd visited and walk the twenty-five minutes back to our homestead. As we passed the last hut to our right, a voice called out to us. An elderly woman sitting on a mat waved us over.

The woman was Sarafina. Through our interpreter we learned that she hadn't walked in two years and that she hadn't eaten in five days. She was alone because her son, her only remaining relative, lived far away. She couldn't walk to the river to draw water and had to rely on the generosity of neighbors to give her leftovers from their own meager meals.

As she looked up at us with cataract-filled eyes, I saw my own grandmother on her knees before me, asking for food. My heart broke and I began to pray silently, "Lord, what can I do?"

And then I heard an internal answer: "Get on your knees."

"What?" I asked again silently, not sure I'd heard correctly.

"Get on your knees."

As I knelt in front of Sarafina, the movement startled her. She turned and looked me in the eyes.

Then I heard another internal voice. "Stretch out your hand."

When I reached for her, Sarafina took my hand and began to laugh. For the rest of our visit, we sat holding hands. That became an anchor for us from then on.

Sarafina struggled with dementia and many days she couldn't remember her own name, let alone details about her life. When her mind began to wander, I'd squeeze her hand, say her name, and she'd come back to the conversation.

I visited Sarafina several times a week for the next few months. Sometimes I brought her "pap," an African staple food of cornmeal mixed with water, but usually I came empty-handed. We'd sit and laugh together, just enjoying the relationship we'd built. It was a beautiful thing.

One of the biggest frustrations was not knowing Sarafina's spiritual beliefs. As a missionary, I wanted to know if she knew Jesus… if she believed He could forgive her sins… if she believed He had the power to heal.

Around her wrist and ankle, Sarafina wore black bracelets from a witch doctor. I told her that I believed there was another way. "God has the power to heal you, Sarafina. He can make you walk again."

"Oh," my gogo (Siswati for "grandmother") said, staring at her bracelets intently.

The conversation went on from there, but as I left that day, I couldn't forget it. And I began to pray that Sarafina would remove those bracelets as a sign that she believed God could heal her. That it would be an act of faith.

Two days later, it happened. Sarafina took off her last bracelet, threw it as far as she could and then looked me in the eyes and said, "Please pray that I will walk again."

I swallowed. The thought was incomprehensible. "Okay, Sarafina, I will pray," I promised her.

For the next week I prayed silently night and day. "Lord, my faith is so small. I know that you have the power to heal. I know that you can and have made the lame walk. Please, Lord, touch Sarafina. Let her walk again. Don't let my small faith get in the way. But please, let me be there to see it. Let me see you work a miracle."

One day just as the sun began to set, a small group of us decided to visit Sarafina. It was an impromptu trip, something I felt very serious about but wasn't sure why.

When we arrived at her hut, she was sitting outside on her mat watching the road. "Where have you been?" she demanded. "I have been waiting by the side of the road for you all day. He told me you were coming."

I was surprised. "Sarafina, I did not tell you that I was coming today. Who told you that we were coming?" I recalled some children we'd met along the way. "Did a child tell you?"

She shook her head. "No," she said, placing a hand on her chest. "He told me in my heart."

And then I knew that God was about to do something extraordinary.

Sarafina was completely different that day. She was lucid; her memory was completely clear. She recalled previous conversations that we'd had, conversations about the gospel. "Yes, Sarafina!" I was excited. "God does have the power to forgive. And He does have the power to heal."

Sarafina said something to me, looking me directly in the eyes. I had to wait for the translation, but when it came, my heart stopped.

"When am I going to walk again?"

I stared at her, stunned, with no idea what to say. When my

mouth moved and when words came out, they surprised even me. "Stand up."

Sarafina stared at me for a moment after she heard the translator speak. No one moved. I couldn't even breathe.

Then she stood.

And then she walked.

Because of the years she'd spent crawling, her legs were weak and she needed people to keep her from falling over.

But she stood and walked with her own strength.

By the time I left Swaziland a few weeks later, Sarafina's legs had grown quite strong. She could walk taller, steadier, and for longer periods of time. The last time I saw her walk, it was in front of five hundred people. They all saw what God could do.

Whenever I think of that summer, I think of Sarafina. I think of how God did the impossible and healed an old woman with broken legs simply because she believed He could.

~Kristen Torres-Toro

12

Warts and All

And he said, "I tell you the truth, unless you change
and become like the little children,
you will never enter the kingdom of heaven."
~Matthew 18:3

In the hot summer sun of the Texas Panhandle, where there are
few shade trees, it takes time to dig a hole, especially if you're
a nine-year-old girl and the shovel is bigger than you. I don't
remember who suggested that I bury a dishrag to get rid of my warts,
but I was willing to try anything.

The warts looked awful. They spread under my eyes in bumpy
waves and popped up all over my fingers. One in particular was like
a bully, a big angry-looking thing as large as the head of a six-penny
nail. Embedded deep inside the second joint of my middle finger, it
was one wart that other people could not see. But I was aware of it
every time I bent my finger, even to hold a pencil. My mother had
taken me to the doctor to get rid of them, but the warts were stub-
born. They just multiplied.

Just before the end of summer, though, something happened.

I've forgotten every single Vacation Bible School of my life except
this one. I remember carving open Bibles from bars of Ivory soap,
making small saddle bags from brown felt, and the last day, wearing
a costume representing a character from one of the week's stories. I
wore one of my father's suit coats, so big it hung past my knees, the
sleeves rolled, a baggy white shirt, and rolled up trousers gathered

around my waist with a belt. I'd dressed myself as John Wesley, traveling preacher.

There was lots of horsing around that day since we were all in costumes, but the teacher managed to read a story. It was about healing, an ordinary person's prayer.

I had never said a personal prayer. I never realized God might be interested in me, a girl who mostly aggravated her mother, who thought cap guns were much more fun than baby dolls, who thought making noise was more fun that being quiet. When I went home that last day, though, I found a quiet place to be alone. I got down on my knees and I begged, "Please, God heal me of my warts."

The next morning, they were gone.

To this day, I can see myself looking into the bathroom mirror. I see my short hair, crooked bangs, and my fingers touching the smooth skin under my eyes. I put my face closer to the glass. There was not a wart in sight. I stepped back and looked at the tops of my hands, searching around my fingernails.

Nothing.

There was only one place left to look.

I took a deep breath and slowly turned over my right hand, palm up. There was nothing but a smooth joint, no sign of a blemish, no redness, just pure, smooth skin. It was as if the wart had never existed. God's love flooded over me.

Almost fifty years have passed, and the memory has stayed with me like a beacon. I've hung onto it many times.

Some might ask, "Why would God bother with little warts and not all the huge hurts of the world?"

Was it my childlike faith? I don't think so. I think it was all about Him. He wanted me to always remember the scars were inside His hands, not mine. He sees me as his child, unblemished. To this day.

~Martha Moore

13

The Miracle of Mariette Reis

This will bring health to your body and nourishment to your bones.
~Proverbs 3:7

I n 1942, when I was only six years old, the world outside my house in Nazi-occupied Winterslag, Belgium was filled with dangers. But inside our home, my three siblings and I felt protected in a cocoon of happiness and faith.

We were devout Catholics who were often forced to worship at home. During the war, there were few priests available to say Mass. Even when Mass was offered, it was too dangerous to walk the streets. The Hitler Youth were known to shoot people for no reason.

In our home, my mother, whose name was Mariette Reis, and my grandmother encouraged great devotion to the saints. They taught us that each saint had a specialty. My grandmother visited us on the Feast of St. Andrew and insisted we girls pray to him for worthy husbands. We also prayed to St. Anthony for help finding lost things and to my favorite, St. Therese, the Little Flower, for assistance in anxious times.

One day, my mother was taking my baby sister for a walk and my mother cut the back of her hand on the old stroller. The cut became infected. She had not yet recovered her strength from the birth, and she was undernourished because of the wartime food rationing, so her body was unable to fight the infection. It spread up her arm.

At that time there were no antibiotics to administer. Wet compresses were applied in an attempt to drain the infection, but my mother's health deteriorated. The local medical clinic sent a nun who was a nurse to care for her and to feed and clean us children. She was a Sister of Charity, the ones with the big white hats. She was a petite woman named Sister Elizabeth; we called her Sister Babette.

Despite Sister Babette's care, gangrene set in, and the tissues of my mother's arm died. She ran a high fever, suffered delirium, and fell into a coma. My father took us in to see her and told us to say goodbye because she was going to heaven. I was frightened to see her lying there, not moving. I didn't want to lose my mother!

My mother's doctor, Dr. Reynaert, was well known in the town as an atheist. He was a rough speaking man, prone to swearing. He examined my mother and decided that her arm had to be amputated to save her life. He would operate the next day.

Sister Babette objected, "You can't do that with a woman who has four children. One is a baby, too."

But the doctor just said, "Well, I'm coming tomorrow to amputate her arm."

That evening, Sister Babette placed a picture of Fr. Damien face down on my mother's arm and wrapped bandages around it. The nun had been raised in Fr. Damien's hometown of Tremeloo, Belgium and had been told the inspiring story of his life many times. Fr. Damien was just thirty-three years old when he traveled to the island of Molokai in Hawaii to minister to the exiled leprosy sufferers in the Kalawao settlement there. He cared for the ill both spiritually and physically. Fr. Damien literally embraced his flock. He dressed their sores and anointed them with oil during the Sacrament of Extreme Unction. With his own hands, he helped his parishioners build proper houses. He fashioned coffins for the dead and even dug their graves. Then Fr. Damien contracted leprosy and died at the age of forty-nine.

Over the years, Sister Babette had developed a special devotion to Fr. Damien. So that night, after she placed his picture on my mother's bandaged arm, she prayed for his intercession on Mom's behalf.

Dr. Reynaert returned the next morning with surgical instruments, including a saw to cut off my mother's arm. He removed the bandages, saw the picture, and really swore. "What the hell is this piece of junk on her arm?" he shouted.

"It's Fr. Damien," Sister Babette told him.

The doctor tore off the picture, but Damien's face remained imprinted on my mother's arm. Her wound had opened, and the infection had drained. The gangrene was gone; the tissues of her arm, healthy.

Dr. Reynaert turned to Sister Babette. "Well, it looks like your saint did the trick."

My mother was completely cured. She filled our home with music as she played the piano. She was not disabled in the slightest.

Fr. Damien not only healed my mother, but he also touched Dr. Reynaert's heart. The doctor proclaimed throughout the town that my mother had been miraculously cured. From then on, he became a regular parishioner in the Catholic Church.

After the war, in 1946, my family traveled to Louvain, Belgium, the site of Fr. Damien's religious order. I get chills when I recall the small room there, with piles of crutches leaning against the altar and the walls covered with items from people who had been miraculously cured through Fr. Damien's intercession.

In Louvain, my mother was questioned by priests about the miracle. Formal papers witnessed by Sister Babette and Dr. Reynaert were filed. My mother's cure would be one of the miracles officially listed and considered to support the beatification of Fr. Damien.

Some day soon, the Catholic Church will make it official. But ever since the night he cured my mother, I knew Fr. Damien was a saint.

~Gisele Reis as told to Marie-Therese Miller

Editor's note: Fr. Damien was beatified on June 4, 1995 by Pope John Paul II. On July 1, 2009, Pope Benedict XVI certified the final miracle required for Damien's sanctification. Fr. Damien was declared a saint on October 11, 2009.

14

Five Weeks to Live

He sent forth his word and healed them;
he rescued them from the grave.
~Psalm 107:20

"It's malignant melanoma," the doctor said. "You have five weeks to live." She was thirty years old, with two children under the age of five. How could this be happening? She had so many plans. Giving up a career to stay at home and raise her children, she looked forward to each day that she could give them—teaching them how to read, playing games and baking their favorite cookies.

And now this.

All that she had planned would come to an end in only five weeks.

My mother was going to lose her life.

After visiting the dentist, Mom had used two mirrors to look at her dental work, and in doing so she found a dark spot on the roof of her mouth. Concerned, she made an appointment with her doctor, who announced, "I'm afraid I have some bad news, but I want another doctor to confirm my diagnosis."

The second consultation revealed the worst. The doctor sat down next to her, put his hands on her knees and said, "It's malignant melanoma, and it's not treatable because of where it's located. We can't remove it all, and we can't do chemotherapy. We'll do surgery right away to cut out the spot and hope that it doesn't spread. The diagnosis isn't good, JoAnn. You have five weeks to live."

Mom and Dad went out for dinner that night and had the gut-wrenching talk about how my brother and I were going to be raised without her. Then they started making arrangements for her funeral. They quickly put plans in place for how to handle the next five weeks.

One item left on the back burner was the importance of prayer during this time. Mom had become a Christian only the year before and didn't fully understand how important prayer was or how it worked. As she tells it, "This is the part where God carried me when I didn't know what to do on my own."

On the morning of her surgery, before she left for the hospital, Mom's friend, Neva, called and read Isaiah 43:5 over the phone. "Do not fear, for I am with you," the verse said. Mom clung to that Bible passage all the way to the hospital and through the halls to the operating room. Once there, she quietly and repeatedly recited Psalm 23 because that's all she could recall from her childhood. "The Lord is my shepherd, I shall not be in want. He makes me lie down in green pastures, he leads me beside quiet waters, he restores my soul.... even though I walk through the valley of the shadow of death, I will fear no evil"... then the anesthesia kicked in.

When Mom came out of surgery the doctor said she would be in a great deal of pain and wouldn't be able to eat solids for several days. Miraculously, within an hour of her surgery she ate a complete meal of solid food. The doctor was shocked—and that wouldn't be the last time.

A few days later, Mom went to the doctor's office for a post-operative check-up. The surgeon, normally a man with a harsh bedside manner, quietly came into the room, sat down beside her and said, "I can't believe what I'm going to tell you. There's only one answer for this." He pointed upward and turned toward her with tears in his eyes. "We got the tests back and there's no sign of malignancy or any sign that it was ever there. JoAnn, your cancer is gone. If I didn't believe in miracles before, I certainly do now."

And so does my family!

That was more than thirty years ago, and in those years we've read a lot of books, played a lot of games and eaten a lot of cookies. And in those thirty years, Mom has fully come to understand the power of prayer—and the reality of miracles.

~Heidi J. Krumenauer

15

Heart Problems

Heal me, O Lord, and I will be healed;
save me and I will be saved, for you are the one I praise.
~Jeremiah 17:13-15

"The tests show you have a heart murmur. Have you ever been diagnosed with this before?"

"No, Doctor. I'm not sure what that is."

"Basically, it's an irregular heartbeat. I see from your chart that you are recovering from drug addiction. How long have you been clean?"

"It's going on two weeks now."

"Well, good. I know it can be hard. And what was your drug of choice?"

"Marijuana and cocaine."

He paused as his eyebrows lowered and he tightened his lips. "Well, snorting great amounts of cocaine has been known to cause an irregular heartbeat. Are you taking any medications?"

"Yes. Antidepressants, pain pills for my headaches, sleeping pills, and blood pressure medicine."

"That's quite a bit. There is nothing I can prescribe anyway. We will just have to monitor this. As you leave, make an appointment for a month from now."

As I left the room, I thought about the consequences if I had continued to abuse drugs. Staying away from drugs the past two weeks had been one of the most difficult things I'd ever done. But

I was glad to have made it that far. My previous attempt at quitting lasted six days, so fourteen was a big accomplishment.

I'd been attending Narcotics Anonymous meetings and did my best to follow my sponsor's suggestion of ninety meetings in ninety days. When I called her, she told me she was headed to a Christian recovery meeting that night.

"Would you like to go? They serve dinner and you can bring your Bible."

"I'd love to go."

I looked forward to this because the NA meetings would use the term "Higher Power" to represent their God. I wanted to freely say "God," my Higher Power, and not feel as though I was offending anybody.

I met her in front of the building behind the church where the meeting was held. With my Bible in hand, I met the people standing outside with great anticipation. Everyone seemed friendly and welcomed me into the gathering. People were everywhere, catching up with friends, and carrying plates of food to share at the meeting. You could see everyone's story in their faces. They may have looked beaten down and broken on the outside, but each person possessed a light that shone from the inside. I wanted that light.

After introducing myself and sharing with everyone how many days I had been clean, I sat back and listened. We sat in a circle as people took turns telling the group how God had helped them through the toughest times in their recovery. I was at home and comfortable there. And although I didn't speak that night, I knew I would be back.

I went back and forth between the NA meetings and the Christian meetings. I was torn between wanting to receive my key chains for NA attendance and wanting to declare the name of God loud and clear. Finally, I came to the conclusion that there was nothing wrong with going to both. I grew stronger in God's Word and began to ask questions when I didn't understand. I knew I needed the Word to stay away from the weed. And with each meeting at the church, I dug deeper into God's Word.

Then one night a man named Chuck gave his testimony about what God did in his life. He asked for prayer because he was traveling overseas on a mission trip. He couldn't believe how his life had changed. He went from using to being used. Everyone prayed for him and praised him for being available for God's plan.

After that session was over, my sponsor asked Chuck to pray over her. She had pain in her body and knew he had the gift of healing. I patiently sat and waited, not knowing what to think.

He picked up a small bottle and poured its golden contents on his hands. He then put one hand on her head and the other he raised high in the air. He closed his eyes and spoke with great confidence to God.

My sponsor swayed back and forth as tears flowed from her eyes. I didn't understand what was going on, but it was real to me. A few seconds passed, and then she fell back on the floor. She lay there for a minute. And after about a minute more, a bystander and I helped her off the ground.

She smiled and said, "I know I'm healed."

I wanted this. I wanted to be healed. I walked over to Chuck. "Would you pray for me?"

Without hesitation, he answered, "Of course."

He held his bottle and said, "What's your health issue?"

"I have a heart murmur."

"Okay. Let's pray."

Again, he extended one hand to the heavens and he placed his other hand over my heart. I wasn't sure what would happen, but I kept my mind open. My stance was tense. I could feel my body start to move in minute circles, but my legs resisted. I heard my sponsor speak. "Let it go, Keisha. Trust God. Let it go."

Before I knew it, my legs gave way and I was on the ground. I could see nothing but a white flash of light that almost blinded me. I sat up, but then froze. I took everything in. I could feel God all around me. I had peace and felt refreshed. I stood up and looked at my sponsor. "What just happened?"

"You experienced being slain in the spirit. I am going to tell you what someone once told me. Look up scriptures on it, study them, and pray for full understanding. Also, enjoy and accept God's powerful way to heal."

That night you could not have dragged me away from my Bible. I prayed and cried, and cried and prayed. The following day, I called the doctor's office to confirm my appointment. I was overly excited to see if they'd be able to detect the irregular heartbeat. I knew in my heart of hearts that it wouldn't be there. I just wanted the proof on paper. I told everyone even before the appointment that I had been healed from a heart murmur and it was an incredible experience.

By the end of the week, I was in the doctor's office awaiting the results. The doctor entered the room with my chart in his hand and a smile on his face. He spoke what I already knew. "Well, Keisha. I can't seem to find the heart murmur at all on the EKG. It has only been a few weeks. That's amazing."

"That's God," I smiled. "Amazing."

~Keisha Bass

"You must have been in your Bible study
again. Looks like you had a faith lift."

Reprinted by permission of
Jonny Hawkins ©2010.

16

Miracle Girl on Loan

You are the God who performs miracles;
you display your power among the peoples.
~Psalm 77:13-15

The pediatric nurse scurried down the hall shouting in Dutch, "Critically ill child, critically ill child! Get the pediatrician!" I felt sad for that child's poor mother. Within minutes, nurses and the pediatrician rushed into the examining room where my daughter lay. I realized my five-year-old daughter, Olivia, was that critically ill child and I was that poor mother.

In light of her severe condition, the specialist opted for a painful spinal tap. I tried to quell the panic welling up in me and began the first of many desperate prayers pleading for my daughter's life.

My husband Frank arrived in the midst of all the chaos. His presence made the situation seem that much more real. We hugged and buried our fear in each other's arms. Our daughter writhed in severe pain and there was nothing we could do but wait and pray as they started the intravenous antibiotics. No pain medications would be administered until the diagnosis was definite.

When the doctor returned to the room, he avoided eye contact. He seemed to look through us and out the window as he reported the news. Although I understood basic Dutch, Frank repeated it in English, "Olivia has bacterial meningitis. It's called HIB and they'll start steroids, pain medications and a specific antibiotic to attack the bacteria immediately. He says she'll probably end up on oxygen and her kidneys could shut down. She may end up blind or deaf." He barely could get the last words out.

"God, this isn't happening. Please take me out of this nightmare," was all I could think. I wanted to turn back the clock. What could I have done differently to change this outcome? Could haves, would haves, should haves. How could she have become so sick? Why did this have to happen only six weeks after our move to a new country? Why couldn't this have happened in America where I spoke the language and understood the healthcare system? Here we had no friends, no church, no network.

Panic ripped through me like a knife. Frank enveloped me in a tight hug. Our fear and disbelief bonded us. I looked at him and wondered if we would be strong enough to survive Olivia's death… or her recovery.

Frank left briefly to make the dreaded international calls, while I remained at Olivia's bedside. I felt so alone.

They bombarded her tiny body with more antibiotics, steroids and pain medications. They would do all they could, but the prognosis was bleak. She was too critical to be moved to a specialized children's hospital; she wouldn't survive the journey.

Olivia moaned in pain and seemed semi-conscious. Dark half moon circles shadowed her eyes and her dry peeling lips remained partially open. I stroked thin wisps of blond hair from her forehead. She looked at me with her glazed-over puppy dog eyes, pleading for me to do something. "I love you, Livvy. I'm going to stay right by you. I won't leave." That was the best I could offer her.

In the middle of the night, as I helplessly watched Olivia suffer, I prayed to God that He would either take her quickly or heal her. In that moment, I experienced a life-changing revelation; Olivia was not mine, but His. She was God's child and He had complete sovereignty over her life. She was merely on loan to us. Immediately I knew God answered my prayer: she would live. From that moment on, she did indeed slowly show improvement.

We felt lifted up in prayer by all of our friends and family across the ocean. We experienced a strength and peace which was not our own.

After a month in the hospital, Olivia returned home unable to walk, partially deaf in one ear and weighing a mere forty pounds. Several times a day she was plagued by severe headaches that triggered crying and screaming fits. Progress was slow, but she was alive. That was good enough for us.

In August, four months after leaving the hospital, we traveled from Holland to southern France to get some much needed sunshine. We decided to visit Lourdes, where in 1858 the Blessed Virgin Mary appeared eighteen times to Bernadette Soubirous, a fourteen-year-old peasant girl. Olivia knew about the thousands of miracle healings that had happened there since and she insisted on entering the healing baths. We explained to her that there might be a long wait since there were many ill people on stretchers and in wheelchairs. She would not be swayed; she expected a full healing.

We waited over two hours before our turn. As a lanky five-year-old, she looked kind of strange waiting in a stroller, but she didn't mind. The atmosphere was quiet and serene as her turn arrived and the aides whispered prayers in French as they submerged her in the stone bath.

Upon exiting the water, Olivia declared, "The water felt holy. God healed me."

And He did.

Within days, she began to hold her head upright and walk better. When we returned to Holland, the therapist reported that her short-term memory was back to normal. Her headaches disappeared, and so did her tantrums. Much to the astonishment of the hearing specialist, her "permanent" hearing loss returned to completely normal.

Olivia spent month after month attending physical therapy to regain her walking and fine motor skills. She received speech therapy to speed up the process of learning Dutch. By February, she passed the Dutch standardized kindergarten tests with all A's.

Today, eleven years later, Olivia is a vibrant sixteen-year-old honor student who loves to sing, play classical guitar and eat ice cream. We cherish each moment of her precious life… our miracle girl on loan.

~Johnna Stein

Baby Loren

Seeing Jesus, he fell at his feet and pleaded earnestly with him,
"My little daughter is dying. Please come and put your hands on her
so that she will be healed and live."
~Mark 5:22-23

Baby Girl Loren was born in Paris, France. Less than one hour after her birth, she was rushed to the neonatal intensive care unit with a heart rate of 280 beats per minute, twice the norm. A rate this high eventually stops the exhausted heart.

Loren's heart was cardioverted, or shocked, back into a normal rhythm. She was placed on intravenous medication to keep the heart rate down and the rhythm normal. But she did not respond to any of the various medications and she received cardioversion several times a day during her first month of life.

After spending one month in the NICU with a rapid, lethal and uncontrollable heart rhythm Loren's doctors decided to send her to Texas Children's Hospital in Houston.

The baby was airlifted and admitted to the pediatric intensive care unit which would become her home for the next four to five weeks. The cardiac catheterization lab found the cause of the rapid heart rhythm, though during the procedure she was shocked numerous times again. Diagnosis... multiple heart tumors. She was scheduled for open heart surgery, an extremely high risk, not only because of Loren's small body mass, but because this type of heart surgery had only been done a few times in the past. Part of the heart muscle would have to be cut away to remove the tumors.

Baby Loren went into surgery the next Friday morning, less than one week after arriving at Texas Children's Hospital. I went about my day taking care of the children who came into the cardiac clinic. My mind was on Baby Loren and I offered up prayers for her all day as I worked.

The baby's parents stayed at the hotel. They had been told at birth that her chance of survival was very slim. They flew over with her, admitted her to the hospital, and then went to a hotel. I'd learned that some parents just couldn't tolerate the heartache. Hers occasionally talked to the doctor on the phone, but did not come back to the hospital for a week.

At 3:00 p.m. on the afternoon of her surgery, the pediatric cardiologist came out of the operating room instructing me to call and ask Loren's parents to come. The doctor said that the surgeon had cut away close to forty percent of the heart muscle to try and remove the tumors. He said that Baby Loren would never come off the heart-lung bypass machine that was used to keep the blood flowing throughout her body and lungs while the heart was opened.

I made the call to Baby Loren's parents, telling them very little about Loren's grave condition, only that she was not doing well and that they needed to come.

As soon as I hung up, the pediatric cardiologist came in with his head down and said, "They can't get her off the heart pump. So they are going to unhook everything and let her go."

I went to an old broom closet that had been converted into a bathroom, where I spent many minutes of my day in prayer for the sick and hurting kids and parents. There, surrounded by soap, antiseptic, and paper towels, I prayed fervently, asking God to give Loren a chance to know what it was like to live outside a hospital, free of pain and with her parents who could hold her and love her.

I was there for Loren's arrival at the open heart recovery room, where tubes and wires covered her body. She was barely visible through the doctors and nurses surrounding her, but I saw a heart-beat on the monitor. She was still alive.

The surgical nurse reported that when Baby Loren was taken off the heart-lung bypass machine, she had no blood pressure. Then, remarkably, as the last sutures were placed, her blood pressure slowly rose to an acceptable range. Her heart started beating on its own. The rhythm was a normal regular rhythm, no racing.

The chief surgeon walked into the recovery room at that moment and called every nurse and doctor over to Loren's bedside. "I want you all to see a miracle right here. This child should not be alive. Someone was watching over her."

As the days passed, Baby Loren got stronger and began acting like a normal baby. After one month in our hospital, Loren's parents came to take her home. It was joyous to see Loren being held and hugged by her mother and father after almost three months of living with tubes, lines and wires.

When I watched them leave the hospital, it occurred to me that God had answered my bathroom prayer exactly as I had asked. Baby Loren was going home to live. She was free of pain, and carried by her parents who loved her.

~Kim D. Armstrong

Weekend Miracle

Heal me, O Lord, and I will be healed;
save me and I will be saved, for you are the one I praise.
~Jeremiah 17:13-15

That Friday morning my husband Louis and I were in the doctor's office, waiting to see him. The doctor had repaired a huge tear in Louis's retina and for several visits now no scar tissue had formed to heal that repair. We were worried because Louis's father had become blind from exactly that same problem.

"Don't worry," I tried to reassure Louis. "By now some scar tissue will have formed."

I was wrong. A few minutes later, the doctor looked into Louis's eye and said, "I must schedule surgery for you on Monday and go into that eye again." He shook his head. "I hate to do that but I've waited as long as I dare for scar tissue to form and none has. Instead, the repair is starting to unzip."

He took a deep breath. "I'd like you to continue to eat meals high in protein and to get as much sleep as possible this weekend. I doubt the eye can lay down enough scar tissue in a weekend when it hasn't up to now. Come in at 9:00 Monday morning and I'll give it a last look before surgery. When surgery is needed a second time on the same retina repair, even when everything goes perfectly, sometimes it results in a considerable loss of vision."

I saw Louis's shoulders tighten.

On the way home, he decided to call members of the adult

Sunday school class he taught and ask them to pray that the eye would show the needed scarring by Monday.

Then he said to me, "You know, for the first time in my life, I'd like to have a laying-on of hands over that eye but I know that our church and pastor have never been involved in faith healing."

"But Pastor would lay-on hands if you asked him, dear," I said.

"True," Louis said. "He's so considerate he wouldn't turn me down, but I wouldn't want him to maybe feel pressured that way."

When we reached home, we knelt bedside and we prayed earnestly to God for a miraculous healing of the eye. I asked also that Louis be able to sleep in spite of the uncomfortable position he needed to stay in to facilitate the healing.

"I'll call the Sunday school class president to pass on the word for prayer as soon as I change into pajamas," Louis said.

But the phone rang before Louis was in his pajamas. It was Robbie from the Sunday school class. "I have half a beef roast left from company last night and wondered if you could use it. If so, I'll bring it over," she said. "Alone, I'll never eat it all."

How did she know Louis needed protein?

Robbie had scarcely hung up when the doorbell rang. I opened the front door to Red and Lucy from the Sunday school class. "But we haven't called anyone from class yet," I thought.

Red said, "I was packing for a business trip and the thought just came to me to come see Louis, so I told Lucy and here we are. What's up?"

Robbie arrived with the roast just as Pastor and his wife drove up. "We were overcome with a strong feeling that Louis needed us," Pastor said.

After Louis and I explained his situation to all five arrivals, Pastor said, "Let's hold hands around the head of the bed, surrounding Louis with love, and ask for scar tissue to form abundantly on that retina repair."

All eyes closed. Pastor led us in a wonderful prayer, with each of us contributing and Pastor ending the prayer. I came close to asking him to lay-on hands but I didn't go against Louis's decision.

While Robbie sliced and heated the roast for Louis's sandwich, I walked the Pastor and his wife to their car. I thanked him for the great prayer and confessed that I almost asked him to lay-on hands.

He jumped back and looked at me with delighted surprise. "How amazing! Because I did lay-on hands over Louis's eye! I just had the strongest desire to, so I dropped Louis's hand and cupped my hands over his eye as we prayed. It was a great feeling."

I hurried back inside to Louis. Tears of joy shown in his eyes as he told me, "Pastor did lay-on hands over my eye. I want you to know that I will not feel one less whit joyful than I do now that I asked for healing, whether healing results or not."

That wonderful series of mysterious blessings that started with Robbie's phone call did not end there. The rest of that weekend, Louis peacefully "fell into a deep sleep" that the Bible mentions several times, even though he was lying in the awkward position that was required after the surgery. From Friday noon until Monday morning he awoke only when I carried meals to him. As my feet walked across the threshold of the bedroom, he awoke and sat up. He used the warm washcloth I'd brought, then took the plate of food, heavy with protein, ate and went right back to sleep.

Monday morning our wonderful doctor said, "Now, I know scar tissue can't have formed over the weekend, but I can't help looking, so let's see." He bent his head close to Louis, looking into is eye.

The doctor straightened up, looked again and shouted to his nurse in the next room, "Cancel the surgery! It's a miracle! We've got lots and lots of beautiful scar tissue!"

~Jeanne Hill

19

The Empty Room

By faith in the name of Jesus, this man whom you see and know was made strong. It is Jesus' name and the faith that comes through him that has given this complete healing to him, as you can all see.
~Acts 3:15-17

On a Friday morning in July, we arrived unexpectedly at my father's house in Browerville, Minnesota. I told Dad that our eighteen-year-old son, Vaughn, had decided to stay home with friends and work instead of attending the family reunion.

The phone rang.

I explained why we'd come to Dad's rather than keeping our original plan. On the trip from Fort Collins, Colorado, our twenty-eight-foot motor home overheated every time we drove over fifty miles per hour. It would die and not start again until it cooled off. We'd dropped my aging mother-in-law in a nearby town at her brother's. By the time we arrived at our hosts, they weren't home so we'd come to Dad's.

The phone rang again.

Dad answered it. "It's a miracle you found them. I didn't expect them to come here today." He handed the phone to me.

My daughter, a student at the University of Northern Colorado in Greeley, was sobbing. "Mom, the hospital called me. Vaughn's been in a serious motorcycle accident. He is in emergency surgery now and the insurance company says I have to get your permission to sign all the papers. And he needs more surgeries!"

I fell into the nearest chair. "Wait a minute. What accident? What surgeries?"

"He rode his motorcycle up the canyon to Estes Park for breakfast. On the way down the mountains, he hit gravel and careened off a bridge. He's in emergency surgery now and will need lots more."

We hadn't thought twice about leaving Vaughn at home. After all, he was a very responsible high school senior.

"It's bad. You need to come home," pleaded my daughter.

"We're on our way." Shaking, I hung up. I wiped tears from my face as I relayed her message to her father. Then I began to pray.

Gordon's clock-like mind ticked off everything we needed to do… call the hospital, pack, pick up Mom… FAST!

But neither Mom nor her brother answered the door. How we guessed the right restaurant on the first try and found them, I'll never know.

With the bulk of the drive at night, we avoided the mobile home overheating. I called the hospital each time we filled up with gas. "He's still in surgery."

Next they said, "He's listed in critical condition."

One hundred miles from home, the motor home sputtered and slowed. "I've never run out of gas… until now." Gordon pounded his palm on the steering wheel and pulled to the shoulder.

No sooner had we stopped than a knock came on the driver's side window. "Do you need help?" a stranger asked. He drove Gordon to a gas station and back.

Gordon was surprised. "The attendant loaned me a can, filled it with gas and told me to pay when I come back."

Miraculously, the motor home started. From the gas station, I called the hospital again. "He's still critical." I closed the door to the motor home's bedroom, knelt and continued my prayers.

We pulled into the Fort Collins hospital parking lot Saturday afternoon around one o'clock and waded through a crowd of high school students to Vaughn's room.

The doctor explained, "We removed his spleen, mended a broken femur and repaired other organs." They'd also wrapped his broken ribs, cleaned his own blood and given it back to him in addition to eight donated pints. "We're giving him every medication we know to help him live."

Vaughn woke up and was obviously glad to see us. Then he said, "Mom, feel my stomach." His bloated, hard-as-a-rock abdomen alerted us to more problems.

Within minutes, doctors hurried into the room. "Vaughn needs more surgery. Now! He's literally bleeding to death inside." They whisked him away.

After surgery, Vaughn lay in a coma. "The meds don't seem to be working," said the doctor. "If he doesn't make a turnaround during the night, I'm afraid there is little hope."

Gordon and I sat by the bed with Michael, Vaughn's "blood brother." Gordon nodded off. I tapped his shoulder. "Why don't you go home and get some rest? Michael and I will stay."

Gordon hugged me goodbye and promised to relieve me later.

Around wires and tubes, I kissed my son's forehead and prayed harder than ever before in my life.

At two or three in the morning, I felt suffocated in the dim, stark room full of beeping monitors. Before he'd left, my priest said, "I keep Hosts in the chapel." As a Eucharistic minister, I knew the protocol. I hurried to the chapel, found the Hosts and cradled one in my palm.

Back in Vaughn's room, I told Michael, "The doctors have done all they can. The rest is up to God."

Trusting the miracle of the Eucharist, I broke the Host into three pieces. One piece I placed on my comatose son's tongue. I gave the second to Michael. The last I placed in my mouth and prayed. "Dear God, will You heal Vaughn because the doctors can't? Please take over so we can have our son back."

Then, having done all we could, Michael and I went home. I told Gordon what I'd done. He showered and left for the hospital to replace me.

I'd barely changed my clothes when he called. "Hurry. Come back."

I imagined the worst.

Gordon said, "When I walked into Vaughn's room, it was empty, the bed half stripped."

I fell into a chair; sobs choked me.

"I panicked," he said. "I believed our Vaughn had died."

I gripped the phone with both hands. "Believed?"

Gordon answered, "A scream rose in my throat and I fell to my knees. Finally, I left the room. That's when I saw the miracle."

"What miracle?" I stammered.

"Outside the empty room, I saw Vaughn pushing his IV stand down the hall. He wasn't connected to any monitors. A nurse walked beside him. She said she wished they'd videotaped his rapid recovery because they can't explain it."

I can.

~Elaine Hanson as told to Linda Osmundson

Reprinted by permission of
Steve Barr ©2010.

20

Trapped Beneath a Tombstone

"But I will restore you to health and heal your wounds,"
declares the Lord...
~Jeremiah 30:16

"Mama!" my six-year-old daughter Blake's scream shattered the tranquility of the March afternoon.

Somehow I knew that this was not one of her come-look-what-I-found or let-me-tattle-on-my brother outbursts. Something was wrong. Really wrong. Heart pounding, I bolted toward the corner of the yard where the children had been playing. Nothing could have prepared me for what I saw there.

Our two-year-old son Matthew lay in the damp grass of the small cemetery located at the edge of our property, his body wedged beneath a four-inch-thick tombstone. His head was pinned to the ground by the massive granite slab. He wasn't moving. And he wasn't making a sound.

"Please, God, no," I prayed aloud. "This can't really be happening. Let this be some terrible dream, God. Please!"

"Tim!" I screamed for my husband. "Hurry!"

Tim vaulted the low fence that surrounded the cemetery. Though he's big and strong—6'5" and 250 pounds—it didn't seem possible that one man could possibly budge the enormous grave marker. But with a single adrenaline-powered heave, Tim rolled the tombstone off Matthew. Then he charged toward the house and the telephone.

I scooped my son off the cold ground and cradled his limp body in my arms. His eyes were closed and his breathing was shallow and ragged. Blood trickled from his nose, eyes, and mouth.

"Don't die," I begged, hugging him close. "Please, Matthew, don't die."

That day in March had brought the first warm temperatures of the year and spring fever had hit our family in a big way. I washed windows while the children played outside. Tim declared the afternoon perfect for painting some old wicker furniture. Knowing that wet paint and small children don't mix, I had shooed Blake and Matthew out of temptation's way.

"Is it okay if we play in the cemetery?" Blake had asked. I had nodded consent.

The cemetery had been a source of fascination ever since we'd bought our five-acre piece of rural property a couple of years earlier. Abandoned and overgrown, no one seemed to know who was responsible for maintaining its eighteenth and nineteenth century graves. And so we became its unofficial caretakers. Sometimes we'd walk among the graves, reading the inscriptions on the tombstones. Blake was fascinated by the large number of children's graves.

"Why did so many children die in the olden days?" she asked.

"People didn't have good medical care back then like they do now," I explained.

Those words came back to me now as I held Matthew's frail body in my arms. In a century filled with medical miracles, could doctors fix a little boy whose head had been crushed by a tombstone? And would he even live long enough to make it to the hospital where they could try?

I closed my eyes and once again began to pray. "Please, God, let Matthew live. Don't take my son away."

As I opened my eyes, a strange peace descended upon me. "Have faith. Everything's going to be okay. Matthew is in my hands." Those words filled my heart as I stroked my little boy's soft hair and waited for emergency personnel to arrive. "Have faith."

A Life Flight helicopter touched down just minutes after an ambulance screamed onto our property. "We've got a hot load," the driver shouted to the pilot. "Get him to the hospital as quick as you can."

Hot load? I'd never heard that term before. And yet the words caused no panic in my heart. The peace I'd felt earlier remained. "Matthew is in my hands."

Because we weren't allowed to ride in the helicopter, we jumped into Tim's truck and gunned it for the hospital. But Matthew had already been taken to surgery by the time we arrived. Friends and family gathered in the waiting room. With each tearful hug or handshake, I felt myself grow stronger.

"Matthew's going to be okay," I kept saying. "I know he is."

Five long hours later, Tim and I were allowed into Pediatric Intensive Care. Lying in a stark white crib, immobilized by a neck brace and with tubes connected to various parts of his body, Matthew bore no resemblance to the boisterous child who'd been frolicking in the yard and climbing on gravestones only a few hours earlier.

"He's not going to die. Right, Doc?" Tim stammered. "Tell me my boy's going to be okay."

"We can't know that yet," the doctor answered softly. "It's a wonder he's alive at all. There's some possibility of paralysis. Maybe brain damage. And a strong chance that his hearing or vision will be affected."

The color drained from Tim's face and he collapsed into a chair. I went to him and put my arms around him. "Matthew's going to be fine," I said.

"How can you say that?" he asked, tears streaming down his cheeks. "How do you know?"

"I have it on good authority," I told him. "The ultimate authority."

As He is one hundred percent of the time, that authority proved to be right. Exactly one week after the accident happened, Matthew was discharged from the hospital. He went home with a fractured facial bone, a crushed ear, a broken nose, and a shunt in his lower back to remove fluid from his spine.

"I never expected that baby to make it," one of the Life Flight nurses confessed to me the day we left the hospital. "It's nothing short of a miracle."

Today, Matthew is a happy, healthy teenager. He loves sports and video games and does well in school. The only reminders of his accident are the eyeglasses he wears to protect his "strong" eye and a compromised sense of smell. Though he has no real memory of the accident, he has heard the story re-told so many times that he claims to remember it in great detail.

So what saved Matthew from death that fateful spring afternoon?

Some say it was the fact that the ground was so soft that it gave way just enough under the weight of the tombstone that the child beneath it was not crushed. Others credit our county's 911 location identification system for allowing emergency workers to reach our home so quickly. Still others point to the fact that our yard was large and flat enough for the helicopter to land.

All those factors, no doubt, played a role in Matthew's miracle. But I know what really saved his life that afternoon. Matthew does, too. "Dad lifted the tombstone off me and a helicopter flew me to the hospital so the doctors could operate," he says. "And God saved my life."

"Matthew is in my hands. He's going to be all right," God whispered to me that horrible afternoon. "Have faith. Have faith."

I did. And I still do. Now more than ever.

~Mandy Hastings

21

God's Little Miracle

Jesus said to them, "I did one miracle, and you are all astonished."
~John 7:20-22

My husband and I were expecting our fourth child. I had a normal pregnancy up until about thirty-one weeks when the doctors noticed there was a problem in the baby's growth; he was only in the tenth percentile for his gestational age. Because of this, the doctors began monitoring me more closely, doing non-stress tests and ultrasounds twice a week. At thirty-four weeks, they noticed that I had excessive fluid around the baby, that the baby's limbs were shorter than they should be, and that the baby appeared to have a "double-bubble" stomach. My doctors here in southeastern New Mexico decided to send me to a maternal fetal medicine specialist in Odessa, Texas (about eighty miles away).

In Odessa, the specialist performed another ultrasound. He confirmed the problems that the doctors at home had stated, but he was able to give these problems a name. The "double-bubble" in the baby's stomach was a condition called duodenal atresia, where the tube leading from the stomach to the small intestine is not present or is blocked. Because he wasn't able to pass any of the fluid, the baby's stomach and kidneys were bloated beyond normal. As long as the baby was in the womb, the doctor assured me he was fine and not in any pain, but that he would need surgery to correct the duodenal atresia shortly after birth. Because the baby had this condition, short-ened arms and legs, and the fact that I had so much fluid surrounding him, the doctor also informed me that there was a great possibility that the baby would be born with Down syndrome. Because of all of these complications, he wanted to send me to Dallas (about 400 miles from home) to deliver in order to be close to some of the best NICU departments and pediatric surgeons in the world.

Of course, my husband and I were devastated. We were worried about the life expectancy of our child, and about the things that he might not be able to do if he were born with Down syndrome. However, although we both felt like having a child with Down syndrome would be a challenge, we knew that it would still be rewarding and that we could give him the best life possible. We weren't really upset about Down syndrome; we were terrified of the surgery and the recovery. Plus, we had three school-age children who we would have to leave at home with family while we were away in Dallas.

I had almost a week to get ready to go to Dallas, so I prepared my kids at home and my husband and I tried to prepare ourselves. We called all of our family, and we were put on prayer lists around the country. My husband, children, and I prayed every night at the dinner table like we always did, but we really focused on praying for our unborn baby. I cried often, but I knew God would help us through—he always had before.

We went to Dallas when I was thirty-six weeks pregnant, and met with a maternal fetal medicine specialist and the surgeons at Children's Medical Center. They did another ultrasound and confirmed the previous findings. The day after we arrived, they induced my labor. After three days there was still no baby, not even close. In the meantime, everyone continued to pray for us. We missed our kids, they missed us, and we were worried about the new baby. However, God heard the prayers of our friends and family, and even though the circumstances were trying, God gave us a peace that I cannot explain in words. We just knew everything was going to be okay, and we continued to pray. After the third day of labor, the doctors let me go back to the hotel for the weekend and they said we would try again on Monday. Monday morning we returned to the hospital but I didn't progress, and they finally took the baby by C-section.

My little Jacob Stewart Rich weighed four pounds fourteen ounces, and appeared to be doing well. Almost immediately after birth, we were told that he did not have Down syndrome. That night, the nurses in the NICU gave Jake a bottle, and lo and behold the next morning he pooped! He was never supposed to be able to do that until after surgery because his intestines weren't attached to his stomach. My husband and I had never been happier to see a dirty diaper! They transferred Jake to Children's Medical Center to run tests to see what happened. They ran X-rays, upper GIs, lower GIs, did blood work, you name it. After four days of extensive testing, they finally told us — not only did Jake not have Down syndrome, they could not find any evidence of the duodenal atresia. Our little boy was small but perfectly healthy.

We returned home after spending two weeks in Dallas. All the doctors apologized for their "mistakes," but I told each and every one of them, "I don't believe that the four doctors at home, the doctor in Odessa and the doctor in Dallas all were mistaken — God healed him." I believe that God wasn't finished with Jacob the first day they induced my labor, and that's why I was in labor for three days without moving close to delivery. God was still working on him, healing him, and He wasn't ready for Jacob to be born yet! I know without a doubt that God healed my son, that He heard all of those wonderful people that remembered us in their prayers. I am a firm believer that God makes miracles happen every day, and that He does hear prayers. I feel extremely blessed not only to have a healthy son, but also to have experienced firsthand one of God's miracles.

~Kelly Stewart Rich

A Book of Miracles

Love from Beyond

*And now these three remain: faith, hope and love.
But the greatest of these is love.*

~1 Corinthians 13:12-13

22

From Sarah, With Love

*Ask the Lord your God for a sign, whether in the deepest depths or in the
highest heights.*
~Isaiah 7:11

Every Thanksgiving hundreds of families arrived at the county fairgrounds to pick up free bags of groceries, and all the trimmings for a delicious Thanksgiving feast, provided by area churches. A gift certificate was included for a plump turkey.

Several smiling high school youth handed out cups of delicious soup or hot cocoa, and politely carried the bags of food to the parking lot for those who were wheelchair-bound or weary from life's daily struggles. Children created brightly-colored holiday cards to place inside each bag.

As I watched all these wonderful volunteers, I noticed an elderly woman heading in my direction. Tears streamed down her cheeks. Rushing to her side I gave her a hug, assisting her with the groceries at the same time. "Are you okay?"

"Oh yes. I just need to sit down for a minute."

I helped her onto a bench nearby and sat beside her.

"Something amazing just happened and my knees buckled right under me!"

I waited as the woman regained her composure. "You see, my precious little granddaughter died this past spring. I have been so sad. Sarah was only five years old.

"Every year she made a beautiful Thanksgiving card, placing it in the center of our holiday table. I didn't know how I was going to get through the holidays without somehow knowing Sarah is okay and is with Jesus." She paused, wiping tears from her eyes before continuing. "I asked God to please give me a sign to let me know my sweet granddaughter is with Him." She dabbed more tears with her handkerchief. "Just a few minutes ago, a kind young man handed me my bag of food. He told me that someone special made me a card that I'd find in my grocery bag."

I nodded, smiling brightly. "Oh yes, aren't they beautiful? The children from area churches made hundreds of cards for our Thanksgiving bags."

Trembling, she clutched my hand. "But you don't understand. My granddaughter's favorite thing in the world to draw was a rainbow. And that's not all. Please, take a look at this card."

It was my turn to cry, as I glanced down at a perfect rainbow painted across a clear blue sky. Underneath were the words,

"Jesus loves you, and so do I... Love, Sarah."

~Mary Z. Smith

23

Roses for Wendy

So they asked him, "What miraculous sign then will you give
that we may see it and believe you?
What will you do?"
~John 6:30

I lost both of my parents in a tragic car accident when I was five. Fortunately, at that age a child doesn't comprehend the finality of such an event.

Many years later, at age twenty-three, I was planning my wedding to Shelly (actually Sheldon), a wonderful twenty-eight-year-old who came from a complete loving family, the type I envied. Shelly and I had already purchased our first home with a spacious, beautifully landscaped yard and patio, perfect for an outdoor celebration. As the date grew closer and we took ownership of the home, we began to clean, arrange, trim, and discard inside and out. However, neither of us had any expertise in landscaping. We only knew how to cut grass, so we learned pruning, trimming, and plant care.

The day before our wedding we were putting the final touches on the yard. Flowers had been planted, the grass cut, and the hedges trimmed. We were so pleased with the neatness of it all. But one plant perplexed us. A rosebush located just outside our front door, obviously carefully chosen for such a place of prominence, was completely barren of leaves or buds. It looked like it might be dead, but since neither of us could be sure, we reluctantly decided to keep it for the time being.

That same evening, after the traditional rehearsal and subsequent dinner, I was too excited to sleep. Instead I decided I needed some quiet time to reflect on the next day. I got up and retreated to the backyard and sat in the warm, clear, star-filled night. It was there I realized the only thing missing from my wedding day would be my parents. There had been no time to think of this up until now and the thought filled me with sadness. After all, every girl dreams of having her father walk her down the aisle and her mother there to comfort her nerves. Overcome with emotion and alone in the yard, I began speaking to my mom and dad, just as if I knew they were listening. I asked them for a sign, something I had never asked from them before, but now felt compelled to do.

"Give me a sign on my wedding day to let me know you're with me."

The next day Shelly's excited voice repeatedly called my name. I rushed to join him at the front door.

"I can't believe what I'm about to show you!"

He stood aside. The barren rosebush had two huge roses in full bloom.

There was no doubt in my mind we were witnessing a miracle… a miracle of love.

~Wendy Delaney

24

Chain of Love

Show me your ways, O Lord, teach me your paths
~Psalm 25:3

I have always believed in God and prayer and when people said God talked to them, I never doubted them, but I wondered what it was like. What type of voice is heard? Why didn't God talk to me? Maybe some people were more blessed than others.

Then something happened to me a few years ago as I was praying for my granddaughter. At first, I thought I was losing my mind.

My son Leo and daughter-in-law Celeste had a beautiful child they named Felicia. After a few years, they divorced and my son received custody of his daughter, but Celeste stayed close to her too.

When Felicia was nine years old, her mom went to South Carolina to visit friends. Celeste called Felicia to say she would be home in a few days and that she was mailing Felicia a key chain with her name on it.

But Celeste didn't come home.

Celeste's mother had been receiving calls from Celeste every day, but the calls stopped. Her mom became very concerned and called several state police stations, but no one had any information. A couple of days later, a state trooper from North Carolina called, asking if Celeste had any identifying marks on her body. Her mom described a flower tattoo on Celeste's wrist and a butterfly on her ankle. The trooper delivered the heartbreaking news. Celeste's body had been found in a field on the side of the highway. She'd been murdered and left there for three days.

Poor Felicia went through all the emotions no child should have to endure. I visited in her bedroom where she was sitting quietly on the floor. I sat down on the floor too and we began to talk. Felicia mentioned that the last time she had talked to her mom on the phone, she sounded happy that she was on her way home and would see her in a few days. Through tears Felicia recalled her mom telling her that she was mailing a key chain with her name on it. But Felicia never received it.

A few days later I left work to visit Leo and Felicia again. I drove, continuously praying for Celeste's family, but mostly for my grand-daughter. As I got off the exit to my son's house, I heard a voice... not of human nature, neither male nor female... telling me, "Get a key chain for Felicia."

"What?"

"Get a key chain for Felicia."

I was so confused. Where would I even begin to look?

Again, "Get a key chain for Felicia."

By this time I started to cry out loud, "Where God, where?"

I was close to my son's driveway when I heard the voice say, "Follow and you will see."

I was told to get on the turnpike, and through my tears, I obeyed. I was told which exit to get off and I did. I was told to turn into the mall, where to park and where to walk. As I passed several stores, I was told to turn left and to enter the next store. The next store, I realized, sold costume jewelry for young girls. I walked in, looked around and did not see anything like a key chain.

I looked at the cashier. "You don't have any key chains in here, do you?"

She said, "Yes, right there," and pointed to an entire round rack of key chains of all types, shapes and colors. Now I was really con-fused. Which one should I pick? I was told, "Get the blue one that has the word ANGEL on it."

I questioned, "Why this one? Why one that says ANGEL?"

Obediently, I took it to the cashier and was surprised that it only cost a couple of dollars.

With the key chain in hand, I got into my car and headed back to my son's. I parked in his driveway and I heard the words, "Write on the back of the key chain."

"With what?" I wondered. I started looking in my glove box for a permanent marker. But, I heard "Use a pen."

I grabbed a pen from my purse and was told to write on the back and what to write.

The metal was soft enough to engrave. I was shocked when I found myself writing, "To Felicia. Be Good. Mom."

Then I went into the house.

My son was in the living room. I asked, "Where's Felicia?"

My heart was pounding with excitement as I held the key chain behind my back. Leo wanted to know what was going on. I told him I needed to see Felicia and I winked. He called for my granddaughter and she rushed out yelling "Grandma!" and hugged me.

I told her, "I have something for you that is very important."

She just stared at me with no expression and asked, "What?"

I reminded her about her last conversation with her mom and about the key chain. I said, "I think I found it."

"Where?" she asked, clearly confused.

"It doesn't matter where, I was just told to get it."

I handed her the key chain and she started to cry. She showed it to her dad.

I said, "I don't know why it says ANGEL on it. Didn't your mom say it had your name on it?"

Leo said, "Oh dear God, Mom. When Felicia was born, Celeste wanted to name her Angel, but I talked her out of it."

That's when I started to cry. I knew the Holy Spirit spoke to me to deliver Felicia's key chain from her mom.

~Paula J. Coté

25

Luke 16

And he began to say to them, "Today this scripture is fulfilled in your hearing."
~Luke 4:21

As I sat in the pew, listening to the pastor became increasingly difficult. I continued to push back scenes from that horrible day as I prayed for God to help me listen to the message.

It had only been a few weeks since the accident and, honestly, I was exhausted. I tried to focus, but flashes from that day kept pressing in, when Max, my husband of just two years, was killed in a car accident. I didn't understand why God had allowed it, but I knew He was still in control.

I continued to try to listen as I held my ten-month-old sleeping daughter, Breeanna, and prayed for peace from the terrible memories.

As I sat praying, those memories were replaced with a nudging to open my Bible to the sixteenth chapter of the book of Luke. I wasn't sure what I would find "new" in the book of Luke as I had read it many times.

Nevertheless, I decided there must be something that God wanted me to see at that moment so I flipped through the pages to the book of Luke.

I cried and laughed when in the right margin beside Luke 16, in my husband's handwriting were the words, "I Love You! Max."

~Lisa Jo Cox

Reprinted by permission of
Steve Barr ©2010.

26

Graveyard Spirits

He will yet fill your mouth with laughter
and your lips with shouts of joy.
~Job 8:20-22

It had been over a year since I'd been to the Ten Mile countryside cemetery. I used to visit once a week but as time had passed and my heartache lessened, so did my visits. As I stepped out of the car, the hot summer sun blazed against the nape of my neck. In the distance I could hear a lawnmower and I smelled the fresh-cut grass. Across the road a few straggling cows halted their lumbering march towards the feeding trough to stare at me. I stared back until the smell of cow dung assaulted my nose, then I turned and continued on through the front gate and into the well-manicured graveyard.

A strange mixture of emotions churned inside me. Since it had been so long since I'd been here, a part of me was excited to say hello to my old friends, while the other part remembered the grief that I'd carried so heavily for so long. But I was there to pay my respects, so I swallowed hard and marched on, one foot in front of the other, towards the three graves that I used to visit so often.

That's when I spotted the sprinkler. A very large, farm-like sprinkler stood four feet tall, rotating in a circular motion to water the cemetery. Round and round it went, shooting long, straight, ten-foot shots of water every thirty seconds or so. It looked awfully close to where I was headed so I stopped and stood watching to see just how far it shot and just how close it sprayed to where I was going. I watched it go round four to five times before determining I would be safe. Its spray could not reach me at the three gravesites.

As I stepped forward I unconsciously found myself following my old routine. I always started at my boyfriend Shannon's grave, then took two steps to the right to his mother Becky's, then lastly, three steps back to his grandmother "Nanny's" grave. At Shannon's I started with my usual greeting—"Hello baby. How ya doin' up there? It's a really beautiful day down here today,"—and whatever other small talk I could think of to delay, for just a few more seconds, what I knew was coming… that same old, familiar, sadness. I lowered my head as I felt it rising up towards my chest and that second it happened. BAM! I was shot with a blast of water from the sprinkler. Yes, that very same sprinkler that I had just watched go round and round shooting short of my spot every time.

I shouldn't have been surprised really. Shannon had always been a comical person so he would do something like that. But he was dead after all. When he was alive though, he could make people laugh no matter where we were. He could even make perfect strangers laugh, and did so with ease. He could have the person at the other end of the drive-thru speaker laughing while ordering fast food, or people in line at the grocery store, bank, video store, anywhere. In a matter of minutes he'd have the clerk busted up laughing.

I remember one night he decided to go down to the neighborhood tavern in his bathrobe and slippers just for fun. Well, as usual, everybody there loved it and at two in the morning he paraded home with half a dozen people following him from the bar. They danced, laughed and sang for hours!

He was twenty-three when I was eighteen. He was my first true love. We planned to be married and start a family—the whole nine yards. So naturally I was devastated when the state trooper came to my door and told me he'd been in a fatal accident. Even more devastated were his uncles and his very dear Nanny. They shared a very special bond since both Shannon's mother and father had died before he was nineteen. It was so hard on Nanny that she died three months after Shannon.

So at the age of eighteen I began this routine, one that hopefully not too many eighteen-year-olds have… once a week I went to the Ten Mile countryside cemetery and visited my three friends. I always walked in with churning emotions. I always went to Shannon's grave first. I always started with a short greeting, always lowering my head as I felt the sadness well up inside me. Then I moved on to his mother and grandmother's graves.

But never, ever, on any such occasion had something like this happened to me.

I was a bit startled at first, thinking that it must have been some kind of fluke. So I stayed exactly where I was, not moving an inch, and turned towards the sprinkler to watch it go around. It didn't hit or even come close to me again. After a minute or so, I turned back to Shannon with another short greeting, and lowered my head as the sadness filled my heart. BAM! I was shot with water again. Mopping my wet face, I looked up and watched the offending sprinkler go around without a hit. I shook my head in disbelief and stepped to the right to Shannon's mother's grave.

I stood for a moment, watching the sprinkler go around, spraying far away from me, then said, "Hello Becky." As I lowered my head, the sadness began to fill me and would you believe it? BAM! Wet again!

This time I chuckled to myself, wondering how in the world this was happening. I scanned the entire graveyard trying to see who could be doing this to me. A real practical joker this must be, picking on a grieving person. Who could do something like this? But there was no one else around. Just me, the cows across the road and that darn sprinkler!

I still had one last grave to visit, directly behind Shannon's. I shook my head and chuckled my way back there, watching the sprinkler go round far from me. I said my hello, then lowered my head and… BAM! Soaked again!

Exasperated, I threw my hands into the air and yelled, "Well, I guess you guys don't want me to be sad today!" I laughed and giggled and shook my head as I walked right past the sprinkler, without getting hit, right out of the cemetery and had myself a fantastic rest of the summer day.

Now when I visit the cemetery I come not with sadness but with gratitude for having loved such a wonderful family.

~Bobbie Clemons-Demuth

27

A Golden Gift

Isaiah answered, "This is the Lord's sign to you
that the Lord will do what he has promised."
~2 Kings 20:9

W hile my husband Doug and I were vacationing at a time-share resort in Alabama one summer, the chlorine in the pool sent us shopping for protective swim goggles. Fortunately, there was a small sporting goods store at a little strip mall ten miles away. Luckily, they had two pair, one for each of us. As we were leaving the store, I felt compelled to go into a little jewelry store at the other end of the mall.

It was highly unlikely for me to be drawn to that type of store because I hadn't shopped in a real jewelry store since the long ago day we had purchased our wedding rings. Doug urged me to follow my whimsical impulse. It was totally out of character for him to want to shop, or to want me to shop. But, since we were on vacation, had no time constraints, and were on an adventure, we lightheartedly headed for the jewelry store.

Upon entering the quaint little shop, I was immediately attracted to a rotating display case that held gold earrings. I certainly didn't need another pair of earrings. I couldn't believe how I instantly spotted an adorable pair shaped like dolphins swimming in a circle. I smiled fondly remembering how our son Jay was always fascinated with dolphins, from the time he was a little boy to manhood. Sadness welled up in me as I contemplated the approaching anniversary of our beloved Jay's death.

"Why would a store hundreds of miles from an ocean carry a pair of dolphin earrings?" I wondered out loud to Doug. Seemed like serendipity to me, so I rationalized why I wanted the dolphin earrings; they would be a fond reminder of Jay, or possibly a birthday present to myself. Maybe the earrings could be considered a reward for all the hard work I had been doing in physical therapy to recover from my recent serious back surgery. If those weren't good enough reasons, I would simply purchase them as a vacation souvenir.

When the clerk showed us the pricey sales ticket, I quickly returned the unreasonably expensive gold dolphin earrings to the showcase and put the thought of purchasing them out of my mind. Doug was relieved.

Our mood returned to "we're on vacation" and we realized we were wasting daylight and swimming time. We headed back to the pool to put our new goggles to good use.

A vigorous workout provided us with a peaceful rest that night. I was slowly awakening at dusk, in a blissful state of semi-consciousness, startled by a voice. It was a familiar voice that sounded like Jay. I strained my eyes, but couldn't see where the voice was coming from.

"How ya' doing, Mom?" The unmistakable greeting shocked me; that was the way Jay always greeted me when he came home for a visit. "I want you to know I'm really happy here," the voice continued. "I want you to buy the dolphin earrings for your birthday."

Jay's voice persisted. "Use the money in my wallet in my briefcase behind the boxes in the workroom closet. Then, when you wear the dolphin earrings, you will be happy like I am."

The voice was gone as suddenly as it had come. I felt disconcerted, confused, yet warmed by what had just transpired.

I was reluctant to tell Doug about this extraordinary encounter because I wasn't quite sure myself what had happened. It was so precious, yet too unbelievable to share.

I reasoned that he would attribute it to my understandable stress at this time of year. I made the firm decision not to tell him, and felt relieved.

And then, before I knew it, the tale of the unusual experience poured forth uncontrollably. Taken aback by the outpouring and obviously skeptical of my story, Doug carefully assessed the situation with his trained legal mind and asked me very specific probing questions.

Satisfied that something miraculous had occurred, he calmly and assuredly said, "God often does amazing things in the lives of faithful followers to show them His love."

My levelheaded hubby reflected that the mysterious event might have been the delivery of a special love note from God and Jay.

Unbeknownst to me, Doug said he'd hidden Jay's briefcase in the back of the closet soon after his death eight years ago, without looking inside it. Doug reminded me that at the time of Jay's death, I was too inconsolable to deal with his belongings, so he put Jay's property out of sight. The briefcase had long since been forgotten.

Then, my usually frugal hubby suggested an extravagant plan. He wanted us to go back to the jewelry store and purchase the dolphin earrings with the understanding that if there were any money in Jay's wallet, it would help offset the cost of the purchase. I felt loved and warmed by Doug's thoughtful gesture.

That afternoon, the day before the anniversary of Jay's death, we returned to the little strip mall jewelry store and made our golden purchase. Surprisingly, the next day, as I wore the beautiful earrings, I realized that for the first time in eight years I actually felt warmed, peaceful and happy on the anniversary date of Jay's drowning.

When we returned to San Diego after our restful vacation, Doug and I headed straight for the workroom closet. There, behind some dusty old boxes, was the briefcase. We cautiously opened it together. Jay's battered brown leather wallet was in there, inviting our visit. We opened the cash compartment and removed the money.

I held my breath as Doug counted out the bills.

The total of the cash equaled the exact purchase price of the shiny gold dolphin earrings! Instant tears of gratitude stung my eyes for my miraculous posthumous birthday gift from my son.

~BJ Jensen

28

George

As a fair exchange — I speak as to my children —
open wide your hearts also.
~2 Corinthians 6: 13

I couldn't take my eyes off the wriggling new baby cradled in her mother's arms. She was so tiny, enveloped in blankets and diapers, her dark eyes sparkling brilliantly as if an irrepressible light burned there. Nestled in the hospital bed, the mother and child looked so clearly joined to each other. Could the baby and I make the same connection?

I felt uneasy. If only George were here. He'd be sitting in a chair, puffing away on his favorite pipe. As much as I didn't enjoy smoke, the aroma of his cherry tobacco always calmed me. Adopting a child was a huge step in a life full of strange twists and turns. If my mentor George were here, he'd back me up and I'd know for certain that this adoption was finally the right one. As if reading my thoughts, the birth mother, Kelly, extended the baby. "You'll make a great mom," she said. I folded little Mariah into my arms.

Seven years ago, the idea of hugging my own newborn was nothing but a cruel dream. I yearned for a family, but marriage eluded me. At age forty, I started the long adoption process, only to be thwarted for different reasons ten separate times. I wanted to give up, but George insisted the adoption was what I needed to do. I needed to keep pushing, he said. This eleventh time, I spent hours speaking with the mother and father, an unmarried couple in Las

Vegas—she still in love with him, he in love with someone else. At the end of their visit to my home, Kelly offered the gift for which I'd so longed. "I'm sure I've made the right decision," she said, gazing out the window where a forest screened mountain and lake views. "This is a great place for a child to grow up. I could never give her this."

Now, with visiting hours ending, I reluctantly handed Mariah to Kelly and watched as she rocked her child to sleep. Then the doubts crept in. Kelly had seventy-two hours to change her mind. My visitation hours were limited, and Kelly had oodles of time with Mariah when I wasn't around. For me, the waiting period would be agony.

Three days later, as the clock ticked off the final minutes, a social worker arrived and asked to speak privately with Kelly and the birth father. As I stood outside the closed door nervously toying with my pen, George surfaced in my mind again. My parents didn't support the adoption—my mother insisted I was too old for it. It was George I needed, my dearest friend. Just a year and a half ago, he'd calmed my worries that the adoption would never happen. "Be patient and you'll get her," he'd said. "When you do, I'll be there." He was like a sage, a man of wisdom, always puffing on his pipe, his clear eyes shining with insight. Neither of us guessed his promise might be broken, but to my horror, a few weeks later, he suddenly died of cancer.

When he was gone, I had no one to tell my dreams to. George was more than just an average friend. He was a father figure, my mentor, even my wise man. He always gave me hope. We met in 1970 after I won the Miss Hawaii contest. In the lobby afterward, he approached me and said, "You deserved to win." How did he know that? It was my fifth time running. I'd tried again and again, but this last time, after hard work and with lots of determination, I had succeeded.

George asked me to meet him the next day. We became immediate friends. During our conversation he shared incredible insights that changed my life. He said life holds more possibilities than we can ever, ever imagine. We can achieve our dreams if we focus on success and have self-confidence.

George intrigued me. He lived in Oklahoma and I lived in California, but that didn't stop us from phoning or having an occasional meal together. He helped me to find my way in difficult times. After I survived a traumatic fiery DC-10 crash, George was my lifeline, talking to me on the phone, helping me to understand just what had happened to me. Months after the crash, on his advice I faced down many fears and testified in court about airline regulations. My testimony led to changes in airline safety procedures. Later, George encouraged me to start my own business. When I broke up with a man I'd dated for years, and then determined it was too late to have a child, it was George who encouraged me to adopt.

During the twenty-three years I knew George, we developed lots of jokes and jibes, but what I looked forward to most were the snippets of wisdom I called Georgisms. Always, before delivering a Georgism, George would sit back, puff his pipe, and think. George and that burnt-cherry aroma were inseparable. Now I was alone. I was scared to death.

The social worker emerged from Kelly's room. "We can proceed," she said. Her words squeezed the breath out of me. "You and Kelly go down to the nursery and bring the baby back into this room."

Kelly signed Mariah out of the nursery, and together we wheeled the bassinet toward the room where we would sign the adoption papers. Walking on eggshells was an understatement. I feared that Kelly might have a million conflicting emotions. What if she changed her mind in these last minutes? But I already considered this baby mine, my Mariah, so tiny in this bassinet, one little being engulfed in a world of pink blankets and the swirling desires of people around her. I giggled as her little fists punched the empty air. "A pistol," George had predicted. He was right; I'd be adopting a pistol of a child. If everything went well… if Kelly signed…

Suddenly Kelly stopped. Oh, no, I thought. She's changing her mind. Tears welled in my eyes.

Frowning, Kelly sniffed and said, "Someone's smoking. It's a strange smell, a cherry tobacco smell." Then she noticed my tears and tenderly handed her baby to me.

I inhaled, smelling burnt cherry.

I kissed my baby. "Mariah, our friend George is here, just like he promised."

~Donna Hartley

29

Snapshot from the Other Side

*And again, "I will put my trust in him." And again he says,
"Here am I, and the children God has given me."*
~Hebrews 2:13

My granddaddy came to see me the night before my mama died. I was so happy to see him that I gushed like the pump in the yard of the tenant house where he lived in Georgia when I was a little girl. It had been years since I had seen my granddaddy, not since his funeral.

"Granddaddy, what a surprise!" I called out to him. "Where have you been? You must be doing well; you look great!" He looked rested, relaxed, and young. "I'm so glad to see you. I can't believe it's you. Is it really you?" I prattled on.

Granddaddy beamed as though he couldn't smile big enough. I sensed his presence, as if I were standing next to a warm heater on a cold day. He hugged me close, and I felt sheltered in his loving arms.

"Granddaddy, why are you here? You've been gone so long."

"I wanted to tell you that everything is going to be all right," he said.

"Of course, it is," I agreed, always the eternal optimist. "Everything's great, even better now that you're here."

He glowed with delight. "It's going to be okay," he soothed.

"Everything's going to be okay." Over and over he assured me while he petted me like a child. "Everything's going to be all right. You're strong," he insisted. "You can handle this, and I'll be here with you. You're a strong woman."

I was so happy to see him that I didn't ask what he was talking about. Still smiling blissfully, he said, "We'll all be here with you."

I suddenly realized that my granddaddy was not alone. My grandmother, who died when my mother was seven years old, was with him. My daddy, who had been dead for eleven years, was there. Sick when he died of cancer, he now looked young and healthy. My great-aunt and uncle and other aunts, uncles, cousins, and people familiar and unfamiliar were crowded around. All were joyous and wearing idyllic smiles of eternal blessedness.

As my eyes scanned the relatives who crowded around my granddaddy as though they were having a snapshot made at a family reunion, I saw my mama on the edge of the crowd. I woke up instantly and looked at the clock. It was 2 a.m. I felt wonderful, totally wrapped in love and extremely blessed that my granddaddy had paid me a visit. I did not allow myself to question, nor did it register, that everyone in my dream was dead, except my mama.

I later learned that at the same time that my granddaddy came to see me in Murfreesboro, Tennessee, my mama, who lived on an Alabama mountaintop and had no apparent health problems, sat up in bed, turned on the light, and insisted on planning her funeral. Though Ben, her husband, objected and grumbled that he didn't want to talk about it, especially in the middle of the night, she was adamant that he listen to what she wanted done upon her death.

She told him where she wanted to be buried, what she wanted to wear, who she wanted to speak, the songs she wanted sung, and those she wanted notified. She even made him promise to put hay bales around her grave so that her funeral would be like a family reunion and everyone could sit and talk and laugh and visit with one another. She cautioned him not to waste a lot of money on flowers.

When she was sure that Ben understood her wishes, they lay down to sleep.

When my brother Ronnie called later that day to tell me that our mama had dropped dead of a massive heart attack while frying cabbage and making cornbread, I suddenly realized that the dream had been a premonition. "I know," I said, when he shared the shocking news. "Granddaddy was here. He told me."

I knew her spirit had been whisked away for a family portrait to be sent to me in a dream, then returned for a few hours until the exact time of her departure.

I knew why my granddaddy had come, why all my relatives had appeared in my dream, why they were so happy. They were anxiously awaiting the arrival of my mama. They were ecstatically looking forward to seeing her again after many years.

My grandparents were going to be reunited with their baby daughter, my grandmother with the child that she left at a young age, my aunt with a sister that she never met on earth, my daddy with his sweetheart of forty-six years. He had loved her since he first saw her playing paper dolls in a dry creek bed when she was a little girl. My mama's people were gathered to joyfully escort her to her heavenly home and celebrate her homecoming.

My relatives wanted me to know that they loved me, and that they were with me, surrounding me, supporting me. They wanted me to know that everything was going to be all right, that they would comfort and console me in my grief.

To this day I have not lost sight of their loving message. Often I replay the video of my dream and gaze upon the family snapshot that my granddaddy sent to me. It brings me comfort to know that someday we will all be reunited, and I too will be included in the picture from the other side.

~Judy Lee Green

30

Love Never Dies

I will declare that your love stands firm forever,
that you established your faithfulness in heaven itself.
~Psalm 89:1-3

My mother had not been feeling well for a couple of days. We all assumed it was the summer flu bug that was going around. Mom insisted she would be fine in a few days. I noticed she started wearing a wristwatch that was in need of repair. The hands were permanently set at 1:00.

"Mom, you have other watches that work. Why are you wearing this one?"

The watch had special sentimental value, she explained. It was the first watch my dad had given her for Christmas the year they were married.

"Let me take it to the jewelers and have them fix it for you."

She declined my offer; the watch remained on her wrist day and night.

Mom still was not feeling well after a week. Dad wanted to take her to the doctor, but she refused.

That evening, while I was preparing for bed, Mom walked into my room to kiss me goodnight. I asked her if she would make my favorite breakfast of waffles in the morning.

"If I'm here, honey," she said.

"Are you going away?"

Chills ran through me as I awaited her answer, but she just smiled and walked out of my bedroom.

I tried to banish all the unsettling thoughts from my mind as I struggled to make sense of what Mom said. I finally dozed off to sleep.

Then I was awakened by a voice. My dad stood there in the darkness. "I think Mom is gone," he said.

"Where did she go?"

"Honey, she died," he replied.

Since I was the oldest, he explained, he didn't want to wake my two younger brothers. He would break the news to them when they woke up.

"This is a dream, right?"

How I wished it were, but I was wide awake.

I looked at the clock on my nightstand. It read 1:00.

Throughout the next week time seemed to stand still as my family grieved. How long before this pain would ease?

Then one evening, a week after Mom's funeral, we were watching TV when we heard the springs squeaking on the sofa. There in Mom's favorite place to sit was an indentation in the seat cushion, as if someone were sitting there. I thought perhaps my mind was playing tricks on me, but my dad and brothers saw it too. Her visit was short, but it offered the reassurance that we needed.

I believe Mom was letting us know that she would always be near, watching over us.

~Terri Ann Meehan

31

Mom's Music

Music is well said to be the speech of angels.
~Thomas Carlyle

Four years ago my sweet mom went to be with her Lord. She did it her way, mind you. She died in her sleep, in her bed, in her own home.

I got the call at work, and I headed home quickly. Home was well north of Toronto, in the snow belt. Mom and Dad lived on a small farm that they had owned since I was seven. It had started out as a weekend place for my dad to "get away from it all." I hated going there every weekend. There was nothing for a young girl to do but watch the one station on the old TV set, if the weather allowed reception.

My mom, on the other hand, loved the peace and quiet of the land and loved to work in the garden among her flowers and vegetables. The place was rustic, with no indoor plumbing or heat. We had a big wood stove in the kitchen that did its best to heat the little farmhouse, but it always seemed cold and too quiet to me.

In the evenings, my mom and I would sit for hours singing in the little kitchen. I sang the melody and Mom harmonized. Her favorite song was "Moon River" and we sang it over and over. Mom told me stories about how when I was a little girl, I could sing before I could talk. She loved to tell how my playpen sat in the kitchen next to the radio and there was one song I particularly loved called "Ivory Tower." Mom would laugh when she told me how I'd get excited whenever the song came on. I knew the melody, but not the words, yet I tried to sing along with it. As an adult, I didn't remember this song, but Mom took great pleasure in reliving that childhood memory over and over again.

As time passed, Mom and Dad renovated that little farmhouse and they went to live there permanently when Dad retired from his job as a butcher. By then I had my own children and went to visit every week or two. The kids loved the farm and the tractor rides with my dad. Me, well, I still hated the silence of the farm. While my mom loved to sit at her kitchen table and look out at her garden and flowers and retell all the old stories, I missed the hustle and bustle of my life at home. But I sat there listening quietly as she reminisced.

After her death, I sat in her chair at the familiar kitchen table, looking out at her garden that was now covered in snow, feeling a terrible ache inside. No matter how old you are, losing your mother is traumatic. Even though I knew she was in heaven, I missed her. I missed her gentle manner and I longed to hear just one more old story. Why hadn't I listened more carefully when she told them over and over? If only I could hear her voice one more time, tell her I loved her and thank her for all my childhood memories.

I sat back in the silence and asked God for a sign that my mom was safe with Him and that I would be all right. The silence was deafening so I finally leaned over to turn on an old radio that sat in the corner of the counter. Music always comforted me.

My heart skipped a beat. "Moon River" was playing on the radio. I sat there stunned, with a tear running down my cheek, as I listened to every last familiar note.

Then the radio announcer of this oldie station came on. "Here's one we haven't heard in a while," and an unfamiliar song began. I began to cry harder as I heard the words sung over the airwaves. "Come down, come down from your Ivory Tower...."

~Yolanda Mortimer

32

Hear the Angels' Voices

Pay attention to your dreams—
God's angels often speak directly to our hearts when we are asleep.
~Quoted in The Angels' Little Instruction Book *by*
Eileen Elias Freeman, 1994

Snow, the kind that is soundless and brings stillness to the crisp air, rarely falls in Southern Nevada. Even though decorations and lights adorn my neighborhood, this year the spirit of Christmas seems to be more than a breath away. The passing of a loved one can do that to a person. Especially when the one departed, my mom, brought the spirit of Christmas alive early every season.

Boxes of decorations stay hidden in the hall closet, way back under the stairs and out of plain sight for when the door is open. Christmas carols play on the car radio and television commercials offer enticing buys, and still the ambiance of the season escapes me.

In late November, I bought a box of Christmas cards, which still sits on my desk next to a book of holiday stamps and return address labels. I glance at them every so often without one ounce of enthusiasm. I know my mom would want the spirit of Christmas to fill our home, for us to sing carols and give praise to our Lord for all He has given us. Knowing this, still the power to embrace the season eludes me.

Yesterday, I heard her angelic voice whisper in my ear, "I am always with you. Rejoice, for you are all blessed." Then her voice faded away before I could capture it in my grieving heart.

Today I wonder if I'm simply wishful, hopeful that she is near and watching over us. If I doubt her presence, then the strength of my faith is questionable. The memory of her beautiful voice singing in the church choir on Christmas Eve resonates. "Ave Maria," her solo, hums through the recesses of my mind and restores my beliefs.

My grandson, Zack, enters the room and stands next to my desk. I look up with questioning eyes. His vibrant green eyes hold my gaze. I sense he's unsure and full of concern.

"What's the matter?" I ask.

"I want to ask you about a dream I had last night. It wasn't bad or anything... I just don't understand."

"Why don't you tell me about it maybe I can help you figure it out."

"I was asleep and the phone rang. When I got up and answered it, the woman asked for you. I recognized her voice, but I was afraid to say anything. She asked, 'Zack?' I said, 'Grammie!' I told her she couldn't be calling because she was in heaven. She said she was so happy there and she had a dog. She could see all of us and a miracle was gonna happen to our family. She promised that we'd always be together and for me not to worry so much. Then I woke up."

My heart flutters. The room goes still.

"So what do you think? Was it really Grammie?" I ask, hoping to encourage him to talk more about his experience.

"Yes, it was."

"She gave you a gift then. You were chosen to tell us her message, maybe so we'll stop crying in her absence. She wants us to be happy, happy as she is in heaven."

"Then I'm glad I had the dream. Grandma?"

"Yes?"

"She's really, really, happy."

"I'm so glad you told me about this."

Zack's eyes mist over and he offers a half grin. He leaves the room and heads back into his bedroom. I glance at the box of Christmas cards: the embossed Virgin Mary holding baby Jesus in her arms, angels in the background looking down on them. The television is on and yet the sound trails off. Above me, from a distant place, I hear a choir of angels humming "Ave Maria." One voice sings louder. Her voice is clear, her words distinct, and offers a tone so familiar and missed. The true meaning of Christmas resurrects in my heart.

I address my Christmas cards and hold my mom's love of this special time of year in my heart. I embrace her memory and all the love she showered upon each and every one of us over the years. I have received the most precious Christmas gift. I am truly blessed and grateful. Come Christmas morning, surrounded by family, I will look upon the tree strung with tiny white lights and know my mom is right beside me.

~Cindy Golchuk

A Book of Miracles

His Messenger

*In the visions I saw while lying in my bed, I looked, and there before me
was a messenger, a holy one, coming down from heaven.*

~Daniel 4:13

It's Okay, Marcia

The Lord bless you and keep you;
the Lord make his face shine upon you and be gracious to you;
the Lord turn his face toward you and give you peace.
~Numbers 6: 24-26

I gazed out the window into a cold, black sky at the blinking red lights on the three distant radio towers as they warned aircraft of their presence. They seemed to me like fireflies signaling distress, and they mirrored the alarm in my soul.

I was eighteen years old and my father had just died from brain cancer. It was the middle of the night and I stood alone in the center of the dark kitchen. A small light over the stove was the only illumination. My mother and sisters slept. I couldn't.

As I stared out the window into the blackness, the woe that consumed me finally crystallized into one overpowering thought: I will never feel safe again.

Why had it happened? The seizure two days before Christmas. The ambulance, the emergency room. The brain scan. "Epilepsy," the doctors said, and they gave him medication. But he didn't get better. Instead, he got worse. He became cross and critical and hard to please. More tests were run and the painful truth emerged: a tumor, probably malignant. Surgery was needed—immediately.

I remember my mom sitting in the hospital room during Dad's recovery my senior year, patiently stitching tiny white sequins on the bodice of the dress she'd made for me to wear to a spring dance.

With each stitch I knew she was saying a prayer, and Daddy did get better. He was even able to come to my graduation in a wheelchair, head swathed in white bandages. For all of us this represented a huge milestone and the hope for better days.

That summer I worked at my first job and prepared to go away to college. Dad regained enough strength to return to work. He still couldn't drive, so Mom chauffeured him all over town as he made his business calls. He'd always been the one in charge. Now he had to wait to be waited on. We all knew that was hard.

The summer passed quickly and at last the day arrived when it was time to pack the car and head up the road to the campus where I would go to school. Just to go to college was a dream come true. But it was hard to leave.

Dad's decline accelerated that fall. The tumor came back. By October he was unable to work. By Christmas he was bedridden. By February he was gone.

Not only did I lose my father, but a big part of my mother left then too. She had been a great full-time mom and he had handled everything else. She had so totally depended on him that, in many ways, once he was gone, she was like a child. Simple decisions were so hard and paying the bills overwhelmed her. Nevertheless, she rose to the occasion and insisted I return to school after the funeral.

As the oldest, I assumed a new sense of responsibility that summer. At times, it seemed almost more than I could bear. How would we manage? One day at a time. That strategy seemed to work well. We pulled together and gradually carved out a survival plan to compensate for the void that overshadowed every part of our lives.

In September I was even able to return to school. It was good to be back among my peers and away from sad reminders. Here I could immerse myself in study, forget the pain, and believe I could control some things in my life—even if it was just academic goals. Surely this was the pathway to financial security. I didn't ever want to feel so helpless again.

So I studied—long and hard. One particular night in mid-

October I had been up late cramming for a French mid-term. At 2 a.m. I woke and realized I had drifted off to sleep in bed, sitting straight up, holding my book on my lap. It was time to call it a night.

As I switched off my overhead lamp, through my dorm window a full moon brilliantly bathed my bed in luminous silvery light. Even the desk was casting bold shadows on the gleaming white tile floor. But groggy as I was, not even daylight could have kept me from the promise of sweet sleep. The surrender was complete... until a short time later when I realized I was not alone.

My eyes were tightly shut, but my mind was fully awake and my heart was pounding. I felt the approach of a dark shadow that entered the room and came to rest directly over my bed. The sensation that someone was bending over me was undeniable. Garbled words were spoken. Soothing words, comforting words that made no sense, but conveyed an unmistakable message: "It's okay, Marcia. Everything's going to be alright."

It was as gentle and benign as a parental tuck-in and absolutely terrifying at the same time. The voice was my dad's and it was so like him to see a need and go to whatever lengths were needed to meet it. Maybe that's why I couldn't open my eyes. Perhaps I was afraid of what I might see. Maybe I was prevented from seeing. All I know is that after the assurance was delivered, the shadow withdrew.

For hours, it seemed, I lay on my bed, stiff as a board, pulse racing, unable to move. This was no dream. Finally, the paralyzing fear subsided and I managed to open my eyes. The room was still bathed in light. Gradually, I climbed out from under the covers, crawled to the end of my bed, and peeped around my desk to make sure I was really alone. Once I was sure, I fell into a deep sleep, exhausted.

The next morning the previous night's episode still haunted me. I needed to tell someone, but how? What would my roommate think? I decided to try. I learned that, unfortunately, some things, suffer in translation. They can't be explained.

To some it may sound like nonsense, gibberish.

But if we listen with our hearts, the message can become crystal clear: "It's okay. Everything's going to be okay."

~Marcia Swearingen

Believe

I pray that our Heavenly Father may assuage the anguish of your bereavement and leave you only the cherished memory of the loved and lost...
~Abraham Lincoln

Two weeks before Christmas my father passed away. Never did I think when I had forced everyone into yet another family photo that it would be our last complete one. I loved my father dearly as he did me. We told each other often.

One night in my inconsolable grief I turned to God to help me find but one bit of solace to make losing him bearable. I needed to find some peace and comfort to start my healing, as my father would have wanted. Pop often told me not to stand around crying when he was gone, but to enjoy life as he did. He had endured many personal struggles and still managed to possess strength and humor. I needed to honor that. A realization dawned on me at that moment of prayer. My father had loved his own dad as much as he and I had loved each other. My prayer was that my dad was now in the joyful presence of his dad, this time with immense happiness where they were eternally reunited. That was my comfort as I wept and prayed.

I reminded myself that I was truly blessed to have had my dad throughout my entire childhood and the childhood of all of his grandsons. They grew to be honorable men with many of his qualities. Pop also had the opportunity to experience great-grandchildren budding out the leaves of his family tree. I was a forty-eight-year-old woman, not a child, when my dad was taken from me. I had no regrets. I just needed to know he was now with his dad in heaven and that he was fine.

At about 10:30 p.m. I ended my prayer. I stopped the tears and felt a warm flow of comfort, then slept soundly and dreamlessly, my first restful sleep since his death. Maybe healing would start.

The next morning I went to work, the last day before Christmas break. I was dreading this upcoming holiday without Dad. It was also exceedingly painful for me to put on a party face for the fun at school, but the staff and students were sympathetic and supportive. We had about an hour left until buses came and students would be sent home for the vacation. The school nurse joined our classroom festivities. She and I had only known each other since the start of that school year, but instantly had a comfortable friendship and bonded over family tragedies.

She asked, "Does the word 'lollipop' mean anything to you?"

My mind screamed, "What?" but my mouth uttered, "I'm Lollipop."

"Excuse me?"

"Lollipop; that's my nickname." With tears welling in my eyes, I continued. "My dad called me that my whole life."

She said, "Well, I have a message for you."

I felt a little weak and suggested we go to her office. As we walked she explained. The night before, she had a dream in which she was at our school. She had punched in the digits to our keypad code and entered through the front door. There were no staff or students, just a vacant building. Completely alone, she started moving down the hall when she heard a firm but gentle man's voice say, "Find Lollipop. Believe." She awoke and tried to figure out what had happened in her dream. The vision was vivid, a sharp picture. Her dreams were usually not so clear. It didn't make sense to her, so she shook it off and returned to sleep. In her dream she again returned to school with the same sequence of events and the man's voice repeated, "Find Lollipop. Believe." The second time it stayed with her.

On her way to school she couldn't connect lollipops and Christmas. It was a candy cane holiday. "Believe." Was it Santa or

Jesus? Was a lollipop a person, place or thing? She had to make sense of it. She asked all the staff if lollipop meant something to them. They all said no. Eventually she found me. Through tears, I shared my night's prayer and the comfort I felt. I could see in her eyes, she was making the connection.

She said, "Your dad is with his father. You need to believe it."

I nodded. "I already believed it last night. You're just confirming it." Then I asked, "What time did you have this dream?

"The first one was around 10:30." She added, "The voice was kind but persistent."

As was my father.

"I just knew I was supposed to find Lollipop and say, 'Believe.'"

The night before Dad died we ended our talk with, "I love you, Pop," and he replied, "I love you too, Lollipop."

~Laurel A. Smith

Divine Delivery

Maternal love! Thou word that sums up all bliss.
~Channing Pollack

In World War II my father, Henry, a Southern small-town boy away from home for the first time, was stationed on an obscure island in the South Pacific. Mail call was a highlight of each week, something he and his fellow Marines eagerly anticipated. The letters they received were their only links to loved ones at home, and they read them over and over, sharing key passages with their buddies. Even the mundane details of life back home were appreciated, for hearing about small everyday matters made them feel connected and in touch with their families and friends a world away.

Henry's mother wrote regularly about anything and every-thing—that the black and white barn cat had given birth to six kit-tens, that she had sewn new plaid curtains for the living room, that Dad had trimmed the pear trees, and that she had somehow lost her wedding ring. She was praying it would turn up somewhere.

Even more eagerly anticipated than letters were the care pack-ages, boxes of home-baked goodies the mothers and sweethearts of servicemen sent. Many such packages were lost at sea when the ships bearing them were attacked. Those that made it through were celebrated. Whenever boxes arrived, the recipient always shared the contents with his tent mates and buddies.

Henry's favorite treat was homemade divinity, a Southern spe-cialty of decadently rich white candy chock full of pecan pieces. One day when Henry was feeling especially discouraged and homesick he received a care package, battered on the outside but with the contents intact. He ripped through the tattered paper wrapping and, with his mouth watering, opened the tin he knew would be full of divinity. There were several layers separated by wax paper... just enough divinity, he thought, to serve all the fellas, with a piece or two left over for him.

The box was passed among the men and the divinity quickly disappeared, piece by piece. At last the box came back to Henry. He picked up the last remaining creamy, white square and bit into it with a sigh of pure pleasure.

But pure pleasure was quickly punctuated by pure pain when his teeth chomped down on something hard and unyielding. He removed the offending object from his mouth and saw... his mother's wedding ring.

God had gone to great lengths to meet Henry's need for comfort and encouragement that day. Henry survived the war and personally returned his mother's treasured ring.

~Lynn Worley Kuntz

The Carpenter's Son

That night God appeared to Solomon and said to him,
"Ask for whatever you want me to give you."
~2 Chronicles 1:6-8

A life built around a full-time job, three children, and a husband who worked the midnight shift was wearing me down. There had to be more to my life than paperwork, potty training, and ridiculous factory schedules. And then there was that nagging thought that kept tugging at my skirt like a whiny child: "There's something else you should be doing." It refused to stop begging for attention.

When I read the announcement in my church bulletin, I knew it was just what I needed: a retreat. Maybe there God could answer the restlessness in me.

The weekend retreat was to be held in a convent. I had never been to one. Walking onto the grounds, I passed towering brick buildings that stood like soldiers guarding holy ground. Standing regally in the center of the compound was an elderly oak tree. Years of rain, like holy water, had blessed it with a long life. Its massive bouquet of branches reached for the sky like hands lifted in charismatic prayer. I stopped for a moment under their gesture of praise, letting the holiness of this place enfold me.

Later, having navigated to my room, I lay my suitcase on the bed and surveyed my surroundings. The room was stark and simple: a bed, desk, Bible, and dresser. A crucifix hung on the gray wall.

"Things look pretty bleak around here," I thought. Peace may have escorted me in, but I wondered if simplicity and I would be good roommates.

That night I crawled into bed and cocooned myself in blankets, trying to make myself cozy. Silence crept around the drab space. The quiet made me uncomfortable. But, in spite of my uneasiness, exhaustion tucked me in and I quickly fell asleep.

I don't know how long I had been slumbering when my eyes sprung open. I gasped, then yelled. Looming before me was a goliath ghostly figure of a boy standing as tall as the ceiling! A thin band circled his head like a leather halo, holding his long, curly hair away from his face. His body was wet with sweat. His head tilted upward with an affectionate gaze aimed toward heaven.

In the second it took to open my eyes, I was infused with knowledge, a holy résumé introducing my spiritual intruder: "This is Jesus, the Carpenter's Son. He has been working long grueling hours helping his father build."

And then I heard the words, not audibly, but inside me. "It's hard work building the Kingdom."

I sat upright in the bed and speedily brushed my hand over the figure like I was erasing a chalkboard. And, just like that, He was gone.

Bewildered, I lay back down and tried to assimilate what had just happened. I stared at the dull gray wall that had been the backdrop of this mysterious visitation. My heart pounded like a hammer. "If that was Jesus, then why am I so afraid?"

The answer came to me in the memory of a Bible passage I had read. The disciples were on a boat in the middle of a storm when Jesus headed their way, walking on the water. At first they didn't recognize him. "It's a ghost!" they screamed out in fear.

I knew just how those guys felt. I was terrified. Evidently, holy fear is a very scary thing. But, the revelation that Jesus had scared the devil out of his disciples, too, comforted me. The consoling thought wrapped its arms around me, calming my fear until I drifted back to sleep.

The next morning was Sunday. I went to Mass with the previous night's encounter on my mind. As Mass started, I was distracted by my thoughts, but praying nonetheless. "Lord, was that really you last night?"

When the time came for the priest to deliver the homily, he paced slowly at the front of the church. Stroking both sides of his chin, as if engrossed in deep thought, he said, reverently, "Jesus the Carpenter's Son. What a beautiful name for Jesus."

I was stunned.

"This is no coincidence," I told myself. "God is definitely trying to tell me something!"

I felt like someone had plugged me in; electric currents surged up and down my body. I was vibrating. Goose bumps sprung up all over me. The phenomenon reoccurred in waves throughout the sermon and did not stop until Mass ended.

Thoughts of Jesus traveled with me on the long drive home. Trying to understand why He would appear to me as the Carpenter's Son, I asked myself questions: "What does a carpenter do?" He builds things. "What does Jesus, the Carpenter, do?" He builds lives.

As soon as I got home, I sat down at my computer and wrote about Jesus, the Carpenter's Son, the builder of lives. On a whim, I submitted what I had written to the editor of my diocesan newspaper. To my surprise, he invited me to write a monthly column for the newspaper. I heard the Call. I started writing.

A short time later, I was asked to be a cantor and music minister at my church. Again, I heard the Call. I started singing.

One thing led to another and suddenly, I had plenty to do. Seems there's a lot of heavenly work out there. The floodgates opened and I just went with the flow.

My visit from the Carpenter's Son was over twenty years ago. Not one day since then have I been idle; I always find something worthwhile to do for Jesus. Like writing, singing, visiting nursing homes, or teaching catechism to my grandchildren. Often, I get tired. Sometimes I want to quit. But, for the most part, when weariness comes a-calling, I just take a break. Then, I look to heaven and wipe the sweat from my brow, remembering that Jesus once told me that it's hard work building the Kingdom of God.

~Teresa Anne Hayden

Pumpkin Pie

*We must not allow the clock and the calendar to blind us to the fact
that each moment of life is a miracle and mystery.*
~H. G. Wells

Christmas morning was my favorite time of the year. Soon our two sons, three daughters, their spouses, and our ten grandchildren would arrive and fill our house with the sounds of ripping paper, squeaking toys, and giggling children. While kids and dogs chased through the rooms, the women would gather in the kitchen drinking coffee and offering advice on everything from preventing migraine headaches to locating a good babysitter. As usual, they'd volunteer to help with the cooking and, as usual, I'd refuse. The men would huddle in front of television sets — my husband and most of the others watching the History Channel in the living room and two sons-in-law cheering for football teams in the bedroom. Occasionally someone would yell, "Quit picking on your little brother," or "Leave those poor goldfish alone."

For now, the elderly calico cat and I were the only ones in the kitchen. With a contented smile, I ran my bare foot across her soft fur.

I loved this quiet time alone, up to my elbows in flour, surrounded by the smells of coffee and cinnamon. Four freshly baked pies lined the counter and two more were in the oven. The turkey was waiting to be stuffed; bread dough was rising. Outdoors,

Bing Crosby's dreams were coming true. Wind-driven snow tapped against the windows and drifted across the roads.

The oven timer dinged and I picked up the worn potholders, taking care to avoid the thin spot. Yes, the pumpkin pies were perfect, filling set around the edges, fluted crust brown but not burned. As I set them on the cooling rack, I felt a sudden, overpowering urge to take a pie to our neighbor, nicknamed George.

George, whose real name was Beulah May, had lived around the corner from us since our children were babies. Like me, she felt the best part of the holiday was baking. Normally we compared notes, but this year had been even busier than usual, and I realized I hadn't spoken to her in weeks.

"Take George a pumpkin pie," a voice said. It sounded like a Charlton Heston parting-of-the-clouds, thunderous rumble. Not a voice to be ignored.

"George doesn't need a pie. She probably has more than I do," I said out loud.

The need to give George a pie persisted. "It's snowing out," I said. "I'll feel foolish. I'll fall on the ice and freeze to death." I was full of arguments. Then, without realizing what I was doing, I grabbed a coat, slid into flip-flops, and carried a still-warm pie wrapped in a white dishtowel out my back door and down the street to George's house.

Nine-year-old Annie saw me coming and opened the door. Her grandmother was right behind her, a worried look on her face.

"Come in out of the snow," George said as she pulled me into the house. "Where are your boots? Are you crazy?" I realized with surprise that I had no hat and my feet were all but bare, yet I wasn't cold.

"I brought you a pumpkin pie," I said. "You'll think I'm crazy but I heard this voice telling me you needed one." I could feel a warm blush spread across my cheeks. "You probably have six already."

Instead of laughing at me, George covered her face with her

hands and started to cry. "No," she said between sniffles, "no pies at all. I didn't make any this year."

I was stunned. George didn't bake for Christmas? Then I noticed how quiet the house was. "Where is everyone?" I asked. George's holidays always involved at least twenty people packed around her dinner table. I looked out the window. "And where are all the cars?"

George rummaged through her pockets for a handkerchief. "There's no one here but Annie and me. We were planning to go to Sue's. You know, with the new baby they couldn't come home like they usually do. But the weather's really bad in Chicago and our flight has been canceled." She abandoned the handkerchief search and brushed the tears from her cheeks with her fingertips. "Oh, I know it seems silly compared to other people's problems, but everyone's pretty disappointed. This will be the first time we haven't all been together." She stared at the floor, bottom lip quivering. "John's going to Iraq. Who knows when we'll have another chance?"

No family for Christmas? That might not sound like a crisis to some people but I knew what it meant to George.

With a sigh, George took the pie from me and set it on the round kitchen table. "We'll be okay," she said, raising her chin with a determined expression. "Christmas dinner won't be the same but I have a canned ham."

"Come to our house," I said. "You're practically part of the family and, heaven knows, there's plenty of food."

George shook her head. "Thanks but no. Annie wants to watch The Christmas Story on TV and the kids are going to call at dinnertime." She took a deep breath and then chuckled a little, trying to make light of the situation. "You know, I told the Lord I could manage if I just had a pumpkin pie."

She paused and grinned at me. "And now I do."

Annie jumped up and down, her dark curls bouncing. "Grandma, your prayers have been answered. Is this a miracle?"

"No, no, not a miracle," I said, embarrassed. After all, why would God pick me to be his messenger?

"Not a miracle," George agreed with a little smile. "Now, if she'd brought whipped cream, then it would be a miracle."

~Mary Vaughn as told to Sally O'Brien

38

Miracle in the Clouds

Say to those with fearful hearts,
"Be strong, do not fear; your God will come…"
~Isaiah 35:4

I stared into the sun-drenched sky. The heat of a mid-July day pressed against me. The pillowy clouds shifted, playing hide-and-seek. I was drawn back to long-ago childhood days when my imagination had run rampant and I found pictures in the clouds… an elephant, a bear, fish.

Despite the oppressive heat, I had stepped outside moments earlier, needing the soothing quiet of aloneness. The double demands of caring for my sister while she underwent six grueling sessions of chemotherapy, and keeping the household, which included our eighty-seven-year-old father and my sister's mother-in-law who suffered from crippling dementia, had diluted my strength, both physically and spiritually.

My sister's diagnosis of ovarian cancer had shaken every part of me. I had spent many hours upon my knees, pleading with the Lord for His mercy upon the sister who was, in many ways, the other half of me.

I looked for a sign to restore me, to bolster my wavering courage, my lagging faith, my weary heart. I lifted my gaze upward once more, staring. Could it be? I squinted against the haze of sun and smog.

There in the clouds, the Lord appeared. Arms outstretched, He seemed to beckon me. I blinked, certain that my eyes were playing tricks on me.

But, no, He remained, a quiet Presence, a gift to my battered spirits.

"Dear Lord," I prayed, "take this cup from my sister, and, if it be Thy will, heal her."

Head bowed, I remained there. Waiting. Striving to listen. Willing my rebellious soul to submit to His will.

A quiet voice in my mind said, "Child, your sister is in My arms. How can you fear?"

"Now I don't."

The moment passed. The image disappeared, and I was left wondering if I had imagined the entire episode.

No! I would not doubt. The Lord had appeared, had given me the precious gift of reassurance of His sustaining love, both for my sister and for myself.

Strengthened, I returned to the house, renewed, ready to serve, knowing my sister… and I… rested in His arms.

~Jane McBride Choate

39

Did You See that Boy?

Jesus turned and saw her.
"Take heart, daughter," he said,
"your faith has healed you."
~Matthew 9:22

Easter Sunday was the day the doctor took my three-day-old son off the ventilator and placed him in my arms. His lungs were collapsing; a tracheotomy was no longer an option because a CAT scan showed no brain activity. A nurse dressed in scrubs speckled with teddy bear prints wheeled us into a blue room, a private room off the neonatal intensive care unit, and left us in front of a large window. Below was the parking lot. Beyond was an old, stone church. Its steeple reached toward the heavens. My son, Jeffery James, struggled and drew his last gasp of breath and his little body went limp.

All was silent and I wept.

I don't know how long we spent together in that blue room, but as I think back now, it seems an eternity. I looked down at the body of my baby. I looked toward the church. I thought, "How ironic. My son was born on the anniversary of Jesus' death. I sobbed, "And he died on the same day Jesus rose from the dead."

I cursed the church. I cursed Jesus. I cursed God.

I spent another eleven days on the maternity ward battling an infection. IVs pumped powerful antibiotics into my body. And every morning, afternoon and evening, mothers and fathers strolled the hall outside my room, holding healthy babies.

Upon my release, I held a dark lock of my son's hair.

A few days after I got home, a small funeral, planned by my mother, was held in the cemetery up the hill from my house. My only request: no Catholic priest. An Episcopalian minister delivered a short service, calling our son "The Littlest Angel." And when his small casket was lowered into the ground, my husband filled the spade with dirt and tossed one pile of earth in before falling to his knees.

That first year was the most difficult of my life. I felt lost. That first week, I sat alone in the decorated nursery, refusing to receive any callers. But people came, attempting to offer condolences. For a while, weeks or months maybe, I'd wait until the house was asleep and walk up the hill to the cemetery to sit by my son's grave. His father and I were young and poor, and though his site had no marker, I could even find my baby in the dark.

Later that year I was pregnant again, and the following year I gave birth to a beautiful healthy baby girl. Although she would never replace the ache I'd always feel for our lost son, I loved her with all my heart and soul. I would never tell her about the brother she almost had. My mother asked if there would be a Christening for her. I answered, "No." I would never set foot inside a church again. And despite the lack of God and church in our lives, my daughter grew and thrived.

Years passed by delightfully, and when my daughter was about ten, she asked me why we never went to church. We were sitting at the kitchen table and the snow was falling lightly outside when she asked, "Do you believe in God?"

She said her best friend went to church every Sunday, and she wanted to go too. I simply told her I didn't believe. I told her that religion was once a part of my life, I had been raised Catholic like her best friend, Megan, but that I had had a crisis of faith many years before.

She shrugged, then asked, "Would it be okay if I went to Mass with Megan and her family this Sunday?"

I sighed, but agreed. Who was I to deny her the right to make her own decision regarding religion?

For two years, weekly Mass with Megan and her family became a ritual for her, and as she learned more and more about the Catholic faith, her desire to belong to the church grew. My mother planned her baptism that spring, and over a glass of wine one evening, my mother asked me if I had given any thought to my daughter's confirmation. I hadn't. But apparently, my mother and daughter had.

"Confirmation classes begin in the fall," she said. "They last throughout the year. She needs a sponsor." I knew what "sponsor" meant to my mother. "Sponsor" meant me going to classes with my daughter. "Mom," I answered, "I know where you're going with this. You've been after me for years to return to the church." I got up from the table. "The answer," I said, "is no. And you know why."

For an hour we argued about blame. "Do not blame God," my mom insisted. "God is there for you whenever you choose to return to Him."

Finally, from exhaustion, I agreed. "I'm not returning to the church," I said, "or to Him. But if the Catholic religion is what she really wants, I will go to classes with her."

My mother thought she had won. "You'll have to attend weekly Mass with her," she said. "A sponsor needs to be a role model."

So when September rolled around, and the leaves began changing, every Sunday morning my daughter and I attended 10:30 Mass together, and every Sunday evening, she and I sat through an hour and a half of religious instruction. And although I was regularly in the pew in body, my mind and spirit would drift consistently elsewhere.

On Easter Sunday that year, my mother, daughter and I attended the service together. We filed into the pew and I, at the end, knelt to say hello to God. We stood for the gospel. We sat while the priest delivered his homily: the story of Jesus' resurrection. I wasn't really listening. I'd heard the story a million times. I was thinking… thinking about the Easter Sunday that I lost my little boy. I looked up at the cross behind the priest, and silently asked the crucified Jesus why God took my son from me. There was no answer, just the monotonous drone of the priest's words echoing throughout the otherwise silent church.

And then there were soft footsteps from behind. And a boy of about thirteen years approached and stood in the aisle right next to me. I peered at him and almost gasped aloud. He looked almost exactly like me: dark hair, green eyes, a spattering of light freckles across his nose and cheeks. Tears filled my eyes and he responded with a soft smile that seemed to say, "Everything's okay."

By the time I turned to my mother and daughter, tears were streaming steadily down my face. They looked at me with concern, and when I turned back toward the boy, he was gone.

"How silly," I thought on the ride home. "Ridiculous." I shook my head and never mentioned the moment to my mother or daughter. I forgot all about it.

In May, my daughter's confirmation came and went. Summer arrived with its warm mornings and I took to having my coffee in a chair out on the porch. Most mornings my daughter would rush out, plant a kiss on my cheek, relay her plans for the day, and run to meet her friends in town. But one gorgeous July day, she shuffled out still in her pajamas and slippers, her hair tossed from the night's sleep.

She sat on the porch steps. "I had the strangest dream," she began. "A boy a little older than me was in my bedroom last night." She rubbed the sleep from her eyes. "He said everything was going to be okay, that he was watching over me. He said he was my brother."

She looked up at me. "He looked like this boy I saw standing in the aisle at church on Easter. Weird, huh?" she said. "Did you see that boy, Mom?"

Her bright blue eyes lit with brilliance and awe.

"Your brother," I whispered.

At that moment, I knew that God had sent my son, not once, but twice, to find me. And at that moment, I knew without question, that I would never be lost again.

~Kristen Hope

Angel Babies

I asked, "What are these, my lord?"
The angel who was talking with me answered,
"I will show you what they are."
~Zechariah 1:9

M y sister Michelle and I were so excited that we were both pregnant with our second children. Our due dates were just six weeks apart. My son Blake was born seven weeks early, and he was perfect. My sister delivered a precious little girl, Kennedy, who, tragically, did not make it.

That was the hardest event my family and I have ever encountered. The healing process was long and slow.

Blake was four months old when Kennedy died. Every time he went into the nursery at my sister's house, he went to one spot in her room and laughed, talked, and pointed. We always said it was probably Kennedy coming to play with him.

Then Michelle and her husband moved. At their new house, Blake didn't seem to see or talk to his cousin like he did in her room at the old house. I was a little sad.

Then, one evening, when Blake was about two and a half, we were alone in the living room where I was rocking him to sleep.

All of a sudden he sat up and started frantically waving at the wall, laughing and talking. He was clearly not talking to me, so I put him down. Blake ran across the room to where his eyes had been fixed when I was holding him.

"Blake, who are you talking to?"

"The baby," he said, and continued to talk.

He then came back to me, excited. "Mommy, see that baby? See that baby? Right there!"

It was like he was seeing his long lost best friend.

I asked him, "What's the baby's name?"

"Baby Kenny."

I got goose bumps! I thought maybe I wasn't hearing him correctly or that he was saying and hearing what I wanted to believe.

I asked him three more times and he gave me the same answer, "Baby Kenny."

I knew at that moment that she was there in our house, playing with our son. I sat watching Blake through tear-filled eyes, thanking God for sending Kennedy to watch over us. I didn't want the experience to end. Ten minutes later, just as quickly as Blake saw her and began talking, he stopped and came back to me.

It was a bittersweet moment.

Kennedy still comes to our house, though not nearly as often as I wish she did. I will be forever grateful that God has allowed me to "see" the miracle of angels through the eyes of a two-and-a-half-year-old boy.

~Monica Matzner

A Book of Miracles

His Saving Grace

*From the fullness of his grace
we have all received one blessing after another.*

~John 1:16

Out of the Darkness

Heal me, O Lord, and I will be healed;
save me and I will be saved, for you are the one I praise.
~Jeremiah 17:13-15

Sleepless nights. No appetite. A gray face reflected in the mirror. These defined me during that year of depression. Some melancholics have called it, "The Dark Night of the Soul." I called it "The Closest Thing to a Living Death."

Some days I curled into a fetal position, unable and unwilling to move. Other days I seemed to function, making peanut butter and jelly sandwiches for my son. But no laughter resonated in my kitchen. Life and food were tasteless.

Sunsets had been my favorite time of the day, but not during that dark year. I could no longer enjoy the oranges and golds of Kansas dusk. Sunset meant the night was coming, and I dreaded the loneliness. Everyone else slept while I rocked myself in a corner of the bathroom. Was I crazy? "A clinical depression," the doctor said. "Chemicals out of whack. No one knows how it starts or how it ends."

My usual routines didn't happen. Music held no joy. The piano sat in the corner of the living room, its ivory keys mocking me. No songs echoed through my house. I filled my journal with dark and discouraging words—"sad," "apathy," "useless." Nothing in my life seemed to matter, and I hated feeling so worthless. I grieved for my little son. I couldn't play with him or read his books. Every crayon in my box was gray.

I tried to pray, but God was silent. Friends came to visit, but no one had a solution. Others prayed for me, but nothing happened. The days seemed thirty-five hours long, the nights endless. Hours stretched into months and still no relief. I begged God to let me die.

Then one day I sat at my desk, hoping some creativity would filter into my "lostness." I longed to write again, to make paragraphs that made sense, to live within my fictional characters. I closed my eyes and pleaded with God to help me. "Please, I can't take it anymore. I don't know what to do."

Out of my darkness came a light that beckoned me into the living room. I traveled out-of-body and saw God standing beside a Christmas tree. His face was indiscernible, His body an opaque vision. Although I could see no features, I just knew He was God. But more exciting than His appearance was the large gold box He held out to me. The fog in my brain lifted as I focused on the white gift tag. Fastened to a shimmering bow, it read, "Health."

Then I was back at my desk, awake and sharply alert. Afraid to breathe, I closed my eyes and waited. A presence stood behind me—Jesus. His graceful carpenter hands touched my head, and a pulse of power reached inside my shattered brain. Like a slow-moving syrup, the warmth of his touch spread from my head to the tips of my toes. Damaged synapses snapped back into place. Dead emotions felt alive, surging through personality and will. I felt that miraculous glow in every tissue of my being, filling me with the incredible gift of healing.

I sat at my desk for hours, repeating "Thank you" in every language I knew.

The darkness had retreated, and in its place was the light of sanity. I wanted to live and be a good Mommy again.

I touched my jeans and felt each denim thread. My stomach growled. Pent-up tears released the poison of condemnation.

No longer worthless, I felt loved with the divine intimacy of my Lord. I stretched my fingers toward the computer and wrote a complete sentence, "God is my healer—Amen."

~R.J. Thesman

Malachi Surprise

"Bring the whole tithe into the storehouse,
that there may be food in my house.
Test me in this," says the Lord Almighty,
"and see if I will not throw open the floodgates of heaven
and pour out so much blessing that you will not have room enough for it."
~Malachi 3:9-11

I received the notice in the mail from the bank. Make at least one mortgage payment by the next Monday or foreclosure proceedings would be initiated.

I had no idea what to do. My wife, Joan, had recently quit her job as a registered nurse to be a stay-at-home mother to our two young sons, Michael and Daniel. We had met with our pastor and he reaffirmed our decision for Joan to concentrate on raising the boys.

"There may be financial problems, but the Lord will provide," he had said. "Taking care of children is not a hassle, as some parents seem to think. It is a ministry to the Lord."

I had a good job, but not an executive position. It was during the late 1970s, and the economy was a mess. Double-digit inflation; double-digit interest rates; long lines to purchase gasoline.

I did not earn enough money from my salary to support a family of four.

All that week, I grappled with the problem. It burrowed into my mind like a mole. "You made a big mistake. You are going to lose your home."

I spent most of my time worrying. I knew the Bible advised: "Be anxious about nothing." But no matter how hard I tried to climb the hill of faith, I kept slipping back into the mire of apprehension.

The situation seemed hopeless. I could not come up with the money or even a clue of how to get it. Within a few days, legal action would be initiated that would take away my family's home.

Friday was payday, but most of that money had to be committed to necessities such as food for my family. The rest did not constitute nearly enough to make a mortgage payment.

I told no one, not the pastor, not the associate pastor, nor anyone else at the church, about the financial plight of my family as I struggled with a new problem. As a Bible-believing Christian, I felt it was my duty to God to contribute a tithe of my income to His church. But suppose I skipped a week? I could make up for it some other time. If I kept the tithe money in my wallet, I'd be that much closer to being able to make the mortgage payment.

I turned in my Bible to the book of Malachi and read: "Bring the whole tithe into the storehouse, that there may be food in my house. Test me in this," says the Lord Almighty, "and see if I will not throw open the floodgates of heaven and pour out so much blessing that you will not have room enough for it."

My decision was made. On Sunday morning, I placed my tithe check in the offering plate.

Then I went right back to worrying. I worried through the rest of the morning. I worried all afternoon. In the evening, Joan and I returned for another church service and I managed to worry all the way through it.

After the evening service, the associate pastor came up to me with a smile on his face and handed me an envelope. "The Lord told me to give this to you," he said, then turned and walked away.

In the envelope was a check for precisely the amount needed for the mortgage payment.

I don't know how the associate pastor became informed of my problem, or how he decided he should do something about it. But I do know this: I tithed and God kept His promise by pouring out a blessing.

From that Sunday thirty years ago, to the present time, my family has not encountered serious financial difficulties of any kind.

~David Heeren

43

Defying Death

So that your faith might not rest on men's wisdom, but on God's power.
~1 Corinthians 2:5

I was working a sixteen-hour shift one Saturday in ICU. It was my turn to take the next admission. When I got the assignment and report, I knew it was going to be an emotional evening. Mr. Smith, a seventy-six-year-old gentleman, had suffered a massive stroke confirmed by a CT scan. He arrived on the unit around 3:00 p.m.

I learned that he'd been an active man with a wife, four adult children, and several grandchildren. He was very close to his family even though three of his children lived in different states. Mr. Smith was an avid gardener and kept busy all hours of the day.

When Mr. Smith suffered his stroke, he had a large amount of bleeding into the brain, and this resulted in a respiratory arrest. The family was given the news that his condition was grave. He had seizures almost continuously. His heart rate and blood pressure were unstable. He would not live through the night.

His wife asked us to do whatever we needed to do to keep him alive until her three children could come say goodbye. One daughter lived close by, and she remained at her father's side. Mrs. Smith called a son in Delaware, a daughter in New Jersey, and another son in Virginia.

Two hours later I was hanging the fifth intravenous medications to stabilize Mr. Smith's rhythm and blood pressure when Mrs. Smith asked me to pray with her that her husband would awaken and be well, but if he had to die, that he would live long enough for his children to arrive.

"How long before everyone can get here?" I asked.

"About seven hours."

I prayed with her. "God, please stabilize Mr. Smith's blood pressure and heart rate so he can live through the night."

About ten minutes after our prayer, his heart rate dropped to forty, then thirty, and then down to no rhythm at all. The cardiac arrest team was called. They worked on Mr. Smith for twenty minutes. Because of the bleeding into his brain, it was determined that even if we could get his heart rhythm back to normal, Mr. Smith would never awaken from a coma. After talking with Mrs. Smith, the emergency doctor called the code, stopped all resuscitation measures, and pronounced Mr. Smith dead.

Because he was my patient, it was my responsibility to remove all the lines and tubes and bathe him.

Everyone had left the room, and as I removed the intravenous lines and tubes, I prayed again for him to get a rhythm back to live long enough for his children to come to say their goodbyes. Normally the procedure is to remove the EKG leads and turn the monitor off. For some reason I had not removed the leads yet, but I turned off the monitor in the room. As I was beginning to remove the breathing tube, the other nurses came running in.

"What are you doing?" one asked.

Turning around, I told her I was taking out the lines and cleaning Mr. Smith after his death. One nurses flipped on the monitor at the bedside. I looked up at it and got chills. Mr. Smith had a heartbeat again. As I watched, the rate increased from thirty to about fifty.

"It's just the drug effect," said one of the nurses. "We all know this happens sometimes; it doesn't mean anything."

But when I checked for a pulse, I felt one in his neck. I turned the ventilator back on to give him oxygen. As we stood in the room watching the monitor, we all realized that Mr. Smith, who had been pronounced dead a few minutes before, had a heartbeat. He was alive again.

At 10:30 p.m., all four of his children walked into the room. Mrs. Smith smiled at me as we acknowledged that God had answered our prayer.

A few hours later, Mr. Smith died, his family at his side, having said their goodbyes. He didn't get well and make it out of the hospital, but God still performed a miracle. Mr. Smith lived for eight hours after being pronounced dead.

~Kim D. Armstrong

44

Bell of Truth

*And everyone who has
left houses or brothers or sisters or father or mother or children or fields
for my sake will receive a hundred times as much
and will inherit eternal life.*
~Matthew 19:29

I was nineteen years old, alone in a studio apartment in Kansas City. It was the Christmas season and self-pity had gotten the best of me. With no job and the rent barely paid, all I had was a box of cereal, a carton of milk, five dollars in my bank account, and a single one-dollar bill in my purse.

Earlier that year, I'd made a fateful decision. I was forced to quit college due to lack of money. So, I packed up two suitcases and got on a bus with only fifty dollars in my pocket. My parents were getting a divorce, and I had no financial support. My temporary minimum wage job had ended. I was new to town, alone and friendless.

So here I was in Kansas City, sitting on my Murphy bed, staring out the window. I began to think, "No one really cares if I live or die. I could be lying in the gutter somewhere and it wouldn't make a difference."

I thought, "I've got to get out of here, get out of this room, before I do something I'll regret."

I buttoned up my old lime green coat. It had once been part of my new college wardrobe. Now it had holes in the elbow and was torn at the shoulder where white stuffing poked out.

I walked down the five flights of stairs with the dollar in my pocket. I opened the door to bitter cold. The icy wind smacked me in the face, making my eyes tear. I began to walk. And walk. I had no destination. I just knew I had to get out of the apartment. Eventually, I came to a park with benches and a fountain, where I could sit, cry and pray.

With my eyes closed, begging God for help, His wisdom, a sign, anything, I heard a voice. A man was speaking to me. Was it a sign? I opened my eyes to find a homeless drunk sitting next to me and asking me for a date!

I headed back toward the apartment. By now the sky had opened up, delivering a combination of rain, sleet and snow. Without a hat or umbrella, my tattered coat soaked up the freezing rain like a sponge and wet hair covered my face.

Walking past fancy stores that were beautifully decorated for the Christmas season, I felt embarrassed by my "little match girl" appearance. A few steps later I stood outside a small coffee shop, gazing in the window. Here, even in this coffee shop, women were wearing furs and beautiful clothes. What would it feel like to be sitting and chatting with friends over a nice warm cup of tea, looking good, watching the dreary weather outside? I wondered if my one dollar could buy me a cup of tea. Then it occurred to me that with tax and tip, I couldn't afford the tea and I continued homeward.

Cold and wet, I asked myself, "Could life get any more miserable?"

It was then that I came upon a Salvation Army woman ringing the bell in front of a red bucket.

"Well," I thought to myself, "you've got your arms and legs, your eyesight and your health, so you're a lot luckier than a lot of these folks The Salvation Army people are trying to help." So I reached in my pocket and gave my last dollar to The Salvation Army.

Back at my apartment, I opened my mailbox to find one envelope, my bank statement. I already knew what it said. But when I opened it to file it away, I noticed something wrong on the statement.

It did not show the expected $5 balance, but now reflected a $105 balance.

I always knew exactly what I had in my account, balanced to the penny. Something was wrong. I wasn't about to spend money that was not mine. I called the bank. I wasn't taking any chances. The bank employee said it was indeed my money, but I knew better.

Donning the tattered, wet green coat, I marched back out into the cold. My bank happened to be directly across the street from the fountain I had sat at crying just a couple of hours earlier.

I walked in. "May I see the bank manager, please?"

I'm sure I looked an awful sight; well-dressed people were staring at this cold ragamuffin demanding that the bank officer remove the mistaken overage.

While he went into back offices to check out the error, I waited patiently in a leather chair that squeaked when I shifted in the seat, water dripping from my hair. Upon his return, he looked puzzled and sat down, scratching his head. "I can't make any sense of it," he said, "but it is indeed your money."

"That's impossible. I know what I had to the penny, and this appeared out of nowhere."

He said he understood my concern because it had not appeared on previous statements. "Our records indicate that a deposit was made into your account last July and we just now caught it. That's why it appears on your bank statement for the first time in December. But it is definitely your money and you need not worry that we'll be asking for it back."

When money is tight, a person keeps track of each and every cent. I knew without question that I'd never made such a deposit back in July, but I couldn't convince him.

I walked home, thanking God for the extra money, which I used for a discount plane ticket to visit family for Christmas. My spirits healed as I shared that holy holiday with them.

A few months later, I told someone about the mysterious appearance of the $100.

"Hadn't you just given your last dollar to charity?" she asked.

"Well, yes."

"So, don't you see?" she replied. "You were rewarded hundredfold!"

The tiny hairs went up on my arms and a chill moved up my back. I call this the bell of truth ringing my spine. I had just experienced a blessing, a Christmas miracle.

~Morgan Hill

45

You're Not Alone

That night the Lord appeared to him and said,
"I am the God of your father Abraham.
Do not be afraid, for I am with you"
~Genesis 26:24

I was all alone! I stared out the kitchen window. The bright sunshine revealed the streaks I'd left when cleaning it.

"It doesn't matter," I muttered. "No one is going to see it."

I tried to concentrate on my weekend chores. Usually keeping busy would help me get over my depression and bitterness. I tackled everything that needed to be done with a vengeance, but nothing was going right. The vacuum cleaner shorted out, the washer wouldn't spin and there were piles of laundry to do.

I headed for the garage. I'd do yard work. Working outside in the fresh air always soothed me and gave me time to think. I cranked and cranked the old lawnmower. I needed a new one, but couldn't afford it now. I could barely manage the bills.

I had married my childhood sweetheart and we had been blessed with three beautiful daughters. Now, after ten years of marriage, it was over.

After work, I spent all my spare time with my little girls, going on picnics, playing games, reading together, talking and listening as I tried to ease their pain over the divorce. That was all forgotten this weekend.

They could hardly wait to leave. Their father and his girlfriend had picked them up to take them to a Six Flags amusement park. They were so excited about going. I couldn't blame them, I couldn't afford to take them to places like that, but it hurt seeing them so anxious to go. Didn't all the time I'd spent with them mean anything to them?

"Of course it did," I muttered as the mower finally coughed and started. "You should be ashamed of yourself for feeling this way when the girls will have so much fun. They need to be with their father."

I was filled with bitterness and hatred as I thought of him. He could never find time to do anything with them before, even when the girls pleaded with him. He was too busy, he'd say; he had to work.

I kicked a ball away from the mower, pretending it was him. I viciously mowed down anything in my path, weeds and flowers both. All the while I kept thinking, "I'm all alone and no one loves me."

I went into the house exhausted. I tried to do the rest of my weekend chores, but I couldn't find the energy. At suppertime I was too tired and upset to eat. It was Saturday evening and I was alone. I felt so sorry for myself. I burst into tears and threw myself face down on the couch. In my pain and misery, I cried out, "Oh, God, help me! I'm all alone and no one cares; no one loves me!"

The sobs shook my whole body. As I lay on the couch, shaking, crying and whispering over and over, "Please help me, please help me, please…"

I froze as I felt an arm go around my shoulders. My sobs quieted.

As I lay on the couch with the weight of an arm around me, I heard a whisper in my ear. "You're not alone; I'll always be with you. I love you and always will."

I was so stunned, I couldn't move for a few seconds. I slowly sat up and looked about the room, shaken, and tried to comprehend what had happened. I could still feel the warmth where the arm had been around my shoulders and I knew I had not imagined the whisper.

Then it hit me. I wasn't alone. I could feel my Lord and Savior

Jesus Christ in that room with me. Sitting there on the couch, I felt so loved and protected. He loved me and cared about me, cared enough to tell me.

The rest of the weekend, I went about in a daze, overwhelmed at what had taken place. Jesus had told me He loved me, had promised to never leave me and to always be with me. I cried some more. This time they were tears of joy.

My life changed that night. The bitterness and hatred I'd felt was gone. No longer did I fret about being alone or unloved. The girls would leave me many times to go with their father, but now I was happy they were getting to spend time with him. I still struggled to work and make ends meet and to find time to be a single parent. I still had problems to deal with, but I had Someone there helping me all the way.

Anytime I would slip into fretting or feeling sorry for myself, I'd close my eyes and think back to that evening. I could feel His arm around my shoulders and hear that soft voice, "I love you, you're not alone and I'll always be with you."

And He has.

~Pat Kane

46

Saved by the Hand of God

"Do not be afraid of them,
for I am with you and will rescue you,"
declares the Lord.
~Jeremiah 1:8

My good friend Reena and her daughter Nicky are still trying to make sense of what happened to Nicky when she almost died one day in the Himalayas. Reena had planned to accompany her eighty-year-old mother on a spiritual pilgrimage to Badrinath, in the Himalayas, but a severe bout of sciatica prevented her from making the journey. Instead, her twenty-seven-year-old daughter Nicky, a professor of botany, went with her grandmother.

Grandmother and granddaughter set off together… one to offer devotions to the Lord and the other to pick up some interesting plant samples in the pristine mountains. They were part of a tour group that hired a bus for the pilgrims and made arrangements for rest stops and food along the way.

The monsoons were venting their full fury that August. Rains in the hills accompanied blustery winds and a damp chill. Reena's mother was laid low with a severe fever and excruciating body ache. Not wanting to hold up the rest of the group, the tour organizers arranged for Nicky and her grandmother to stay in a rather remote rest house while the others continued their arduous climb. A faithful houseboy Ramu would cook, clean and look after their comfort.

Grandma was distraught. "To come all this way and not see the face of the Lord," she moaned, her emotional anguish as great as her physical one.

"Don't worry, Granny. God is everywhere. If you really wish, you can see Him, for He is in every tree and flower and blade of grass," Nicky comforted her.

The view from the rest house was lovely and both spent hours on the open balcony gazing at the slopes clad thickly with tall cedars, pines and poplars. But after two days, Nicky began to get restless. Even though the rain still came down in misty gusts, she decided to go for a walk on the mountain tracks.

"Be careful," Granny warned her as Nicky wrapped herself in a woolen scarf and set off. The paths were steep and slippery, but she was careful as she picked up several plants. "I'll go back and look them up," she thought.

As she turned to go back she espied a truly rare beauty of a flower. It was a little way down a steep slope, but a faint track made her think it was possible to reach it. She started down, carefully placing her feet. One wrong step and she'd go hurtling down the steep precipice a thousand feet below. She reached the flower, plucked it triumphantly, and cautiously started on her way up.

That is when disaster struck. The ground under her feet started to slip. The rains had loosened the soil. Nicky had heard of avalanches of mud and realized that she was stuck in the beginning of one. She tried to clutch at something, but there was not a tree, not a branch, not even a sapling. As her hands groped desperately at the soil, she scooped up handfuls of grass. She tried to dig her feet into the soft earth to stop her slipping down, but it was in vain. She tried to call out for help, but her throat was dry with fear and only a faint croak came out.

"Bachao (save me)," she begged in her mind, even as she began to slide down inexorably.

Suddenly a warm hand grasped hers. "Here, madam, hold my hand," said a voice above her. Peering down, with arms stretched, was Ramu, the boy from the rest house. He climbed down with the nimble surefootedness of hill people and gingerly pulled her up.

"His hands are so warm," she thought as he helped her to her feet. She thanked him profusely, then headed off again.

When Nicky entered the rest house, Grandma looked at her strained face and asked in concern, "What happened, my child?"

Nicky recounted the entire incident ending with, "If Ramu hadn't come along, I would be lying at the bottom of the valley by now."

"But that isn't possible," said Granny. "Ramu has been here with me all morning, building up the fire and regaling me with folk tales!"

Ramu came in with a steaming lunch. "I was keeping Maaji company and only went to the kitchen when I saw you coming in."

Granny and Nicky looked at each other in stunned wonder.

"Didn't you say that God is everywhere?" asked Granny softly.

~Mita Banerjee

47

The Anniversary Gift

The excellence of a gift lies in its appropriateness rather than in its value.
~Charles Dudley Warner

"Do you realize we've been married for almost nine years?" my husband, Shannon squeezed my hand as he drove into our driveway.

"What do you want to do for our anniversary?" I asked.

Shannon shook his head. "Things are tight, babe. We can't afford gifts this year, but I could get my parents to watch the kids so we could go out to eat."

I knew he was right. For the past several months, every time we turned around something either leaked, squeaked or fell apart. We had depleted our savings on repair bills. Still, I wanted to give him a gift. I always gave him something small on our anniversary, and I didn't want to break tradition. It didn't have to be expensive, but something sentimental would make our day extra special.

Recently, I'd finished doing a study on the power of prayer. So, I silently prayed that God would give me an idea.

Two days before our anniversary, I was making the bed when a penny rolled out from under it. I picked it up and glanced at the date—1996, the year of our wedding.

That's it! Shannon loved collecting coins. We shopped antique stores all the time looking for them. If I could find a 1996 nickel, dime and quarter, then I could give him a complete set. I couldn't wait to get started on the project. It was both inexpensive and senti-mental. I finished making the bed and began my scavenger hunt.

I started in the living room and then worked my way around the house. I flipped over every cushion and searched through every drawer. Later that day I found a 1996 nickel buried in the kitchen junk drawer. Then I rummaged through every old pocketbook in my closet. I found a 1996 dime in an old change purse. Now all I needed was the 1996 quarter. I planned to buy a small inexpensive shadow box to display them, but I really wanted to find all the coins before I bought it.

Where else could I look?

Then I remembered the stash of change that I kept in the car. Armed with a Ziploc bag, I headed for the garage.

Car change is disgusting. I broke several nails trying to pry coins off the bottom of my cup holders, full of McDonald's sesame seeds and gooey Coke scum. If I found a 1996 quarter there, then I'd have to clean it before I could include it in the shadow box. I searched for the rest of the afternoon, but I couldn't find a single 1996 quarter.

Since God had given me the idea, I just had to trust him.

Later that day, I phoned my girlfriend about my plan. She said, "That's insane; just make a card! Besides, God doesn't have time to worry about the little things like that."

I know I must have sounded crazy, but I didn't care. I didn't listen to her. I kept praying. I knew it was a test, and I was convinced God did care.

I put in a load of wash and started supper. Then I remem-bered that I hadn't checked Shannon's nightstand. I raced into the bedroom and pulled everything out of the drawer. When I reached the bottom, I spotted a quarter. My hands shook as I flipped it over to check the date — 1995. I felt like God was laughing. 1995 was the year we got engaged. But that wouldn't work. I needed 1996. I tossed it back in the drawer along with the rest of the junk and returned to the kitchen. With only twenty-four hours left, I prayed harder.

The next morning Shannon wished me happy anniversary and

left for work. After I took the children to school, I called my mother-in-love and asked her to look around her house for the quarter. She said that she would, and I drove to A.C. Moore to buy a shadow box. By the time I finished running my errands, it was time to pick up the children. We returned home and I took out the shadow box. As a last resort, I decided to insert the 1995 quarter until I could locate the one I needed. I glanced at my watch; it was almost five o'clock. Soon my in-loves would pick up the children and Shannon would be home from work. I had about thirty minutes to finish up before I needed to get dressed for dinner.

I was on my way from the kitchen into the bedroom when I remembered that I hadn't run the dryer. I stopped in the laundry room, set the timer, and hit start. I took about seven steps toward my bedroom when I heard a loud clanging noise from the dryer.

No way! Could it be?

I raced back to the laundry room. With trembling hands, I opened the dryer door and removed each article of clothing, shaking every piece, one at a time. When I got to the last pair of jeans, I peered inside the dryer. Stuck to the inside back wall was a clump of fabric softener. How did it get there? Fabric softener goes in the washing machine, not the dryer. But nestled inside the clump of goo lay a quarter. I laughed out loud! I couldn't wait to see its date. I peeled it off the wall and flipped it over. Sure enough, it was 1996.

I cried and laughed at the same time. Not only did I find my 1996 quarter, but I realized that I'd experienced two miracles that day. How does a quarter clang around the dryer when it's stuck inside a clump of fabric softener? I believe there is only one answer. With only thirty minutes left, that was the only way God could get me to look inside the dryer.

I had just enough time to replace the 1995 quarter with the 1996 quarter before Shannon returned home. Needless to say, it was the most sentimental anniversary that we've ever shared. I enjoyed telling him the story even more than I enjoyed giving him the gift. That special shadow box still hangs on a wall in our bedroom. And every time I look at it, I am reminded of God's faithfulness, even in the little things.

~Amy S. Tate

48

In His Hands

The Lord will protect him and preserve his life
~Psalm 41:2

My childhood friend Amy, her mom Peggy, and my mom took a road trip together to the world's largest flea market, in Canton, Texas. The four of us have had many wonderful adventures together, yet I missed out on this particular trip because I was living in Chicago at the time.

After a full day of shopping, Peggy drove them home with the SUV packed with newly acquired treasures, including Christmas gifts, holiday decorations, and an elk-handled meat cleaver—proof that you never know what you'll find in Canton!

Camaraderie was in full swing as the stories flew. Mom, who could not quite hear the conversation from the back seat, contemplated taking off her seatbelt. Having taught driver's education for years, she decided that it would be better to miss out on the girl talk than to be unrestrained.

As the SUV cruised at 60 mph in the HOV (High Occupancy Vehicle) lane, right in the middle of rush-hour traffic, the other four lanes were full of stop-and-go traffic.

Nearby, a white car stopped suddenly to avoid hitting another car. The truck behind it swerved to miss it and crossed the double line, right in front of the SUV! There was nothing Peggy could do. They slammed into the truck, knocked into a cement barrier, and then flew through the air straight towards the oncoming traffic. Midair, the

SUV veered back to the right, flew thirty-five yards, crashed down and bounced on its tires, and then sailed into the air again. It then flipped head-to-toe, landing upside down, windshield to windshield on top of another car. Then it rolled again, finally landing driver-side down three lanes over from the HOV lane. In all, there were six points of impact.

Once they stopped, my mom shouted, "Amy, are you okay?"

"Yes,"

"Peggy, are you okay?"

No answer.

Amy noticed fluid leaking around the car. "We have to get out now!"

Peggy was regaining consciousness as Amy pushed on the door to open it. "It won't budge!"

People rushed over, trying to get the door open.

Then a man appeared, wearing white. He opened the door and lifted the three passengers out one-by-one.

When Peggy first saw him she thought, "Probably a dishwasher or a cook all dressed in white." After he lifted her out, she looked around again… and he was gone.

In the aftermath of the wreck, a policeman who had been traveling on the other side of the cement barrier said, "I knew for sure you were coming over the guardrail and straight at me. Something made your vehicle turn around in midair."

The rescue crew arrived and eventually turned the SUV upright. The door that had been so easily opened by the man in white wouldn't open again.

Another man came over to my mom and motioned toward the SUV. "What did they do with the people in that car?"

"We were in that car," said Mom.

"Really? Wow! I saw the accident and was sure that the people in that car wouldn't come out alive."

Moments later, an EMT approached my mom and pointed to the SUV. "Where did they take the people in that vehicle?"

"We were the people in that vehicle," Mom repeated.

The EMT shook his head. "I've never seen an accident like this where everyone came out alive."

Amy summed it up. "It was a miracle that we're alive."

Not only did all three walk away from the wreck, but the only injury was Peggy's broken finger.

"During all of the bouncing and flipping and rolling," my mom recalled, "I didn't feel any jarring. None of the things we bought hit me. We had a loose meat cleaver in the car, for goodness sake! Throughout the tossing and turning, I felt the unmistakable presence of something holding me—carrying me—until the SUV came to a stop."

To this day, she proclaims, "I am comforted to know that whatever happens in life, God is holding me in His hands."

~Michelle Sedas

49

The Easter Miracle

O Lord my God, I called to you for help and you healed me.
~Psalm 30:1

My sister Sandy was only twenty-five years old when she started experiencing shortness of breath and chest pain. She coughed a lot, but assumed she just had a bad cold. After collapsing on the floor from the pain one night, she went to the doctor for an exam.

"I have bad news for you," he told her, looking down at her chart. A young woman and nonsmoker, she shouldn't have been told, "You have lung cancer. It appears to be spreading."

Sandy looked up in horror. Lung cancer! Her husband smoked, but she had never touched a cigarette in her life. Yet she was the one for whom the sentence had been handed down.

"Only fifteen percent of patients make it five years," the doctor said. He explaining the treatment options, then patted her on the shoulder and left.

Who would raise her baby boy, only one year old?

How would her husband manage?

She drove home, numb to everything around her. "Fifteen percent of patients make it five years," played like a mantra inside her head. She needed to make plans and didn't have time to waste.

She informed her friends and in-laws, then began chemotherapy. Sometimes she went home from treatments, throwing up until there was nothing left inside her. The emptiness assailed her as depression sank in. She tried to cope with the brutal pain the best she could. Her husband gave her haunted looks as he contemplated a life without her.

Finally, Sandy consulted her priest. "Sandy, you need to put things into perspective. If the cancer doesn't get you, a bus might," he said philosophically. "Enjoy each day and try not to fret for tomorrow, for it isn't here yet."

Perspective helped Sandy to realize that maybe he was right. When her energy level allowed, she stayed active in church activities, raised her son and kept busy with her husband.

The doctor was not so positive, however. After another round of tests, he announced that the cancer was spreading even more. "Go home and make out your will. It looks as though you will only have six months to live."

Six months! Sandy couldn't accept this. She told others, "I'm expecting an Easter miracle!"

"Why do doctors think they are God anyway?" she asked herself bitterly. "Only God knows when it's someone's time to go."

As the days ticked off one by one, Sandy anticipated spring with more fervor than usual. She planted bulbs and trimmed the lilacs, as her energy level allowed. The countdown began: three weeks, then two weeks. Finally, it was just a few days before Easter when Sandy went to the doctor for an exam.

He did the usual round of tests, and then left the room in a hurry. He returned with several other doctors as they scanned the results, looking at her and then back at the chart.

Time stopped. My sister assumed the worst. Had the cancer progressed more rapidly than anticipated?

"Sandy, I don't know how to tell you this..." the doctor began.

Her heart dropped into her stomach as she waited for him to finish.

Quietly, he continued. "We can't see any sign of cancer anywhere. It's just... gone. I have no other words for it except to say... it's a miracle."

Sandy looked at the doctors in shock. She couldn't believe her ears. Gone? Gone! She wanted to race home and start making phone calls. She wanted to hug her son.

She ran to her car and looked up at the sky, which suddenly had taken on a deep blue hue. Puffy clouds sailed lazily by, the smells and sounds of spring enveloped her.

Her Easter miracle happened after all.

~Diane Ganzer

50

Speaking from the Heart

Now go; I will help you speak and will teach you what to say.
~Exodus 4:12

M y husband Rich and I decided to add to our family through adoption. There were many different avenues we could have taken, but one called to us in an extraordinary way. There was an article in the newspaper about a local family who had traveled to Romania and adopted there. We wondered if it was something we could do, so we talked to them. The adoption process seemed complicated, Romania was so far away, they spoke another language, and we didn't know anything about international adoption law.

To complicate matters, the government was making it difficult for foreigners to adopt, though the orphanages were overflowing with children. The orphans barely received medical attention, and in some cases did not even get the basic necessities that children need—food, clothing, and a warm clean bed. The orphanage workers did their best with what they had, but it wasn't enough. The children were suffering.

It was a simple decision to fly halfway around the world to a tiny country I knew little about. It was easy because I was doing the right thing. I left for Romania without my husband; we both couldn't afford to take time off work. I hated to leave him and I'll never forget how lonely I was as the plane taxied off the runway.

On the long flight I worried about what I would find once I got there. I had never been to another country and I was afraid I would struggle with the language barrier, especially since I am hearing-impaired and rely heavily on reading lips.

I hired Dragos, a translator, thinking that would be helpful, but it was still a challenge for me. He spoke broken English and I could barely read his lips to understand him. I had to concentrate intently on every word he spoke and I always made him repeat everything and talk more slowly. He was unbelievably patient with my hearing disability.

Days turned into weeks and they all seemed to blend together until I found Adela, or rather she found me. Before I could mother this beautiful child, I first had to complete a ton of paperwork. I had to cut through red tape and jump through numerous hoops to get appointments at the U.S. Embassy, meet with social workers, and translate some of the documents into the Romanian language and others into English. It seemed to take forever and I was worried that something would go wrong. But everything fell magically into place.

When the day arrived to finally meet with Rada, Adela's birth-mother, I was a nervous wreck. I would be receiving my daughter. Excited, scared, and relieved, I couldn't wait to finally hold Adela in my arms again. I felt a total acceptance that Adela's birthmother thought I was special enough to care for and love her baby forever.

Dragos stood off to the side so I could focus on the most precious moment of my life, accepting Adela, my new daughter.

Time seemed to stand still when I looked at Rada and she looked back at me. My heart thumped practically right out of my chest. I wondered how I could tell her that everything would be all right. She only spoke Romanian and I only knew English. At that moment she touched my arm and I felt my heart begin to melt. She gently placed Adela in my arms and I accepted my baby with an outpouring of love. She felt so warm and soft. I placed my hand on Adela's head and Rada placed her hand over mine.

She licked her dry lips and spoke to me in a hushed tone. "You will be able to care for her. I cannot, I am so young," she said.

"We'll love her and protect her with all our hearts. Please don't worry," I said, even though I knew she would.

She smiled warmly. "I won't worry because I see in your eyes how much you love her already. And I know you will give her a good home."

Tears welled in my eyes and rolled uncontrollably down my face. "You have given me the gift of life, love, a chance to be a mom again." I sniffled and she couldn't contain her tears either. "I'm so proud of you for having the courage and love to let her go."

She nodded as if to accept my words and a brief silence fell between us while we stared in wonderment at the child we were both cradling.

"Do you know she looks just like you, so beautiful and perfect? She has your hair," I said, looking right into Rada's dark brown eyes.

She blushed, and smiled, and let her eyes rest on Adela. "You are so kind," she murmured.

At that moment we both looked down at Adela and I placed my hand on Adela's tummy and she seemed to smile at us like she knew it was a special moment in our lives. Rada placed her hand over mine.

"She knows you already," she began. "She's smiling at you."

"No," I said, "she's smiling at us." We were both staring at our baby, studying every detail of her tiny face. I knew Rada was burning the image into her memory. It would comfort her through many years. I felt Rada's hands slowly slip off and she quietly walked away. I knew these would be the hardest steps she would ever take. Watching her leave was surreal and is etched in my memory forever.

Dragos rested his hand on my shoulder and peered into the tightly wrapped bundle in my arms. "I think you've been holding back on me," he said with a lilt in his voice.

I glanced up at him and read his lips. "I don't understand."

"Why did you hire me to be your translator?"

He didn't give me a chance to respond.

"I watched you with Rada. You didn't read her lips and you

spoke to her in perfect Romanian. I thought you didn't know this language."

"I don't know it."

"Then how did you just use it?"

No one could have been more surprised than me. My heart fluttered in my chest. "It was a miracle."

~Denise Colton-D'Agostino as told to Barbara Canale

51

Have a Little Faith

So then, don't be afraid. I will provide for you and your children.
~Genesis 50:21

I don't think my husband and I really understood what we had gotten ourselves into. Sure we knew things would be tough. We were both still in college, newly married, and our first baby had just been born. Life was chaotic, money was short, but we had more than enough love to get us through. What more did we need?

Life soon taught us that love doesn't put food on the table, nor does love magically make baby formula appear.

This reality was all too real as I looked helplessly at the neatly lined-up canisters of baby formula on the drugstore shelf. There were dozens of varieties. Name brand, off-brand, specialty, soy- and lactose-free. The one thing they had in common, however, was that they were all out of my price range.

I opened my purse for the hundredth time that morning and wanted to cry. I had $2.23. Not enough for a can of formula.

My sweet baby boy was sleeping in the shopping cart and at that moment panic set in. What would happen when he was hungry and I had nothing to give him? Sure I could ask my mom for help or my mother-in-law, but considering they were miles away, it wouldn't help me today. An unexpected car repair had taken every extra dime we'd had that month. And now my baby was going to go hungry.

I bought four packages of ramen noodles instead, and silently wondered if they were on the list of "okay foods for a three-month-old infant."

My husband was waiting for us in the car and after securing the baby I plopped into the passenger seat.

"What are we doing?" I choked back a sob. "We are barely making rent, barely getting studying done, and now we can't buy formula for our baby! We don't even deserve him."

My husband took my hand and kissed it, with tears of his own forming.

"Have a little faith, Em," he told me. "We knew it was going to be hard. I'll think of something. I won't let our baby starve, and neither will God."

At that moment something in me just snapped. My husband always had to throw the "faith" card into everything. I had never been one to pin my hopes on such an abstract idea and at that moment it seemed almost comically frustrating to me.

"Faith?" I asked in a snide tone. "You think *faith* is going to, right this minute, feed our newborn? Do you think *faith* is going to magically fill our fridge? If God really wanted to help us He would have never given us a beautiful baby and then allowed him to go hungry. Faith hasn't helped us much up to this point, Ryan. Why should it suddenly help us now?"

Ryan was quiet. He didn't chastise me, or lecture me, or even say anything to make me feel his disapproval. He just kissed my hand again and started the car.

"Well, I still have faith," was all he said.

The ride home was silent. I was worried about the night ahead. I had enough formula for one bottle, maybe two if I mixed it thin. In the morning I would call my mom, swallow my pride, and ask her to transfer money into my checking account. If only I could have bought one can of formula to tide us over until payday. Still, better to put away the ego and ask for help instead of letting my baby starve, I supposed.

My thoughts were interrupted as Ryan pulled into the small post office parking lot.

"Stopping for the mail," he announced. "I forgot to get it yesterday."

Our apartment complex didn't offer mail service so we had to stop at the post office every day and check our P.O. box. It was rainy and cold and I cursed this inconvenience as I hopped out of the car.

I inserted the key into our box and was surprised to find another key nestled among the pile of letters. Attached to it was a note:

"You have received a package that was too large for your post office box. Please use this key to retrieve it in box 40C."

What could the package be? We weren't expecting any sort of large delivery.

I located box 40C and turned the key. When the door opened my heart skipped a beat. I instantly recognized the symbol on the large box as the logo of the baby formula we had been using for our son. With all the excitement of a child on Christmas morning, I tore open the package to find two full-sized cans of formula inside, with a coupon for two more free cans to be redeemed at the store.

Still in shock, I ran outside to my waiting husband. I showed him the precious delivery and began to cry tears of relief. Knowing my child wouldn't go hungry that day or the rest of the week even, was the most uplifting sensation I had ever experienced.

"I don't know what to think," I told Ryan. "I can't believe that today, of all days, we would be so lucky to get free formula samples."

"Do you have faith now?" Ryan asked me with a smile.

That day was the beginning of my own relationship with God. I learned He is always by our side. He never lets us walk alone. We just have to have a little faith.

~Emily Weaver

52

It Can Happen Twice

To preserve a man alive
in the midst of so many chances and hostilities,
is as great a miracle as to create him.
~Jeremy Taylor

Some people are fortunate to have even one miracle in their lifetime. I am truly blessed with not one, but two.

Being a native New Yorker, I, like many others in the "Big Apple," made my career my priority. This can be exciting, not always easy, and occasionally cold and heartless. Working overtime was a regular habit to meet December deadlines. In my industry, fashion, a new line was being created and with spring market week less than a month away, I worked extra hours.

It was getting late one afternoon and the snow was starting to stick. I grabbed my coat and proceeded to my small one-bedroom apartment with work under my arm. I dropped off my handbag and paperwork at home, brushed the snow from my hair, and ran out to the Chinese take-out to get soup for dinner.

On the corner, I waited for the "don't walk" light to change, anticipating warm soup and a long evening of work.

There was very little traffic when the tiresome light finally changed. As I proceeded to the other side of the street, bright lights started racing toward me. I knew that in an instant I would be hit by a car.

A moment later I found myself getting up off the ground.

My first instinct was that the car had stopped and I slipped in the slush. What a relief! But then I realized something was amiss. My glasses were missing. So were my shoes.

Bystanders came running toward me. "Are you all right?" "I called the ambulance."

"I just slipped," I said, picking myself up off the street. "Where are my shoes and glasses?"

One witness motioned to a car parked to the side. "You were hit and your body landed on the hood of that car. Your head smashed the windshield."

I still did not believe I was involved. These people must have been mistaken. The police arrived and insisted that I go to the hospital. None of this made sense to me. Perhaps my body was in shock, but I did not feel any pain and there was no bleeding.

Someone found my mangled shoes… one block away. My glasses were located across the street, contorted like a pretzel. The implications were still not computing. I needed to get something to eat and go home and work.

But the ambulance took me to the hospital. Getting undressed, I found a few black and blue marks on my legs but nothing more. I was poked, prodded and X-rayed. I could walk, nothing was broken and I did not have a concussion. The doctors asked, "Are you sure you were hit?"

"The witnesses and police reports say I was."

As I left the hospital, I reflected that maybe I was saved from an awful fate to have a second chance. Perhaps it was a warning to learn to appreciate the precious moments given to me. I carried that experience as an informative life lesson and never forgot that message.

My life went on with a marriage and then a pregnancy. Like most couples, we were ecstatic. I watched my weight and ate right. In fact my craving turned out to be a healthy choice. I could not get enough fresh spinach.

My tentative due date was June 4th. The obstetrician said I was doing great. In January, I had a sonogram and was delighted to watch our baby bounce, kick and move about within me. The technicians informed me that we were having a boy.

The morning of February 3rd, I felt slightly queasy and noticed some blood. The doctor had seen me a few days before and everything was fine. I called him immediately and he said that this was likely a normal occurrence, but to be on the safe side, I made an appointment for that afternoon.

There the doctor discovered that I had an incompetent cervix. I had to get to the hospital immediately! I would deliver my baby seventeen weeks early. The doctor said sadly, "There is no way to save your baby; it's just too early."

When I arrived at the hospital, I was rushed into a room. My husband arrived within a few minutes and he held my hand as the doctor informed us that we could try to have a baby again in four months.

After I gave birth, our baby was quickly taken to the neonatal ward, alive, weighing 670 grams or one pound, six ounces. With translucent skin and visible organs, he could fit in the palm of my hand. Our baby boy made the neonatal ward his home until June 4th, my original due date. Then we took him home.

My husband and I witnessed his miraculous development each day for four months. He not only survived, but thrived. Today, after fifteen years, he still excels in his endeavors.

I suppose many would say the miracle of medical science saved him. But I believe God saved us both. He gave me that second chance. And I indeed appreciate the precious moments given to me.

~Veronica Shine

53

Mother's Intuition

A mother is a mother still, the holiest thing alive.
~Samuel Taylor Coleridge

I looked at my watch. Almost 4:00... the time I'd promised to leave the hospital. I'd practically lived there since our baby was admitted. Our pediatrician first heard Lisa's heart murmur when I'd taken her in for a lingering cold. "It's probably nothing serious," he reassured me, "but I think she should be seen by the doctors down at Children's Hospital."

Two days later, my husband, our five children, and I headed to Denver for Lisa's appointment. We planned to make a day of it, visiting the museum and having lunch out. Instead we ate in the hospital cafeteria while we waited for the results of EKGs and chest X-rays. When the doctors called us back to his office, we learned that Lisa had a condition called patent ductus arteriosus. "Before babies are born," he explained, "blood flow bypasses their lungs. When a baby begins to breathe, a temporary blood vessel is supposed to close. Lisa's hadn't, so oxygenated blood isn't getting to her body. She needs surgery."

I was terrified, but again the doctor reassured me, saying the condition was fairly common.

Lisa was admitted to the hospital and her surgery scheduled for the following week.

When friends heard of Lisa's hospitalization, they were wonderful, sending food, and caring for our other children. I drove home each night after Lisa fell asleep, then left at 5:00 a.m. to get back to the hospital before she woke. The schedule was taking its toll on our other little ones, and today my husband, a basketball coach, had a game so he couldn't pick up the kids for supper. With much encouragement from the nurses, I'd agreed to leave early.

I looked at my watch again… just 4:00. If I didn't leave soon, I'd get caught in the Friday afternoon traffic.

I knew I should go, but something made me stay.

Five minutes more wouldn't matter much.

At 4:05, I rationalized I could sing Lisa a couple more songs.

At 4:10, I readjusted the blinds and watered the plants.

At 4:15, I bent down to start Lisa's music box. She didn't look quite right. Her lips seemed slightly blue, her breathing shallow. Panicked, I pushed the call button. An aide arrived. She patted my shoulder. "Your baby is fine. You just go along home to your other children. We'll take care of Lisa."

I knew she was wrong. I ran to the nurses' station. "Please come," I begged. "Something's the matter with my baby."

One of the nurses looked up. "Don't worry; we took her vitals less than an hour ago. She was fine then. Someone from the next shift will check on her again as soon as we finish report. You just go along home and don't worry."

By then I was hysterical. "Somebody help!" I screamed as I ran through the halls.

The cardiologist's office was just beyond the patient rooms. His secretary jumped up to try to intercept me as I burst through the door. I grabbed the doctor's hand.

"You've got to come now," I sobbed. "Nobody will listen and my baby is dying."

"She's overwrought," the doctor whispered, "but I'll walk her back."

I didn't let him walk. I dragged him down the hall.

One look at my listless little one and the doctor sprang into action.

The room immediately filled with medical personnel. From the corner to which I'd been relegated, I listened in horror to snatches of their conversations: "heart failure... immediate surgery... touch and go... she'd probably have died... a miracle that her condition was discovered when it was."

It was a miracle, but then God often works his miracles through mother's intuition.

~Ellen Javernick

A Miracle in Greece

"Because he loves me," says the Lord,
"I will rescue him; I will protect him,
for he acknowledges my name."
~Psalm 91:13-15

My friend Steve lived on the East Coast but traveled regularly to Minnesota for business. During one trip, he was dining at his favorite Greek restaurant there when he noticed a waitress staring curiously at him. He engaged her in conversation and learned she was from a small town in northern Greece.

"That's exactly where my twin brother Tom is!" he exclaimed. "He's a Fulbright scholar studying Greek Orthodox icons there."

"I know. I recognized you as Tom's brother as soon as you walked in." She had just returned from an extended visit to her hometown in Greece, where she had met Tom at a local bookstore.

Steve believed things happen for a reason and a few weeks later he learned the reason for his coincidental meeting with the Greek waitress. He was back home on the East Coast when he received word that Tom was severely injured in Greece.

Tom had been walking down a rugged, seldom-used path, near a Byzantine monastery on Mt. Athos. It was the day of the feast of the Ascension of the Virgin Mary in the Greek Orthodox religion. Suddenly, the path, formed by a long-gone waterfall, crumbled and he plunged about a hundred and fifty feet, halfway down a cliff face of the mountain. Tom was knocked unconscious and when he came to he saw blood everywhere. Bones stuck out of his left arm. One of his legs was caught in a thorny bush and the other leg hung over the edge of the cliff.

Groggily he tried to determine what was preventing him from falling further. He became aware that he was being cradled on the crimson-colored shoulder of a woman, her arm wrapped around his midsection. He recognized the colors from his study of icons; the Virgin Mary was portrayed wearing crimson. Tom closed his eyes. When he reopened them he was surrounded by a brilliant white light that vanished after a moment.

Severely injured and in mortal danger, he was unable to move. He could see the tops of trees below him and began considering his options. After some time he began to despair. He was tempted to throw himself off the edge of the cliff and put an end to his suffering. No one would ever find him in that remote place.

A booming voice inside his gut responded adamantly to that temptation. "Oh no you don't! Who do you think you are that you can decide your own fate?"

Inspired, an incredible, uncontrollable survival instinct kicked in and he found the strength to crawl back onto the ledge, away from the cliff.

Tom survived the next three days on toothpaste, moss, and a handful of chickpeas and raisins. For water he pressed the damp soil between his fingers, and then licked his hands to quench his severe thirst. The raisins expanded from the morning dew and provided a tiny amount of additional liquid. He conserved his energy by yelling only when he heard a boat arriving at or departing from the coastline far below. During the darkness of night, his mind filled with the faces of everyone he had ever loved. He visualized those people handing him food and drink; he imagined himself thanking them for helping him survive.

Finally, on the third day, Tom's cries for help were heard. In dramatic and dangerous fashion, Greek villagers, monks, and an experienced rescue team arrived and carried him to safety.

The tending physicians diagnosed a broken collarbone and cervical vertebrae, a partially dislocated shoulder, bruised ribs and a severely injured left arm. They said it was a miracle that, despite his arm being shattered in thirty-two places, there was no infection, nerve damage or cut arteries.

When Steve heard of his brother's accident and the severity of his injuries, he was concerned about the limited medical care Tom might receive in that remote part of Greece. He recalled the Greek waitress he had recently met and she referred him to a wonderful local Greek doctor who helped nurse his brother back to health.

Though his recuperation was difficult, Tom knew it was a miracle that Mother Mary had been his first rescuer that day.

But that was not to be the last miracle.

During his recovery, Tom came across a series of twenty-two paintings he had drawn months before the accident. He had titled them "Out of Darkness." The paintings showed in progression a silhouetted person falling off the edge of something, then sprawling on a platform. The person went from a dark to light form as the scenes unfolded. When Tom had painted them, his intention was to portray life as a pre-game warm up, an interim step toward the end result, which is death and then eternal life. In reviewing these paintings after the accident, he was stunned by the striking similarity to his accident. Perhaps God had been trying to get his attention and he had not been listening. At the time of the drawings, Tom was in a spiritual abyss, depressed and feeling alienated from God.

During his recuperation, he experienced an explosion of personal and spiritual growth. Filled with faith, hope and charity, he aligned himself with those who suffer around the world. He knows he is never alone. God is always with him.

Tom does not view his accident as something "bad." He now believes everything happens for a reason. As he says, "We just need to be ready to listen and act on the messages we receive."

~Mary Treacy O'Keefe

A Book of Miracles

Answered Prayer

*I call on you, O God,
for you will answer me;
give ear to me and hear my prayer.*

~Psalm 17:5-7

55

Miracle on the Hudson

In hindsight,
I think something remarkable did happen that day.
~Capt. Chesley "Sully" Sullenberger III

I t was Thursday morning, January 15, 2009. I was in New York City where I traveled to work on a regular basis. It was about 10:30 a.m. and snow was coming down pretty hard. I had checked the weather forecast because I had a 7 o'clock flight home to Charlotte, North Carolina, and I didn't want to get stuck. The Weather Channel website said the snow was going to quit and it was going to be a nice day.

I went into a meeting with my boss about 11 o'clock and snow was still coming down.

"What are you still doing here?" he asked. "You're going to get stuck up here. You really ought to get home."

So I rebooked for the 2:45 p.m. flight. Seat 16E.

When I boarded the plane, I was on my cell phone, sending texts, talking to people right up until they closed the cabin door. We taxied for about thirty minutes, as is usual at LaGuardia Airport, and we took off.

Sitting back, I felt the steep climb that pressed me against the seat. I opened the newspaper to read the remnants of *The Wall Street Journal* that I hadn't finished that morning.

There was a muffled bang that I could literally feel. The whole plane shuddered.

"What could that possibly be?" I wondered.

The plane went into a really steep bank to the left. It was all going so fast. I thought maybe the plane was out of control and it was over. But the pilot, who had identified himself earlier as Captain Chesley Sullenberger, seemed to get control back. He stabilized the plane.

There was no panic. After the initial gasp from everyone, it was very, very quiet.

I was looking around and listening when I heard somebody on the left say, "We must've hit something. I saw shadows."

Then a little later, someone else said, "The left engine is on fire!"

Even at this point, I wasn't terribly worried. I figured we had two engines, and if need be we could fly with just one.

But as time passed I realized how quiet it was on the plane. There was nothing but the whistling of the wind. It dawned on me—we had no power. We were literally gliding and we weren't very high. That's when I sat bolt upright and grabbed my head. I felt a cold fear like nothing I'd ever experienced.

I prayed intensely. I repeated, "Please God, help us. Please God, forgive me," over and over again. Nothing coherent. There were just too many thoughts going through my head.

Yet I still had hope. If they could at least get one engine going… we just needed some power to get back to LaGuardia. We'd only been up for three minutes; certainly we could turn around and make a safe landing.

That hope went out the window when I realized we were getting lower and lower, following the river. When that realization set in—sheer terror—I realized the likelihood of dying on this plane. There was nowhere, no one to turn to but God.

I prayed intensely. I was there with Him. It was the closest I'd ever felt to Him. I didn't bargain: "If you save us, I will…" Instead, I prayed for my family, my children, my wife.

Shortly thereafter, Captain Sully came over the intercom. "This is the captain. Brace for impact."

There was nothing in those words for me but death and pain. A cold hard reality hit me, and there was nothing I could do about it. I was strapped in my seat, completely and utterly powerless.

In the midst of that utter hopelessness, I was looking forward, as crazy as that might sound. What was death going to be like? Was it going to be just complete darkness? Or a bright light? Perfect clarity? Joy? What was it going to be like in the presence of God? I believe God gives us all hope even in dire moments. It was such a blessing to have that sense of hope and that sense of salvation.

I pulled out my BlackBerry. I wanted to get a message to my children… to give them something to carry with them through their lives, some sort of closure. I was trying to do that as I looked out the window, watching the water come faster and faster. I put the BlackBerry down, closed my eyes, and pleaded, "God, please let me see my children again." Then, "God, this is going to hurt so bad."

I was terrified, not necessarily of death and what comes after that, but I was really worried about the pain.

We hit the water. The BlackBerry came up and hit me right on the bridge of my nose, just about knocking me out.

And we came to a stop.

I knew immediately we were okay.

The impact was not terribly traumatic. I knew the plane was intact and not broken up. No one was going to be severely injured.

I got into the aisle, and the emergency doors were open. I saw a beautiful, clear, blue day, twenty degrees, sun light streaming in. It was the most wonderful feeling I have ever felt. Symbolic it seemed, like it was a new day, a new life. A beginning.

I filed out the doorway to step onto the wing, and turned back around to get a lifejacket. No one had announced that we were going to make a water landing and to remember our lifejackets underneath the seat cushion. Of course all the cushions by the exit row had been stripped away and I found none.

I did absolutely nothing right. I did everything wrong, but I still came out of this. If I had gotten out there on the wing, and the wing was sinking, and the ferries were not there, I would have drowned because hypothermia would have overtaken me in ten minutes.

Be that as it may, I stepped out on the wing without a lifejacket. I already saw the ferry coming and it was like a dream for me. So many things went wrong. But so many other things went right. An amazing turn of events.

After that day, I got at least a dozen e-mails of the drawing of the plane with God's hands lowering it down—"What Really Happened on the Hudson River." I truly believe that.

Certainly for me, I came much closer to God that day. It was probably the only time that I've been intimately, truly wholly there and one with Him.

~Warren F. Holland

56

Sourcing Miracles

Hear, O Lord, and answer me,
for I am poor and needy.
~Psalm 86:1

It had been a painfully long year and in the wake of my divorce
I found myself with fewer than half of the possessions I owned
one year earlier. I focused on what I had... my children, my job,
my faith, and freedom from a difficult marriage. Those were the most
important things, I reasoned. I knew that my faith, coupled with my
ability to find a bargain, would combine to meet my need for a dining room set and a couch. Walking into a home and sitting with kids
on hardwood floors was enough to make the thriftiest shopper head
straight for the nearest mega-furniture store.

But shopping for new pieces was simply out of the question.
My salary kept me only slightly ahead of my bills. After a month of
saving, one Saturday I had an additional $100 to spend. So with my
checkbook in hand and faith in my heart, I set out to local yard sales
and distant thrift stores.

"Lord, I need a miracle today," I prayed before I pulled out of my
driveway. "But if today isn't the right day for a miracle, I would be
okay with that too."

Four hours and countless thrift shops and garage sales later, I
still had no dining room set or couch. I decided to see if I could find a
rug to go under the "miracle" dining room set I knew I'd find one day.

As I walked across the parking lot of my neighborhood home center I reminded myself I was "just looking." Yeah, right.

With the help of a kind young man from the home center, we loaded my new rug into my car and off I went, delighted that the very affordable area rug exactly matched the color scheme of my soon-to-be dining room.

As I drove, I prayed. "But Lord, I still need a table and chairs and a couch. I would love to sit at a dinner table with my kids at the end of a day."

Resigning myself to the obvious fact that today was not a day for miracles, my mind wandered as I drove the familiar route home.

As I meandered past cow pastures and horse farms, I passed a row of long-needled pine trees standing along the side of the road. And there beneath the trees sat a dining room table and four chairs with a sign on the table declaring them "Free!"

I turned my car around and pulled over to examine my dining room set. In beautiful condition, the top needed to be sanded and re-stained, but that was work which I would gladly undertake. One by one, I removed the table legs and somehow managed to fit everything in my little Japanese car, a feat only a determined mother with no furniture could accomplish. Several cars slowed down, inspecting my find.

"Yes, I'm taking it," I replied multiple times.

Leaving three of the four chairs behind, I took the "Free" sign and put it in the back of the car, lest anyone should think the chairs were up for grabs. I planned to return and load the remaining chairs as soon as I unloaded the rug, table, and legs into my garage.

I worked at lightning speed and returned to pick up the remaining chairs within fifteen minutes. I was shocked to find they were gone. Another passerby must have thought I'd left them because I didn't want them.

Disappointed, I got back into my car and headed home, following the same route I had taken moments earlier. And there, a few miles up on the side of the road with a "Free" sign attached to it, was a beautiful, floral couch that perfectly matched the colors of my family room! "This was not here five minutes ago!" I shouted to no one.

I knocked on the door of the home from where I suspected it came and an older man answered. I explained my sorry situation to him and with a smile he promised he'd hold the couch long enough for me to make arrangements to pick it up.

The next day I loaded it onto a rental truck and brought it home. During a few weeks of persistent searching, I found three chairs, all unmatched, which perfectly fit my "shabby chic" décor.

Now, with each meal served at our table and each long chat on the couch, I think of those times when God showed up just at the right moment and met my need. As I explain to my children, God does answer prayer. All we need to do is ask.

~Elisa Yager

57

Miracle on the Mountain

He trusts in the Lord;
let the Lord rescue him.
Let him deliver him, since he delights in him.
~Psalm 22:8

M y name's Doug. I'm a ski patroller at a major California resort. One snowy day I was doing a "hill check," looking for problems. I skied through an area closed to the public because the snow guns were blasting. Suddenly my skis ran across a sticky pile of un-groomed snow. They froze up and stopped dead. I blew out of my bindings. My head hit the ground. My body slammed in behind it. There was an explosion inside me, like a concussion through my entire body. I tumbled downhill, ending up face-down, spread-eagle, looking up the hill.

I couldn't get up or even move. I couldn't feel my arms, my legs, my chest, anything. I couldn't breathe. My training told me the news: a spinal cord injury paralyzing my breathing. I couldn't key my radio. I could only lie there, feeling my life leak out of me like air from a punctured balloon. I knew I was dying.

I glanced uphill, looking for help.

That's when I saw my father standing there. Dad had been dead for seven years.

He did not look ghostly at all. He was wearing his usual old brown pants and yellow windbreaker, as if he'd just come out for a walk. I guessed he was there to guide me over to the other side.

Breathless, I mouthed the words, "What do I do now?"

Dad said, "Just breathe."

I looked down. My chest was beginning to rise and fall. Cold air rushed into my lungs; warm vapor puffed out. I looked up to say thanks, but Dad was gone.

Within minutes, a team of my fellow patrollers arrived, six guys I knew very well — Rick, Josh, Scott, Eddie, Chuck and Alex. Top notch patrollers, best of the best. All six of these guys were devout Christian men, active in their churches. Eddie was an ordained minister.

They went into the routine: C-collar, oxygen, backboard. When they rolled me over, I looked up into their faces and knew I was in good hands. Overhead, the clouds broke. A shaft of bright sunlight hit us. Just then the boys went "off-book." They put their hands on me and prayed that I would be healed, that my healing would be a sign of God's love, compassion and will, that I would forever be a witness to that.

As they prayed, all my fear vanished. I felt I was only playing a part here, that this was something bigger than me, and whatever it was, I was willing to accept it.

After they prayed, they went to secure my hands across my chest. When my right hand touched my chest, I said, "I feel that!" Again with my left hand, "I feel that!" The feeling was far away, but it was there. I felt an immediate rush of gratitude, a sense of divine grace. I knew a miracle was taking place.

Medically, I was a mess: multiple spinal cord contusions in my neck, deep-cord syndrome, and incomplete quadriplegia.

My recovery progressed at an extraordinary rate, mind-blowing even to my doctors. Soon I was able to wheel myself around to share my story with other patients at the hospital. It seemed to truly resonate with people, to inspire them, to connect them with their own faith.

My old friend Vicky came to see me. Her husband, Michael, had died five years earlier from melanoma. We were sitting in the hospital garden under a giant banyan tree and I was telling her my story of how my comrades had prayed over me and saved me. I said, "I know there are angels in this world, and some of them wear red jackets with white crosses."

Then something happened. I looked at Vicky and said, "There's one more angel. It's Michael. He's here."

For the next several minutes, I had the clear sense that Michael was speaking through me to his wife. The words are not important. What is important is that there was a beautiful love, forgiveness, completion. They got to say, "I love you," one more time.

The next day I was in the garden again and Michael came to visit… just like Dad had. He told me something specific to tell his wife. It made no sense to me, but I knew it would to her. I didn't call Vicky right away. I didn't want to dilute what had happened the day before, in case maybe I was just crazy. I held onto it all day, until the last phone call at night.

"Vicky," I said, "Michael came to see me. He wants me to tell you to re-read the letter he wrote to you when the two of you first found out he was terminal, the one you keep in the box under the bed."

Vicky just lost it on the phone. She confirmed the existence of the letter in the box under the bed. She said, "I haven't been able to read that letter for years, but I was compelled to read it again today, after what happened in the garden yesterday."

And the miracles after my accident just kept coming!

There was a very old woman named Macie in the spinal wing. She couldn't walk, wouldn't participate in her therapy, was awake all night and had bedsores. The hospital was planning to transfer her out to a facility where she would eventually die.

One day I wheeled into her room. She was blown away that anyone would care enough to talk to her. I told her my story. She told me hers. We got to be friends.

The next day I was out in the garden again. I held up my hands to heaven and said, "If it's possible for a group of guys to put their hands on me and transmit this healing energy, why can't I do that for someone else?"

The voice in the garden responded, "What makes you think you can't?"

"Oh," I said, and spun my chair around. I rolled back up to the unit, grabbed my friend Pat, an amazing 300-pound Christian woman, a patient who rode around on a little power scooter who had become my friend when she'd heard my story.

"Pat, come on," I said. "I need a witness."

The two of us wheeled into Macie's room and beside her bed. "Macie," I said, "I've been out in the garden and God told me He was going to allow me to heal people by putting my hands on them."

I'll never forget the look of love and soul in those old eyes when she looked at me and said, "Oh, would you put your hands on me, please?"

I put my hands on her and prayed for her, just as the men on the mountain had prayed for me. Pat prayed with eloquence and passion. There was a powerful, moving energy in the room for a half hour or more. When it was over, it was clearly over.

I was drained, elated but exhausted. I headed to my room, fell into bed, and didn't move all night.

The next morning I rolled out into the hall. Pat was just coming out of therapy and we circled up together, talking about last night. Suddenly we heard a small high-pitched voice.

"There he is," she exclaimed. Pat and I both turned around.

Macie was coming towards us, walking on her own down the hall beside her astonished physical therapist. "There he is," Macie rejoiced. "The power of Christ has done come through Doug and I can walk again today!"

I know it was Macie's own faith that healed her. I was only called upon to facilitate that. Macie and I both continued to improve, and on the same day I left the hospital to go home, Macie left the hospital… to go home.

My own recovery has been astounding. Two and a half years after my injury, I completed the L.A. Triathlon at the Olympic distance. I now participate regularly in triathlons and other endurance events, as opportunities to celebrate my recovery and to support charitable causes.

My comrades on the mountain put their hands on me and prayed that day, that my healing would be a sign of God's love, compassion and will.

And I will forever be a witness to that.

~Doug Heyes, Jr.

58

Fueled by Faith

We have confidence before God and receive from him anything we ask,
because we obey his commands and do what pleases him.
~1 John 3:21-22

The night air blew on my young unblemished face as our car lumbered along on the long asphalt road. It was a Wednesday, like many others before. My mom, three brothers, two sisters, and I were on our long trip home from a church youth activity. Although I was not quite old enough to attend the youth socials, my mom worked with the program, so I always looked forward to watching from the back of the room as spirits were lifted and laughs shared.

Perhaps one reason I looked so forward to the Wednesday church nights as a child was not because of my burning faith, but because it pulled me away from the troubles that often waited at home.

During these long hard years, my family of eight struggled financially. It was difficult for my father to keep a steady job, and my mother barely earned minimum wage at a physically and emotionally demanding job. There were many times when we truly did not know where our next meal would come from, but we somehow always survived. And we somehow always made it to church every Wednesday and Sunday.

On this particular Wednesday, we all piled into the car and drove the thirty long miles from our old wood-frame home in the secluded country to civilization, to church. My mother must have known that she was low on gas and lower on money, but her determination overpowered her logic.

There we were on our way home from church on a dark empty road somewhere between civilization and home, and our 1980 Ford station wagon stalled, then rolled to a dead stop.

We sat there for a few minutes that seemed more like hours, while my mother frantically tried to restart the car. I sensed her nervousness and felt fear creep into the car. There we sat, long before the days of cell phones, completely alone. I can only imagine some of the thoughts that crept through her mind. My dad was out of town. No one would even realize we were in trouble. We could sit there all night. Finally, Mom turned around and looked over the back seat to where all six of the children were piled together.

"Kids," she said softly, but intently, "we are going to have to pray."

None of us asked questions. We were a family that relied heavily on prayer. However, in that intense moment, we all knew that this prayer was different from the ones that we said safely kneeling by our beds. Each one of us seemed to take on his or her shoulders the responsibility of the family's safety. As a child, sitting there in that car with my hands folded tightly and tears streaming down my cheeks, I prayed harder than I ever had before.

We pleaded out loud, fully convinced that Someone out there was aware of us. I cannot recall how long we prayed, but I can easily recall the feeling of peace that came over us like a warm blanket. We stopped praying, raised our bowed heads, and looked up at each other.

My mother smiled sweetly and reassuringly and slowly moved her hand toward the key. She clicked the key just enough to make the gauge lights come on. Our eyes locked on the needle that seemed to tauntingly hang there below the "E." Full of hope, we all watched intently, waiting for my mom to try to start the car. Just then, before she could turn the key, the needle on which all eyes were locked began to move up. Slowly, before our amazed and frightened eyes, the needle moved above the "E."

Mom glanced back at us with a look of amazement that soon turned to gratitude and joy. She quickly turned the key, started the car and drove all the way down that lonely road safely to our driveway.

We did not speak of the incident on the ride home or the next day. We did not need to. The next morning, as my mom poured gas from a gas can into the car to get it to start again, I watched, knowing that something miraculous had happened to all of us the night before... something none of us could ever deny. The hope that may have been young and unsteady before was forever embedded in my heart. From that point on, I knew that miracles could happen and that my life would always be fueled by faith.

~Courtney Rusk

59

Summer Faith

But Jesus called the children to him and said,
"Let the little children come to me, and do not hinder them,
for the kingdom of God belongs to such as these."
~Luke 18:16

It was one of those dreary, cold rainy days in February that Portland, Oregon is famous for, and my mood was as miserable as the weather. Some people like rain. I am not one of those people. I had already gotten drenched once that day; taking my three-year-old daughter Summer to her Christian preschool, so the last thing I wanted to do was to go out in it again. But it was two o'clock and she needed to be picked up by two-thirty.

The traffic was terrible. When I finally pulled into the school parking lot, it was quarter to three. I knew Summer's teacher was not going to be happy.

I parked the car, pulled my coat collar tight and buttoned it, then reached for my umbrella, which wasn't under the front seat where it should have been. Someone (it couldn't have been me, of course) had left it in the garage that morning. I muttered a couple of words that likely made my Guardian Angel cringe, and hurried through the lake forming on the concrete.

Inside, Teacher Jennifer lifted an eyebrow at me, obviously annoyed with my tardiness, and pointed down the hallway. Summer was bent over a table, working to finish a painting.

"Hi Mommy," she chirped.

"Come on, honey," I called. "We're late. Teacher Jennifer wants to go home."

She held up her artwork. "Look! I drawed it for you!"

I took the paper and squinted impatiently at it. "Uh-huh. Good." I nodded and handed her coat to her. She put the picture down and folded her arms.

She wasn't going anywhere until I apologized. And it better be believable.

"It's wonderful!" I gushed. "Best one you ever did!"

She finally nodded and obediently held out her arms for her jacket. Outside, the rain was now a freezing, nearly sideways sheet. Both of us were soaked by the time we got to the car.

"It's wainin," Summer observed from her car seat behind me.

"No kidding," I said, drying my dripping hair with a handful of Kleenex before starting the car. I was just pulling out when Summer yelled, "Wait! We gotta go back!"

I slammed on the brakes and turned around. "What are you talking about? Go back outside? Why?"

"My Care Bears mitten," she cried, waving a lonely right-hand Care Bear at me. "My mitten's gone. I musta leaved it in school."

"Oh for heavens… Wait a minute," I muttered, backing the car to the curb. Parking, I turned around to lean over the seat and undo her seatbelt. "Okay, look in your pockets."

"I did!" she wailed. "It's not there!" She turned both pockets inside out to demonstrate their mittenless-ness to me.

"Get up," I sighed. "Maybe you're sitting on it." She climbed out. No mitten. We checked around and under the seat and on the floor-boards. No mitten.

"See!" Summer cried. "We haffa go back!"

"No! Maybe it's outside, next to the curb." I opened the door and stuck my head out. Niagara Falls poured over what was left of my hairstyle. No mitten.

"That's it!" I pronounced with finality. "You have three pairs of mittens at home, for crying out loud. Now, get back in your seat so I can buckle you in."

"I want my bestest Care Bear mitten!"

"Well, I want a week in Jamaica."

Thinking on that kept her quiet for a moment or two, allowing me to get the car headed for home.

But five minutes later, "I want my mitten!"

Looking at her distressed face in the rearview mirror, I said, "You've made that perfectly clear. Now give it a rest. Please."

Eyes narrowed, frown lines deep, she muttered something threatening under her breath.

"What did you say?"

"I say," she pouted, "I ask Jesus. Jesus will get me my mitten."

Rolling my eyes, I said, "Jesus is NOT going to get you your mitten. He's busy with more important things."

"He will too," she stated firmly.

Once we finally got home and parked in the garage, we went into the house. I told Summer, "I've got a lot to do before I get dinner ready. Go play in your room, honey."

I hung up our coats in the laundry room and headed to the kitchen to deal with the dishes in the sink when I remembered the mail had to be brought in—from outside—in the rain. Groaning, I put my coat back on and stomped down the hallway to the front door. Summer followed on my heels.

Opening the door, I looked hopefully up through the rain for any sign of blue sky. A clap of thunder echoed in the distance. "Oh hush up!" I muttered, and prepared to sprint to the mailbox.

Before I could take a step though, Summer squealed.

"What now?" I groaned, spinning around.

"I tode you!"

"Tode me what?"

She pointed out the door, grinning.

I turned, and following her finger with my eyes, looked down at the doorstep.

There, on the welcome mat, was a Care Bear mitten. A left-handed Care Bear mitten.

I blinked in disbelief, my mind scrambling to make sense of what I was seeing.

What? How? My common sense tried to reason that she must have dropped it on her way out this morning. But no, we hadn't been anywhere near the front porch. We'd gone out through the garage. In fact, she and I had not been out the front door in more than a week.

Stunned, I turned to look into Summer's shining face.

"I tode you Jesus would get it for me!" she beamed.

Gathering her into my arms, I whispered, "Yes, you did, little girl. You really did."

Holding her tightly, I was overwhelmed with awe at our God who would perform such a miracle for a little child, simply because she stood steadfast in her faith.

After a minute, Summer pulled away to say, "Thank you, Jesus!" Then she picked up her mitten and skipped off to her room.

I looked up to heaven and whispered, "Amen to that, Lord."

~Tina Wagner Mattern

"Dear God, it's Billy … oh, that's right
- you have caller ID."

Reprinted by permission of
Jonny Hawkins ©2009.

60

Escape from Hell

Answer me when I call to you,
O my righteous God.
Give me relief from my distress;
be merciful to me and hear my prayer.
~Psalm 4:1

"Engine 18, respond to 1637 East 16th Avenue. Report of a fire. Time out 1935."

Cap was away. Brad was in charge. He and I were eleven-year vets. Greg was the rookie.

The address was close by. If there was indeed a working fire, we'd have to handle it. Help would be a while arriving.

At the scene, I noticed brown smoke wafting from the rear roof area of an old yellow two-story house. It appeared to be a bedroom fire. The residents assured us everyone was out. As Brad radioed our situation, Greg got ready to fight his first, for real, house fire.

I entered and climbed the stairs, stopping short of the landing. With my face at floor level, I looked down the hall... two doorways on the right and a closed door at the end. Smoke had banked down about a third of the way. I took a mental snapshot.

Back at the front door, Brad was ready to make entry. Greg was still nervously making gear adjustments. I saw myself in him. I knew he'd be telling this story one day. Without Cap, there was no time for the usual training. We needed to knock this fire down and out. I took the line that would guide us back out from Greg. "Get your mask on and let's go."

Smoke darkened all but a foot from the floor now. Visibility grew worse and heat increased as we moved forward. The door at the end of the hallway had no knob—something was lurking—waiting to pounce. I removed a glove and touched the door. It was plenty hot. We could hear fire consuming the house around us.

Brad hollered, "Get ready, I'm gonna kick it in."

On my knees with Greg in tow, I yelled, "Ready; do it!"

One hard kick set the door ajar. Angry flames reached through. One more thrust and the door flew open.

I leaned in and opened the nozzle full blast. The volume of water should have choked the fire, but it raged on, roaring about my head. "Force yourself to hold and fight this beast," I thought. My head was in the mouth of this dragon and it was about to bite down when the life force within possessed me and I bolted back. "I've got to get out. Get out! Get out!" I commanded.

I left the nozzle running in the doorway. Through my ear tabs and hood my ears were burning and the penetrating heat was taking my breath. When I bolted, I sent Greg rolling like a billiard ball into a side pocket.

Out of the flames and perhaps ten feet down the hallway, I was in total darkness. At that point I heard a desperate voice cry out, "No, No, No!" One of my buddies was charging me to come back because the hose was doing the job, or one of them was in trouble. I turned and after a few steps was back in the blinding flames.

Then the building exploded.

For a second everything went bright white, then slammed together again with a fierce shudder. Orange and black spun like a tornado. The explosion ruptured my store of strength and erased my mental image of the interior. I hadn't come in contact with anyone on my return. I instinctively knew I had to use what energy I could muster to get out of the bowels of this monster.

One step and I ran into the wall. The explosion had turned me sideways.

A hurried over-correction caused me to run into the opposite wall.

My helmet was falling off because it was melting and the straps had burned off. As I grabbed for it, I collapsed. I knew I had only seconds to live if I couldn't get out immediately. I thought, "Where's the way out?" An answer followed. "You're not getting out. You might as well take your mask off and die in a hurry."

I tried to ward off that enemy, but gave out after crawling just a few feet.

Pressed against the right side wall, all I could see was the raging orange and black storm.

All I could hear was the victory roar of the dragon.

All I could feel was my flesh burning.

Like a View-Master picture wheel, the face of my pretty wife rolled before me. I said, "Find our little boy a father. He'll need a man in his life. I love you." Then my older son to whom I said, "Go to college. It's all prepared for you." Next my sweet little girl; we smiled and exchanged love eye to eye. Lastly my little buddy. "I'll always love you, Buddy."

I knew my face piece would melt any second, but my thought was, "I'm not dead yet." My training reminded me that I had an obligation to fight to survive.

I'd had other training as well. As I pushed myself to hands and knees, I drew a hot labored breath and uttered the name, "Jesus!"

In that instant the roaring ceased. The terror dissipated. The pain dissolved. The fear vanished.

Despite the dragon's blazing rage, I was at total peace.

A soothing voice spoke, "Over here," and I began crawling in that direction. As if someone lifted the corner of a curtain, the fury of orange and black turned into white light. I lunged into the light and found myself sliding down the stairs and rolling out the door.

My crew doused me with water and with my first breath of fresh air I exhaled, "Thank you Jesus!"

Brad and Greg had followed my command and crawled out following the line. Once outside and seeing I wasn't there, the same loyalty that drew me back in for him, drew Brad back in for me. He was trying to scale up the stairs at the same moment I was sliding down them. But he neither heard nor saw me rolling out. Back outside, he was astonished to see me. He approached and said, "Herm, I thought we bought it that time."

We soon learned that the fire was a work of arson that started in the basement. I had only been throwing water through the top of the flames. When the first firefighter of the next company opened the back door and stepped inside, he fell through the floor and hurt his back. As his buddy pulled him out of the flaming hole, the back pain had caused him to cry out, "No, No, No!" The rush of air from that back door being opened fed the fire and caused the explosion.

With my burns and bandages, my wife didn't recognize me, but my escape from hell was just a part of my miracle. My healing was swift. Only skin grafts on my arms reveal I was ever burned. It's the badge of the good Lord's miracle that saved me.

~Herchel E. Newman

61

Remembering to Pray

Ask and you will receive,
and your joy will be complete.
~John 16:24

I t was a beautiful Thanksgiving Day, with bright blue skies and unseasonably warm weather. Instead of enjoying a turkey meal with family, though, we were moving for the second time in a year. The previous year we had rented a house while waiting for the farmhouse we bought to be vacated and remodeled. Finally, the remodeling was finished and we were moving into our home.

For several years we had searched for just the right piece of land in the country. As soon as we saw this slice of heaven on earth, we knew our search was over. With more than fifty acres, it consisted of a little of everything we'd hoped for. A peaceful rambling brook divided the lush golden meadow from the dense forest. Tucked inside the forest were lots of winding deer paths, and even a spring on the side of a hill that flowed into a quaint trickling waterfall. Thousands of sweet-smelling pine trees dotted several soft rolling hills. My husband's favorite part was the stocked pond, just a few yards from the back deck of the house, a fisherman's dream come true.

As I lugged yet another box from the bed of the pickup truck, I paused to scan the peaceful serenity of the surroundings. It was easy to feel God's presence here. Birds were in constant celebration from sunup to sundown, and graceful white-tailed deer would stop for a moment to stare at us, flick their fluffy tails and bound away.

I stood mesmerized by the bright sun glistening on the pond, its soft lull instantly relaxing me. Gazing at the water, I recalled a conversation from just a few days before. My husband Chuck and I were strolling the perimeter of the pond with the previous owner Eric, when Eric nonchalantly mentioned, "You need to set some traps for muskrats. They're tearing apart the dam on your pond."

Chuck and I had looked at each other and gulped. "Great," I thought. "Add that to the list of things to do."

Still daydreaming, I heard Chuck speaking to me, snapping me back to the present.

"Ya know," he said in a voice more tired than usual, "we still need to get our washer and dryer out of storage." Then he added with a heavy sigh, "I hope they'll both work."

The washer and dryer were the last items to move. We had purchased them twenty years earlier when we were first married, and now that we'd overspent our budget remodeling, we hoped they'd last a little longer.

Later that day, we wrestled the washer and dryer into the basement and got them leveled. I held my breath when Chuck plugged them in, then turned them on. The gentle purring of their motors was thrilling... yet short-lived. We watched in despair as a puddle of water formed under the washer. Then we noticed the air in the dryer wasn't getting warm.

"No problem," I said, trying to be optimistic. "I'll call my brother Danny. He'll know what to do."

Danny was an appliance repairman and one of the best. So it shouldn't have surprised me when his wife answered and said his schedule was full. It would be weeks before he could come out. My heart sank again.

Exhausted, I plopped down at the kitchen table and cupped my face in my hands. First muskrats, and now appliances. What next? I sobbed. I didn't even know what a muskrat looked like, much less how to get rid of one. And where would we get the money to replace the old washer and dryer?

Suddenly, an image of a special five-year-old Sunday school

student, Tiffany, came to my mind. One Sunday morning while teaching her kindergarten class, I realized to my horror that I'd left the lesson, including crafts, at home. I began to panic, wringing my hands and murmuring out loud about my predicament.

Tiffany had promptly marched up to me, tugged at my dress, and matter-of-factly reminded me, "Just pray about it, teacher. God knows how to fix it."

That's it—prayer! The very message that I had been trying to impress upon those young minds was now a good message for me.

I bowed my head and thanked God for all that He had done for us and for the beauty of the earth. I also asked Him to please help us get our washer and dryer fixed and show us how to deal with those pesky muskrats.

I was instantly filled with peace. So much so that later that evening when my husband mentioned shopping for a washer and dryer soon, my answer surprised him.

"I don't have a sense of urgency about this." I couldn't explain it, but I knew it would be taken care of.

The next day, however, when the phone rang, nothing could have prepared me for what transpired.

The caller was a man named Phil, a friend and coworker of Danny's.

"Uh, Connie," he began a little sheepishly. "I, uh, just finished talking to your brother. I called him to get your number and he told me about your old washer and dryer. Well, I, uh, thought maybe we could work something out."

I was momentarily speechless, thrilled at the prospect of getting the appliances fixed.

"Well, sure," I spoke at last. "What did you have in mind?"

"You see," Phil went on hesitantly, "my teenage son likes to trap."

"Great!" I anxiously interrupted. "He can trap in the forest. No problem."

"That's not what I had in mind," Phil continued. "I heard you have a pond and, well, uh, if you and Chuck let my son trap muskrats on your pond, I'll fix your washer and dryer."

Chills ran up and down my spine as I recalled a precious little girl tugging at my skirt.

Yes, Tiffany, God does know how to fix it.

~Connie Sturm Cameron

62

Late Night Meetings

You hear, O Lord,
the desire of the afflicted;
you encourage them, and you listen to their cry.
~Psalm 10:17

A few years back, I went through an extended period of insomnia. Several times a week, I'd wake between 2:00 and 3:30 a.m. I fought it as best I could. I'd keep one eye closed as I navigated my way across our bedroom and into the bathroom, hoping to fool the other eye into believing we were still asleep. It rarely worked. I'd stumble back to bed, resume my best falling-asleep position, and lie there for long minutes, or an hour... or two... wondering what in the world was wrong with me that I couldn't sleep through the night.

But it occurred to me one night that maybe I wasn't waking up at all. Maybe I was being awakened.

"Is it You, Lord?" I asked. "Are You waking me?"

I tried to come up with a reason why God would want to interrupt my sleep. After rejecting "practical joke" and "health sabotage," I was left with the only reasonable conclusion: He missed me. Perhaps we hadn't had enough us-time during the day, and He waited until dark to get me alone.

I decided I'd go with that. "Lord, from now on, if I wake in the middle of the night... I'll know it's You."

He took me up on that offer.

During this time, my husband and I gave away our mobile home and moved into a teeny travel trailer, which was to be our dwelling for the six months it would take to build our new house. It wasn't the ideal situation for middle-of-the-night meetings, but I long ago gave up arguing with God. If He wanted me to ease myself inch by slow inch across Dave's snoring body and grope around in the darkness for my robe and slippers, then so be it.

I took to keeping a square of tin foil near the dining table so I could mold it around the plastic light cover, allowing only a small directed beam of light to leak downward and onto the pages of my Bible. The sounds of my sleeping family, the slumbering earth, and the burbling water heating in my teakettle collectively created the most peaceful silence I've known.

I'd sip my cocoa and read and listen. God never failed to speak to me in those quiet hours. Sometimes He'd speak to a specific need in my life. Most nights He just told me He loved me. We doubtful beings never stop needing that reminder, and He knows that.

I learned a great deal about the heart of God in those late night meetings—and all the meetings since.

One night several years ago, long after we'd moved into our home and given away that little travel trailer, I felt that familiar nudge and rose to meet with God. But the moment I sat down, before I could even open my Bible, I felt a strong need to repeat a favorite scripture: "When the enemy comes in like a flood, the Spirit of the Lord will lift up a standard against him." Isaiah 59:19 (NKJV)

I didn't know why I felt such an urgency to speak that verse, but I said it anyway. And then I said it again... and again. For an entire hour, my mind was completely trained on that one truth from Scripture, and all I could do was sit in the stillness of my living room and repeat the words over and over. I have never before or since felt an inclination to pray that way, but it was clear on that night that God would have me do nothing else.

It was 3:30 when I stopped. Though I felt completely energized, as if I'd just taken the most wonderful nap and was ready to face my day, I also felt so at peace that I knew I'd fall asleep as soon as I sank down into my pillow—and I did.

The next day, a friend called me. As our conversation progressed, she kept yawning into the phone.

"Tired?" I asked, laughing.

"I am," she said. "I haven't been sleeping well. I keep waking up in the middle of the night."

"Me, too," I said. "In fact, I was up last night."

"I was, too," my friend said.

I then explained what had happened the night before. "It was the strangest thing, but I felt completely riveted, completely focused on repeating those words. 'When the enemy comes in like a flood, the Spirit of the Lord will lift up a standard against him.'"

I heard a long pause on the other end. And then she asked, "Exactly what time were you up?"

"From 2:30 to 3:30."

The pause lengthened, and when my friend spoke again, I heard tears in her voice. "God had you up praying for me."

She said she had awakened at 2:00 with a heart so heavy it drove her to the bathroom floor, where she lay sobbing and trying to pray. She didn't share the exact nature of her grief; she simply said that life felt too hard; hope seemed too distant. She felt utterly overwhelmed, she said, by a flood of worry, fear and despair. Until suddenly, at 3:30, the darkness fled, the heaviness lifted and she felt awash in peace.

And at the same moment that I rose from my couch and returned to my pillow, my friend rose from the floor and returned to hers.

I am often completely taken aback by the knowledge that the God who dreamed up gravity and love, who thought to put spots on a giraffe and loyalty in the heart of a puppy, who named and then scattered the stars in the sky, would watch me sleep… and wake me to meet Him… and invite me to put my two hands next to His on the plow.

~Shannon Woodward

63

The Cycle of Total Surrender

Listen to my cry for help,
my King and my God,
for to you I pray.
~Psalm 5:2

The infertility specialist gave me a sad, heavy look as he shook his head back and forth. "I know this is very hard for you," he said regretfully. "I'm sorry."

After six and a half years of infertility, my most recent test results confirmed a disappointing prognosis—pregnancy looked impossible.

A lump grew in my throat.

I couldn't believe I was hearing this. I wondered, "Is my quest to have a baby over? Can nothing else be done?"

"Let me talk to the doctor and have him give you a call when he returns from his conference," my doctor's partner continued.

Choking back my emotions, I asked to leave a note for my doctor. "I would appreciate a call from him about my chances. I don't want to become addicted to the infertility process and chase after something that's not medically achievable. The shots and all the driving are wearing me out. It's not worth making trips here each month if it's fruitless."

"I understand," he consoled in a gentle voice.

Over the previous year, I had journeyed over 6,000 miles in round trips from my home to the infertility specialist's office. Data collected from ultrasounds, blood samples, and numerous other tests showed more than one problem. While most women ovulated monthly, my ovaries either released an egg too small, too early, or did not release one at all. Also, for reasons unknown, cells from my uterine lining flowed up through my fallopian tubes into my abdominal cavity, then attached and grew on my ovaries and other organs, causing scar tissue and severe hormonal imbalance. The condition, called endometriosis, affects ten to fifteen percent of women during their reproductive years.

I cried the whole way home. I lifted up my pain to God. "I may never be able to be pregnant and have a baby. Oh Lord, is this it? Did I get this far only to learn my body's not cut out to have children? You've allowed me to get some answers, but now what? Help me. I'm turning this situation to You. There's nowhere to go. Nothing is impossible with You."

When I arrived home, my husband noticed the shaken expression on my face immediately. Trying to maintain my composure, I explained the results of the blood work. I could barely blubber out the rest of my words. "I can't take this anymore. It's obvious to me that I'm not getting anywhere. Maybe we're going down the wrong path and should proceed with adoption."

Brian listened quietly and put his arm around me. "I think we should wait and see what the doctor says, Sweetheart, then make some decisions from there," he offered. "I kept thinking they would give you a shot of something and everything would be okay." He swallowed hard. "This is so frustrating and I don't know why it's happening to us, but you have to have hope."

Hope? A solitary word with so much weight. The doctor did not have much of it to give me this morning.

I was sinking and Brian tried to help me hang on. Yes, I have to have hope, I thought, and faith. I have to accept however God wants things to be.

"You're right," I muttered. "We've prayed about this. It's all in God's hands."

Brian held me until I calmed down. My solace, however, lasted only a few minutes. As I retreated to our bedroom, I closed the door, held my drenched face in my hands and cried out, "Lord, please give me a sign to show me if I should go on, or stop and proceed with adoption. We want to raise children to honor You."

I continued to grieve over the next week. I would tell myself, "I'm not going to break down again. I've already sobbed my soul out. There's nothing left. The Lord is in control. I want His will." Looking forward to God's future plan, I embraced a renewed outlook and surrendered to new possibilities. Maybe the baby we were praying for would come through adoption.

Uncharacteristically, my doctor waited to respond to my note until he met with me. "I didn't want to make any judgments until I saw the results of this latest cycle," he explained. "An egg was released this month...."

"I'm not surprised...." I casually interrupted, unimpressed with my body's performance. "It's done that before."

"... and your blood work was excellent for the first time since we've seen you. In fact, we ran it twice because we thought you might be pregnant."

"Really?" My whole body popped up in surprise, stunned at the one response I had not considered. "I've been praying for a sign about going forward," I blurted out. "That's incredible!"

"I think you got your sign," he affirmed with a warm smile. He showed me the radical difference between this month and previous months. The progesterone blood draw results were three times higher than ever before. My chances for getting pregnant were dramatically improving, but still not certain.

Over the next few months, I optimistically tried more treatments to once again jumpstart my body's ability to ovulate normally.

But no pregnancy resulted.

My doctor recommended one last cycle of powerful drugs to stimulate egg production and force ovulation. If my system did not respond, I would end my expensive medical treatment.

At a prayer meeting, I begged God to take control of my body.

As I kneeled, closed my eyes, and bowed my head, I whispered to myself, "Lord, Your will be done over my body, mind, and spirit."

As the minister and others present prayed, a warm wave of calm swept over me. I returned home and told Brian, "I feel completely serene. The burden of having to be pregnant is gone."

After living with our infertility for seven years, my husband looked at me puzzled. "Are you sure?"

"Yes. Whatever the Lord wants is fine with me," I replied confidently.

I completed my final round of fertility drugs and waited for God's answer with peace, yet hopeful anticipation. I got it a few weeks later after a final blood test.

"The results are positive!" the nurse exclaimed. "You are pregnant. Congratulations!"

A shot of energy rippled through my body as I squeezed Brian's hand. Through God's grace, our past season of sadness suddenly moved to a life of new fulfillment!

Over the next four and a half years, His plan of abundance would unfold beyond our wildest dreams. We spontaneously conceived and delivered four healthy children.

When I truly let go and let God take control, He delivered!

~Kimberly McLagan

64

Ask and You Shall Receive

Ask of me, and I will make the nations your inheritance,
the ends of the earth your possession.
~Psalm 2:8

Several years ago my wife of fifteen years and I found ourselves struggling financially. We had gone through college together, started careers and had two children.

As a veterinarian, I had followed what I thought was God's plan for my life. I'd sold my stock in a very successful multi-man practice to go into full-time teaching. The pay as a teacher is not nearly as good as a practitioner's and the cut was the major contributor to our financial worries. So I had three jobs. I was teaching full-time at a college in Dallas plus teaching night classes part-time for a local junior college. To supplement my teaching salaries I had started seeing patients in a back room of one of the college labs on Friday afternoons from 1:00 until 5:00. It was a modest practice at best, and most of the patients I saw belonged to students so I only charged enough to cover my overhead.

Money was extremely tight and we were not able to pay some of our bills. It was so stressful that my wife decided to take our children and go to her mother's house for a few days to try to decompress, leaving me with the house and my jobs.

I called her Thursday night and asked exactly how much money we needed to pay our bills and not be delinquent or have late charges. She told me we needed $311 to make it until my next paycheck. We agreed to pray that God would help us through this time. We said a short prayer on the phone, and then I did something I had never done before. I got down on my knees and asked God specifically for money. I asked Him if He would bring enough animals to me on the following afternoon so I could pay our bills. I told Him I needed $311.

After I prayed, I went to bed and when I woke up the next morning, I had forgotten about my prayer. I went to school, taught my classes, and went to the lab in the afternoon in case any patients might come to my makeshift clinic. It was an unusually busy day; I saw all of the animals and finished up around five. Since my practice was so small, I only had a student assistant helping me. We did business on a strictly cash basis. If the client had the cash, they paid me and if they did not, I told them they could pay me later. I kept the money I made that day in my shirt pocket. I had always focused on service and caring for the animals, not money, so I didn't even think to count it at the end of the day.

When I got home that night, I was extremely tired and fell asleep on the couch. The phone woke me. It was my wife asking if I had made any money at the practice that afternoon. I pulled the wad of bills out of my shirt pocket and counted it while I spoke to her on the phone. I counted out $310. She gasped and reminded me that was only one dollar short of the money we needed to pay our bills. I looked down and saw a dollar bill on the floor beside the couch. When I had pulled the money out of my shirt pocket, I guess a dollar had fallen to the floor. That dollar added to the rest of the wad equaled the exact amount we had prayed for, $311.

That day marked a big turnaround in our lives. We have never been in that dire financial situation again.

I know this is but a small need, but it was a huge miracle when you realize God provided exactly what we had asked for, to the penny.

~Gene F. Giggleman, DVM

65

Ruth and Naomi

A mother's love for her child is like nothing else in the world.
~Agatha Christie

Our son, Lane, and his girlfriend were at odds again. It seemed to me they disagreed about any and every thing. As a mother, I was apprehensive when I heard about their engagement. I liked the girl all right, but I wondered whether she was the right one.

I had been praying for Lane's mate since the day he was born.

Now that he was engaged, I wanted to be sure, and my daily prayer became, "Lord, if this isn't the right girl, please send the right one."

During this prayer one night I had a vision. With my eyes closed, I saw two girls. No mistake about it… the girl on the left was Lane's betrothed. She appeared as a dark silhouette. The girl on the right was a blue-eyed vivacious blonde in living color with a smile that brought joy to my heart. A vision like this had never happened to me before and I guess I just thought that it must have come from me. I tucked it away in my mental file but I thought about it a lot.

As the wedding date drew closer, and the church was rented, I became more apprehensive. I prayed for the Lord to intervene if this wasn't the best decision for our son.

Two weeks before the wedding was to take place, Lane's fiancée fell out of love with him and called the whole thing off. He told us his pain would never stop. I felt sorry for him, but in my heart I knew that God had to be working. Amidst his heartbreak, he continued working on his college degree. Two years passed and I prayed daily for Lane.

With graduation near, Lane called to give us the time and details. His dad and I talked of our pride in him as we drove the two hours to his college campus. We arrived at his apartment and he told us to wait while he went to pick up a friend he had invited. Twenty minutes later, our son walked in with a beautiful blue-eyed blonde. I gasped when I saw her. She was the very same girl I had seen in my vision two years earlier! I could hardly contain myself, but I kept my mouth closed for fear I would scare them both off.

Their friendship grew from May to November, when our son called us one day and said, "What are you doing November 19th? Would you like to go to a wedding?" And the rest is history.

Kari is the most wonderful wife and the mother of two beautiful girls. She likes to remind me that we are like Ruth in the Bible and her mother-in-law, Naomi. So that's what we call each other, "Kari Ruth" and "Joan Naomi."

This blue-eyed beautiful blonde is everything the Lord showed me and more.

~Joan Clayton

66

Summoned to Pray

Therefore I tell you,
whatever you ask for in prayer,
believe that you have received it,
and it will be yours.
~Mark 11:24

"Honey, I'll leave as soon as duty is over; that should be right after midnight," my new husband promised.

I hung up the phone, a newlywed anxiously anticipating our every-other-weekend reunion. At that moment I questioned the sanity of our decision to spend our first year of marriage apart as I completed my teaching degree at UT Arlington and he completed his last year of service at Fort Sill, Oklahoma.

I straightened up our tiny one-bedroom apartment, then went to bed to await his arrival.

In spite of my anxiety, I still managed to fall asleep, dreaming about our weekend together. Suddenly I was awakened from my sound sleep with a summons to pray, as real as if it had just been delivered by a mailman. It was accompanied by an urgent knowledge of what to pray for... my husband's immediate safety.

I thought back to another instance just the year before when I had felt an urgent need to pray for Jim in Vietnam. Later, I received a letter he wrote telling me about a late night trip back from taking a shower when he nearly stepped on a bush viper. Miraculously, he had seen it just in time. He was not wearing his glasses at the time and the only light was from a friend's tent where a prohibited candle burned. I wrote back telling him about my urgency to pray for him on that very same night. We both knew it was the Lord's doing.

So now I fell out of bed onto my knees. I cried as I prayed to the Lord. Then, as quickly as the summons had come, it was gone. My tears dried and I fell back to sleep, remarkably peaceful despite the traumatic awakening. The last thing I remembered was glancing at the clock on the nightstand. It was 2:50 a.m.

There was a knock at the door. I sat up in bed and looked at the clock again. 6:00. I thought to myself, "Jim must not have been able to leave when he originally planned." Then I remembered the urgent call to pray. I rushed to the door, opened it and there stood my young husband… a bit disheveled, his right eye covered with a black patch.

He quickly answered my questions. A car going only thirty miles per hour, with no lights, pulled out of a bar onto the highway just outside Ft. Worth. My husband was driving seventy miles per hour on the highway and there was a collision. Our new car was totaled. The officer at the scene said the other man had been drinking. The only injury to Jim was broken glass in one eye.

"For some reason I felt the need to buckle my seatbelt right before getting to Ft. Worth," Jim said. He'd never done that before. Back then, in 1969, there were no seatbelt laws.

"Thank God!" I gasped, hugging him tighter. "What time did this happen?"

"I'd just checked the time. It was 2:50."

~Sharon L. Patterson

The Power of Surrender

If you believe,
you will receive whatever you ask for in prayer.
~Matthew 21:22

After losing 150 pounds, I was finally ready for surgery to repair two massive abdominal hernias. In order to repair the hernias though, my surgeon first needed the extra skin to be removed from my abdomen, and for that we needed the help of a plastic surgeon. For eight months I jumped through hoops, some of them ridiculous, for the insurance company to meet their requirements for this surgery. I had a secondary condition (hernias) which required the panniculectomy (abdominal skin removal), I had skin issues, I met the weight stability requirement after a massive weight loss, and four doctors said I needed this surgery.

Something folks might not realize is that when someone loses a lot of weight, the resultant empty skin can cause all kinds of problems, especially if you're older and your skin doesn't have the elasticity to snap back. My empty skin hung down mid-thigh. I had breakdowns of skin hidden "in the creases and folds." My back hurt every day, all day, and the backaches were killer. The hernia pain was excruciating at times and the sizes of the hernias made me look beyond pregnant. Sometimes I could hardly stand upright. I jumped through the insurance company's hoops for months, as I was determined to feel good again!

I found the perfect team of doctors. They really "got me." They submitted their surgical plans and photos to my insurance company for approval. A surgery date was selected. We got right up to the eve of surgery, and my insurance company denied the surgical requests once again. They would cover the hernia surgery, but not the skin removal necessary to be able to do the hernia surgery. Even though I met all the requirements they'd earlier set out in writing to me, they denied the panniculectomy, and instead presented a new list of demands. This was the final decision, and all my options were exhausted. I realized this was merely a game to them and they had forgotten that I was a human being. A human being in pain.

On my way to work the following morning, I was still crying over the realization that I would have to live with chronic back pain for the rest of my life. I was experiencing other unmentionable problems and knowing I would have to struggle with those for the rest of my life left me sick with fear. I was only in my fifties. I'd lost weight to improve my health and quality of life, not to pick up a whole new set of insurmountable health problems.

So I prayed. I asked God to teach me how to live with chronic pain, if the surgery really was not going to happen. I prayed, "God, please teach me how I can continue to carry around this skin that is causing me pain." I cried because I'd worked hard in therapy to climb out of a depression and get my peace of mind back, and now I found myself sinking back into a depression. "God," I prayed, "I want my peace of mind back. I need to learn to let this go. You just have to show me how because I can't do this anymore. I'm throwing in the towel," and I surrendered my fears to His care. Then it seemed like God clapped His hands together, cracked His knuckles and said, "Now watch me work!"

Within the hour, Shelley, the physician's assistant from my plastic surgeon's office, called me at work. Forgetting my earlier prayer of surrender, I again picked up my heavy load and started suggesting things we could try, I could take more pictures, I could do all sorts of things. When Shelley finally got my attention, she said that she'd spoken with the doctor and he had said, "Tell Jeri we're not going to go through her insurance. Tell her I will do the panniculectomy for

$500. Jeri has worked so hard and I want to be a part of making her dreams come true."

I was incredulous. Who does this? Who gives so freely, so generously to someone he met only once? I dove under my desk, broke down and sobbed. Alarmed, my coworkers ran over thinking who knows what only to find me under my desk, crying. All those months of playing the "please the insurance company game" and being continually denied had taken their toll. I could have continued the fight and legally forced them to comply with what they'd put in writing to me, but instead I accepted God's gift.

The surgery was back on track and on schedule. The insurance company couldn't argue with my doctor's compassion. I asked a friend why it had to come to that. Why did I have to go through all that game playing with the insurance company? Why after I let go of trying everything in my arsenal to make the surgery happen, did it finally fall into place? "Because," she said, "you surrendered. When you surrendered your will, God's goodness stepped in."

The surgery was a tremendous success. Thirteen pounds of skin were removed from my abdomen and all my organs were put back in place. Imagine carrying around a thirteen-pound medicine ball for the rest of your life that you could never put down. That's what I had. But, today is a new day! I've maintained a 170-pound weight loss for over a year now. I feel like a million bucks and I continually look for ways to pay my miracle forward.

~Jeri Chrysong

A Book of Miracles

Angels Among Us

But the angel said to them,
"Do not be afraid.
I bring you good news of great joy that will be for all the people."

~Luke 2:9-11

68

Angel Guide

Last night an angel of the God whose I am and whom I serve stood beside me
~Acts 27:22

In the middle of a Vermont mud season, my husband, two young children and I welcomed my father into our home. He was hoping for a full recovery from pneumonia so he could go back to retirement and his cabin on the coast of Maine. The pneumonia was brought on by the chemotherapy that wracked his old body.

One evening, while folding laundry in the living room, piling little pairs of tights next to tiny T-shirts with trucks and tractors on them, my dad sat on the couch and watched. The top of his bald head was slightly fuzzy, his stomach was bloated and his cheeks sunken. "You know," he said, like he had just remembered something funny, "there's something we've all been forgetting about."

"What's that, Dad?"

"The cancer!" he said.

Maybe he'd forgotten about the cancer, but no one else had. He had a type of liver cancer for which there was no cure, and because of the pneumonia, he was not able to finish the trial treatment he'd been receiving. Not that it was helping anyway. Everyone but him knew the end was slowly drawing near.

One night while my husband was out grocery shopping and I was putting the kids to bed, my father called to me from downstairs. I could tell by his strained voice that something was wrong. Running down, the children close behind, I found him on the couch. He was breathing like he had just run a marathon. His face was red and his eyes were wide with pain. Even while calling 911, I realized he was not to have a slow cancer decline after all. This heart attack would bring a quick end. "Go in the living room and watch for the ambulance," I told the children, surprised at how calm my voice sounded. I didn't feel calm inside; it felt like a tornado was ripping me apart.

My heart pounded so loudly that I could hardly hear the medic on the phone give me directions for CPR. "I can't do this," I thought, yet I tipped my father's head back, pinched his nose closed, breathed into his mouth and pumped his chest. "This isn't really happening; it's just a bad dream, and where is that ambulance anyway?" The road we lived on was muddy and long; it would be a while until they arrived.

I knew he was dying, but I also knew that for some reason I had to continue keeping him alive. I held my mouth against his, wishing it didn't remind me of a kiss, wishing his breath didn't smell like the chicken soup we'd had for supper. Wishing this wasn't happening. Once while pumping his chest I felt something crack. "I think I broke a rib!" I said to the stranger on the phone. "That's okay," he said. "It happens." I breathed and pumped and was glad the children were spared this strange and horrifying sight. "Don't forget to tell me when the ambulance arrives," I called to them. And please, God, make it soon.

When they did finally arrive, they had machines to do the CPR. A young medic wearing a Red Sox cap looked at me kindly and said, "We'll do all we can, but it doesn't look good." I knew that and never doubted that this was about his death. They also told me I had done a great job; my efforts had saved his life. Whatever that meant at this point.

My husband met me in the emergency room. We watched as my father's breathing slowed. I didn't want him to go. I wanted to cry out, "Come back," but his body lay like a statue on the table, his blue eyes stuck open, seeing nothing. The short gasps of breath were slowing down. It was his time, but I didn't want it to be. I wanted him to get better and go back to his house on the coast where we would visit him and eat lobsters and mussels, watch the sun rise out of the sea, play Scrabble and backgammon, where he would read his mysteries and walk the beaches, content and happy with his sweet life. I wanted him to watch my children change from little to grown, to guide me through all that was still to come.

Even though I was standing right next to him, I felt far away, dizzy and unbalanced, like I was on a ship in a storm. Surrounding the bright hospital lights I saw black dots everywhere and I wondered if I might pass out. Still, I tried to comfort him. "He needs help," I thought. "Should I say something like 'it's okay to go'? But I don't want him to leave!"

Watching over him I became aware of someone standing directly behind me. Strangely, I didn't need to turn around to be able to see her clearly. She was like an angel, a little taller than I, dressed in flowing, golden silk. Her black hair fell around her glowing face and her eyes told me I had nothing to worry about. Ever. She was the most calm, yet powerful, force I had ever known. Although she looked like she was made of light, I found myself leaning into her arms. She held me so completely it felt like I had merged into her. I did not have to hold myself up anymore. As my dad took his last breath, and as I was held by this angel, I raised my arms up and up and up, guiding his spirit with my hands toward heaven.

Late that night, I sat alone at my altar. In front of God I cried for my dad, for me, for the intense feeling of loss. Feeling a sudden need to sit quietly, I became aware of a voice speaking to me. I could feel that it was the angel from the hospital, so I steadied my breathing and listened. "Your father came to you for his death," she said, "to learn about God. You breathed God into him as he was dying." My father had been a strict atheist.

The next day, recounting the sacred experience of watching my father die, I told someone about how I raised my arms up and up, guiding his spirit. My husband, present for this conversation, said, "No, you had one hand on his chest, and the other on your own. Don't you remember?" It sounded familiar, and I remembered my hands in that position, a hand on both our hearts, and feeling the energy pour through me to him, his chest rising for the last time. "Yes," I said, "I do remember that, but I also remember seeing my hands guiding him up. How can that be?"

And then I remembered the angel who held me, and knew it was her hands, reaching around me, lifting my dad to heaven.

~Lava Mueller

Thanksgiving Angel

I do all this for the sake of the gospel,
that I may share in its blessings.
~1 Corinthians 9:23

I was fifteen when my world took a bleak turn for the worst. My mom was diagnosed with cancer... again. The first time had been devastating. She underwent surgery and chemotherapy and she beat the cancer. Then the cancer came back. This time however, there was more to worry about than just the disease my mom was battling. Because of the medical bills she was paying from her previous cancer, this illness left her on the brink of financial ruin. My dad had died years before. It was just Mom trying to hold down the fort. My mom made too much to qualify for any type of assistance and too little to pay the mounting medical bills. I was too young to get a job.

That winter was the worst. We didn't have money to pay for electricity, so we did without. We had a little gas stove that provided heat, and our neighbor let us plug in an extension cord to his home so that we could have one lamp on in our home. The gas stove in the living room was the only heat in the house. I slept on the floor in the living room, as close as I could to the stove without setting myself on fire. Mom slept in her cold room, with as many blankets as we could pile on her.

Every day and every night my mom prayed and often asked me to pray with her. She thanked God for our blessings, thanked God for each other and always asked God to give us the strength to get through the hard times we were experiencing. She was never bitter, angry or demanding. She believed God would see us through it. I, on the other hand, wasn't so sure. If God was so good and great, why were we suffering like we were? Why had my mom, who still walked to church every Sunday no matter how cold it was or how sick she felt, gotten cancer again? Sometimes it was hard for me to pray. I was angry at God; I was angry at the world. Life just wasn't fair.

Thanksgiving Day came. I searched our cupboards for food and there wasn't much. I started slamming doors as I looked through the cabinets for a can of food we might have missed. The more I searched the angrier I became. The noise must have woken my mom, because she came to the kitchen wrapped in a blanket. She looked worried for me and she asked, "Baby, what's wrong?"

I retorted, "I'm hungry. That's what's wrong." I wasn't angry at her. I was angry at our situation. I knew I was acting like a jerk but I couldn't help it.

She opened her arms toward me and said, "Come here. Let's pray."

I rolled my eyes. "Like that ever works." I knew my words had hurt her but I was too upset to take them back.

She looked at me. The sadness in her eyes killed me. "God hears our prayers. We have a million blessings if you just open your eyes to them. Right now things are hard, but God is here helping us through this. Whatever we need, God will provide. All you have to do is have faith. Pray for what we need and God will answer."

"Oh really, is that so?" I turned on her. "If God is so great, why are we starving? If God is so wonderful why are we freezing to death in our own house?" The hurt look on her face was more than I could bear. I was sickened by my outburst at her but I was too angry at God to stop. "Hey God," I yelled up toward the ceiling, "if you are so powerful and almighty why don't you send us something to eat? In fact, since it's Thanksgiving, why don't you send us a fat juicy turkey with all the trimmings? Or are we not good enough for you to send us some food?"

I looked at the table scornfully. "Yeah, that's what I thought. I don't see any Thanksgiving dinner. Do you?" I sassed my mom. She stood there, silent tears running down her face.

I was deeply ashamed of what I had done and said, but I was still extremely angry at God and our circumstances. I walked fast, practically running to get out of the house. I yanked the door open, almost colliding with a stocky man in a blue striped shirt carrying an armful of boxes.

"Oh, just in time!" he said and walked in. "Happy Thanksgiving to you both!" he said cheerfully as he put all the boxes on the table. "This big box here is the Thanksgiving turkey, cooked of course. And this one is mashed potatoes; this container has gravy. Oh, and this one here is pumpkin pie, and this one pecan pie…."

Suddenly my ears felt full of cotton. I couldn't hear a word he was saying. I could smell the turkey, the stuffing, all the food in those containers. I could see our little table piled with boxes of food. "So you all have a great Thanksgiving. Now ma'am, if you'll just sign here for the delivery." He handed my mom a pen.

Mom stared down at the paper, but the entire time the delivery-man was staring at me. He had the bluest eyes I'd ever seen.

He took the pen from Mom, thanked her and as he passed me he touched my shoulder and said, "And God bless you, my child."

I stood there dumbfounded as he walked out of our house and closed the door.

It took a few seconds for me to snap out of it, but I bolted after him. Who was he? Who had sent the Thanksgiving dinner? There had to be an explanation. I ran out to our porch and down the steps, but I slipped and fell because frost covered the steps. I ran to the gate at the end of our cement walkway and out to the sidewalk. There were no cars in sight.

As I turned back towards the house, one thing stood out in the morning sunlight. There was only one set of footprints in the frost that covered our walkway. I stepped closer to the walkway, examining it closely. My footprints were the only footprints that disturbed the frost in our yard.

Whenever God seems far away I remember that Thanksgiving. I

remember the angel God sent to cool my anger. That angel, for I have no doubt that is what he was, showed us that God cared enough to bring us food at our time of need and bring faith back to one girl's heart.

~Cynthia Bilyk

70

Angel in the River

An angel from heaven appeared to him and strengthened him.
~Luke 22:42

My younger sister and I were on a summer vacation with our aunt and uncle. At the time I was still a non-swimmer, and naïve to the dangers of the river. As my uncle and aunt relaxed on the beach with my sister and cousin, I could hardly wait to jump in the cool water. They cautioned me to stay close to shore.

I didn't have flotation devices, and I was unaware that I was slowly creeping away from the beach. All of a sudden I couldn't touch the sandy bottom with my feet. How did I get to the middle of the river? Afraid of getting in trouble for disobeying the rule, and jeopardizing any future camping trips if I survived, I didn't yell out for help. Sounds silly, but I was only seven, and cursed with being too shy.

Within seconds I had already gone under twice, gasping, and running out of air. The far off voices of others in the water and on the beach were now muffled. Just as I was going down a third time, out of nowhere appeared a handsome smiling man with blond hair. He was within inches of me and had hauntingly beautiful blue eyes. Neither of us spoke a word. With his index finger to his lips, I knew he was assuring me this was our secret about me drowning. Strange as that sounds, I was relieved no one would know. In my mind I distinctly heard, "Everything will be okay." No one was near us, and the man never reached out to touch me.

Within a flash I was back at the shore! The moment my feet touched the sand, I could clearly hear the voices of everyone in the distance. My uncle and aunt were still at the same spot on the beach, unaware of the near-tragedy that just transpired. I quickly glanced back at the river, searching for the blue-eyed stranger. He was gone! I couldn't comprehend what had happened. Only a few seconds had passed, and I was no longer in the middle of the river drowning. How could I be back safely on shore without feeling myself move, and why did the mysterious man vanish? I wanted to say thank you.

I kept my secret for forty years before I figured out the blue-eyed man was my guardian angel. I was almost fifty when I finally shared my river experience with Mom. She was naturally upset that I hadn't yelled out for help, and amazed I could keep this secret for so many years.

As a child I had no way of understanding what happened at the river. Over the years though, I've experienced many other close calls, some even life-threatening, with outcomes that didn't always make sense. I knew I wasn't alone. God always sent my angel in the nick of time. He never appeared again as he did in the river, but I felt his presence and heard the voice in my head, "Everything will be okay."

My favorite childhood prayer, long before I met my angel at the river, was to my guardian angel. Even now, as a grandmother, I always end my prayer time with "Angel of God, my guardian dear, to whom God's love commits me here. Ever this day, be at my side, to light and guard, to rule and guide. Amen."

~Connie Milardovich Vagg

71

The Angel

Do not forget to entertain strangers,
for by doing so some people have entertained angels without knowing it.
~Hebrews 13:2

I closed my eyes and daydreamed in the cramped seat of the airplane. While the jet carried us across the Atlantic Ocean, my thoughts went back to when I was four years old living in a tiny English village.

I had admired my brother, Sonny, a handsome sailor in the British Navy away at war in WWII. After the war, he served in Hong Kong, his favorite place in the world, and I lovingly learned to write HONG KONG—the first words I ever wrote—on the envelopes to him.

Over the years, the relationship with Sonny and his family and our parents became strained. I only saw him a couple of times over a period of twenty years. I moved to the U.S., but I visited my hometown in England every year that I could. This trip, my cousins and I chatted as we drove around the cool and windy sea air in the county of Norfolk.

"Sonny is buried somewhere around here," I piped up at one point.

"Don't you know where his grave is?" cousin Brenda asked.

"No. As you know, Mum died earlier in the same year and no one else had contact with him."

"Sad how families drift apart."

"I remember the hospital's name. It's near Cromer, so I suppose he'd be buried near their location," I said.

We spontaneously decided to find his grave. So the day proceeded. We checked with the city's registry office. No James Arthur Goodwin, Sonny's real name.

The wind whipped around us as Brenda, her husband Tony and I methodically read every gravestone in several small cemeteries. No luck.

We drove past thatched cottages and country gardens. "Here's a nice large graveyard," Brenda said, pointing at a black and white sign. Tony drove through the entrance and parked the car in the graveled parking area.

We began our search in a cold drizzle, walking forlornly up and down the neat rows of gravestones and monuments. A caretaker with blond hair rode by us on a small tractor. He stopped, turned off the engine and watched us. "Can I help you?" he asked. He removed his work gloves and placed them on the tractor seat.

"I'm looking for my brother's grave," I offered. "He was nearby in hospital when he died."

The caretaker smiled at me. "I just happen to have the key to the chapel over there." He pointed to a building across the parking lot. "All burials are recorded there. If you know about when your brother died, I can look in the record book to see if he's resting here."

"Yes, I know it was in January 1982," I said, breathless, as we tried to keep up with him. The caretaker stuck a large key in the door lock. It turned with a thunk, and the door slowly opened.

Inside, on a shelf covered in dust and dead flies, was a large ledger book. The caretaker blew off the dust and opened it to 1982. He ran his finger down the columns of names. "Yes, here he is—James A. Goodwin. Grave number 136."

"I'm so relieved," I said quietly. "I've found him at last." My cousins nodded in agreement.

We followed the caretaker out to the grave numbered 136. We stared at the unkempt rectangle. "It's unmarked," I gasped. "I can't believe his family left him in an unmarked grave." A sob caught in my throat. My brother had been dumped here, alone, with no marker. Not even a vase of fake flowers.

We thanked the caretaker and he drove his tractor to the back of the church.

Brenda wiped away a tear. "Why don't we find a monument maker and have something made with his name on it?"

"Just what I was thinking," I said. "I only have a couple of days left on vacation so we have to do that soon."

"We can go to one on the way to our house," Tony piped up.

After many wrong turns through Cromer's streets, we found a monument maker. I chose a marble vase engraved with Sonny's name. It would be ready for delivery to the cemetery in a few months.

I returned to the U.S. where my life plodded on uneventfully.

Then Brenda called me one afternoon. "We just got back from Cromer," she told me.

"Did you go to the cemetery?"

"Yes, but listen to this." She paused. "We were walking toward Sonny's grave and there—wait for it—the same caretaker was at that moment taking the marble vase out of his car."

"No. I'm astonished," I burst out.

"Unbelievable," Brenda said. "We followed him as he walked to Sonny's grave and gently placed the vase in the soft ground."

"Did he say anything?"

"He quietly said, 'Just a coincidence.' Then he walked back to his car and drove off." Tony added.

"We wanted to thank him, so I called the church to see how I could contact him," Brenda continued.

"And did they give you his phone number?"

"They said they didn't have a blond caretaker. The man who's cut the grass for the last twenty years has dark skin and black hair."

We fell silent. My skin crept with goose bumps. I suddenly remembered that I had never told the blond caretaker my brother's name, just the month and year of his death, when he had looked up his gravesite in that dusty ledger.

"I think we've met an angel," I said.

"We think so too," Brenda whispered.

"Amazing. He found Sonny for us."

"Amen."

~Rosemary Goodwin

First Funeral

*The angel of the Lord encamps around those who fear him,
and he delivers them.*

~Psalm 34:6

Rivulets of sweat trickled down my back under my clergy shirt. It was a hot August Saturday afternoon and my first funeral service with my new congregation. The Lord had placed me in a multi-ethnic neighborhood church in Hawaii, in the middle of a rural sugar plantation community.

"We really need a fan up here," I muttered, as the sweat dripped into my eyes.

The men in the congregation were sweltering in their shiny, well-worn, funeral-only suits. I wore my obligatory heavy white clergy robe with a Hawaiian motif stole.

The service was going well as families and friends shared touching testimonies and colorful stories.

My turn came, and as I mounted the pulpit my eyes swept over the congregation. Among the supportive smiles of members I also saw the old-time samurai-type, who attended out of family obligation. They watched me with neutral faces, but their body language, with arms firmly crossed over inflated chests shouted, "Try to impress me, newcomer."

I silently prayed, "Lord I place this service into your hands." Then I proceeded with an evangelical message worthy of the old missionary preacher, Rev. Hiram Bingham himself.

"Nobody knows when death may strike." The words were barely out of my mouth when an elderly gentleman in the center of the third row keeled over. I was stunned, not knowing what to do. The organist, who was also a nurse instructor, rushed over to him, rendering aid. A deacon headed for the office phone to dial 911.

My first thought was, "Don't die here in the middle of my well-planned service!"

There was a commotion as the congregation shoved pews aside to make room for him on the floor. I knew I had to take action. But what kind? People were looking to me for leadership; they were counting on me, yet helplessness and desperation overwhelmed me.

I bowed my head and prayed, "Oh Lord, help me now!"

I looked up and suddenly, to my surprise, I saw two giant figures in the back corners of the church standing from the floor to the ceiling. It was mind-blowing. These were not gentle cherubs. These were experienced warriors in armor worn by Israelites. They had swords, beards, and helmets. I knew they were angels of the Lord, the very same who slew the 185,000 Assyrians recorded in Isaiah 37:36.

These angels radiated power, influence, control, experience and authority. Yet I felt as if they had their glory turned down, as if on a dimmer switch. They could go to full blast at any moment with their blazing presence as they stood watch with their arms folded.

Transformed by the angelic presence, I felt a supernatural ability to take charge of the situation. "Brothers and sisters, we must pray," I commanded with my new authority. Everyone bowed their heads as we reverently prayed for the afflicted man as well as all those deceased.

As we concluded our prayer, the fire department rushed in. They gave oxygen and did an assessment, then determined the man had fainted because of the heat.

People pumped my hand and thanked me as they left the service, praising me for my strength and leadership.

And I praised God and his angels.

~David S. Milotta

73

Four-Legged Angel

May the Lord answer you when you are in distress;
may the name of the God of Jacob protect you.
~Psalm 20:1

Surrounded by rolling green hills dotted with horses and cows, the picturesque ranch town of Waimea on Hawaii's Big Island is a peaceful and friendly place. One afternoon, while staying with friends at their house there, my husband and I decided to go for a stroll along the many, mostly traffic-free, country lanes in the area.

We met a beautiful Golden Retriever, obviously well cared for but with no collar. He seemed exceptionally friendly so we stopped to play with him, throwing a stick which he retrieved several times with glee. When we resumed our walk, he followed us, and although I worried that he might be going too far from his home, I couldn't deny that we were enjoying his company. We felt an immediate bond with this adorable dog and even talked about adopting him if we learned that he didn't belong to anyone.

After about twenty minutes, we found ourselves walking along a dirt road in an unfamiliar area, our golden friend still trotting beside us. Hilly grasslands sloped upward beyond a fence on one side of the road, and houses spaced comfortably apart dotted the other. One house, almost hidden by shrubbery and shaded by tall trees, seemed somehow furtive. I shuddered as we passed it and felt an urge to be as far away from that place as possible.

Just then, the door to the house creaked open and five dogs rushed out, barking and growling as they ran toward us. I felt terrified and couldn't move. There was nowhere to hide and no time to run.

All of a sudden, our new friend appeared, like a genie, between the dogs and us. He faced them—all five of them—growling and baring his teeth. I was amazed to see the attacking dogs stop in their tracks ten feet away from him. Our protector held them there while we escaped, scurrying quickly down the road. At a safe distance, we looked back and saw the five dogs heading back toward their house.

But the Golden Retriever was nowhere in sight.

The road was quiet again.

I felt an ache in my heart; I missed our friend already. Instinctively, I knew he was not hurt.

With a feeling of emptiness, we made our way back to the house, hoping the whole way that we would see our Good Samaritan again. But it was not to be.

When I told our friend about the encounter, her eyes flew wide open as she exclaimed, "It was an angel!"

To this day I have no doubt. A four-legged angel protected us.

~Jennifer Crites

74

The Park Bench

God is the circle whose center is everywhere,
and its circumference nowhere.
~Empedocles

While the natural cycle of life should have prepared me for the eventual death of my beloved grandfather, the thought of losing him was something I never allowed myself to consider. Throughout his life, Grandpa seemed to defy the conventions of the aging process. Hale, hearty, robust and quick-witted, he was my confidant, my mentor, and most importantly, my best friend well into his nineties.

Then, less than five minutes after I had talked to him on the telephone, he died suddenly from a cerebral hemorrhage, leaving me with a hole through my heart, soul and spirit.

I was his first granddaughter, but Grandpa was not one to spoil me. Nevertheless, I did always feel special with him. His eloquent manner of speaking and magnificent carriage attracted attention in every venue. Whether we were in a restaurant, a supermarket line, or a doctor's office, people gravitated toward him, and I loved being at his side. He lived by the Serenity Prayer, accepting what could not be changed, while bravely trying to improve what could. Even as a young child, I always sensed he heeded a Higher Power. His example was his greatest gift to me.

In the weeks that followed his death, I lived a numb existence. I staggered through the days, grieving, only to be tortured with thoughts of him throughout the night. I could not begin to comprehend that he was gone. He would no longer enter a room, answer the telephone, share a meal.

To physically escape the mental anguish, I started walking. For months, my only objective was to exhaust myself physically by day, to ensure my nights would be given over to sleep.

Soon, my walking pattern became routine. I strolled a few miles to our neighborhood park, then rested briefly on a bench overlooking a duck pond. An elderly man sat on an identical bench on the opposite side. Neither of us ever spoke to the other, but I sensed we were both seeking a similar peace in the silence.

Months passed, and eventually these excursions began to quiet my heart. I felt a change happening. The old man smoked a pipe and the tobacco reminded me of a time long ago when my grandfather used to smoke one, too. Perhaps the aroma triggered something, but I was transported back to a happier time. I remembered myself as a child reading the Sunday comics with Grandpa, playing with wooden blocks, and telling stories while eating canned fruit.

Throughout the next few months, other images flooded my memory. School graduations, holiday celebrations, birthdays and summer vacations from long ago were relived while sitting on that park bench. Again, neither I nor that old man ever spoke, but somehow I knew my gradual healing was related to that time on our identical benches.

One day I woke and realized the oppressive weight on my heart had lightened. It was then I recalled a dream I had. My beloved grandfather was there. He looked a little peculiar, though, as if he were a bit disturbed with me, a bit confused. I couldn't quite place the look on his face, but I knew I had seen it before.

It came to me later that day as I sat on that park bench. There, gently surrounded by the aroma of tobacco as my elderly companion puffed on his pipe, I remembered. Thirty-five years ago, my grandparents had taken a trip to Ireland. I hadn't wanted my grandfather to leave me, and I carried on horribly, crying about how much I would miss him. He had been disappointed in my behavior then, and that same look was on his face in my dream.

"Why are you acting like this?" he had asked me before his trip. "I'm only going away for a short time. I'll see you again very soon. Stop that."

Looking back over my behavior the past year, I could almost hear that same admonishment. But there seemed to be a new twist to his message this time. Now he seemed to be saying, "Let me go. I am finally home, and I am happy. But I am disturbed with you. It's not your time yet. When you're ready to come home, I'll be here. I am already waiting for you."

That realization hit me like a thunderbolt. I sat on that park bench for quite some time. Finally, with the sun setting, I buttoned my coat and started home. It was only then I realized the old man had left.

From that day forward, while I continued to miss my grandfather deeply, my heart was not so heavy. I could even smile when I remembered his perfect diction, erect posture, and witty sayings. I continued my walks to the park, but I never saw the old man again.

One day, I asked the park rangers if they had seen him.

The three men looked at each other, and then at me. Finally, one of them said, "We're not sure what you mean, Miss. The three of us have watched you sit on that same park bench every day for nearly a year. But you have always been alone. We never once saw an old man here."

~Barbara Davey

75

My Brother's Keeper

And your children I will save.
~Isaiah 49:25

It happened almost twenty-five years ago, when my brother was three and I was six. We were spending the day at my grandmother's house and I snuck off to her bedroom to play. My brother, Ryan, who followed me everywhere, came along. I didn't need to explore long to find what I was looking for. The small bottle of red nail polish lay in plain sight on the dusty oak dresser.

I sat on the floor in the open doorway and painted my nails. As usual, it was a messy job and by the time I was halfway through, the thick smell of nail polish surrounded me. I had been warned not to do this on several occasions, so every few seconds I looked down the hallway to make sure my grandmother wasn't coming.

Behind me, Ryan amused himself by using the old-fashioned bed spring as a trampoline. "Creak! Creak!" it loudly complained under his assault.

Just as I was finishing my nails, I felt a light tapping on my shoulder.

Ryan and I were alone in the room so I spun around expecting to find him.

Strangely though, he wasn't there.

"Where are you?" I asked into the empty space.

Thinking he had ducked under the bed, I pulled the sheet back and got down on my knees prepared to yell out, "I found you!" But I was stunned when I didn't find him there.

I grew worried and quickly began opening closet doors, frantically searching for my little brother. I'd been sitting in the doorway the entire time so I was certain he had not left the room.

As I got ready to open the last closet door, I felt the tapping on my shoulder again, more urgent this time. I spun around for the second time... and saw my brother's legs hanging over the second-floor bedroom windowsill!

My heart raced. I ran to him, overwhelmed by fear that I would not reach him in time.

But I did. Holding on to him and pulling backwards with a strength I am still surprised I possessed at age six, I hauled him back safely into the room. We landed with a loud thud on the floor, breathing heavily.

I was so relieved we just sat there hugging tight for a long time.

Me, my brother, and his guardian angel.

~Romona Olton

Reprinted by permission of
Steve Barr ©2010.

76

Rain Man

The golden moments in the stream of life rush past us
and we see nothing but sand;
the angels come to visit us,
and we only know them when they are gone.
~George Eliot

I t had been raining hard off and on for a few days, and in San Antonio, Texas, as much as we usually need rain, that much is dangerous. Roads flood quickly, and the number of high water rescues, injuries and deaths go up.

My mother-in-law Marlene had invited us for dinner at her house, and we'd been there for much of the day. Three of our five children were with us: Ryan, our teenager, plus our two little girls, Alana and Rachel. Our other two daughters were spending the night with friends.

As we headed home to the other side of town just as darkness began to settle in, the rain had dissipated somewhat. It gradually began to increase, however, the closer we got to downtown.

"Alan, maybe we should take the 281 instead of going through downtown," I said, thinking that accidents tend to occur when the roads are slick. I was probably a little more nervous than usual because not three weeks before I had been in a rain-related accident which totaled my car. Today we were in our new van.

But my husband was driving this time. "We'll be fine," he said. "Besides, this way is faster, and I want to get home."

There was construction downtown. The walls erected on both sides of the traffic lanes made me extremely nervous. The woman in the truck who'd hit me such a short time ago had come into my lane and knocked me up against one of those walls, spinning our little minivan into the wall and then across three lanes of traffic. Luckily, nobody was hurt.

Looking ahead, I could see water pouring off an overpass so much that it appeared to be a huge cataract before us. Cars were slowing, but nobody stopped. No signs were posted saying this was a "Low Water Crossing." I urged Alan to turn around, but we were on a highway and there was nowhere to go but straight. He assured me that it would be okay.

The water hitting our new Dodge van from the overpass sounded like baseball-sized hail pounding on our roof. I sucked in my breath and held it until we came out on the other side.

No sooner had we crossed under the bridge than we saw cars in front of us stalling out. A few people had already gotten out of their cars and were attempting to push them out of the traffic. Alan got out to help them, but when he tried to open his door, it wouldn't budge. The water had risen quickly and the pressure held the door tightly closed.

Alan rolled down his window and climbed out. In water up to his waist, he moved forward to assist the car in front of us, but within seconds, water began to gush in at my feet.

"Alan," I yelled, and at that moment, the van began to rock, the water lifting it first on one side and then the other. Alana and Rachel were crying. One of them screamed, "We're going to drown!"

I laughed, more out of nervousness than anything, and told them that we were not going to drown. Everything would be fine.

Ryan looked worried, but was quiet.

Alan waded back toward us and I handed Alana out the window to him. Ryan slid out of the side window. With the water rising quickly, Alan needed both hands to hold onto Alana, and I couldn't climb out of the window with Rachel in my arms. Ryan was on the other side of the car, and I didn't have time to get her to him, nor could he get around the car fast enough to help me.

It seemed as though everything was happening in slow motion.

Then, out of nowhere, a tall dark man with long black curly hair and no shirt appeared. He took Rachel out of my arms, and I climbed out into water that was up to my armpits. Luckily, it wasn't fast-moving water and was only contained because of the construction walls.

I have no recollection of this stranger handing Rachel back to me, but the next thing I knew, she was in my arms. I turned to thank him, but he was nowhere to be found.

I asked Alan if he'd seen where the man had gone. He said, "What man?"

I knew I hadn't imagined him, but we had to get out of the still-rising water quickly, so I soon forgot about him.

People were scrambling up the sides of the bridge. We joined them just in time to see the roof of our van go completely underwater.

A hospital was nearby, and though none of us were hurt, we went there to get blankets while our clothes were dried for us. Eventually, we took a taxi back to Mom's house, because cars couldn't get through to our side of town.

The next day, when we were finally able to get home, Rachel said to me, "Mommy, what happened to that man?"

"What man, Rache?" I asked.

"The one who held me in the water."

"I don't know. I wanted to thank him for helping us, but I couldn't find him."

"He kept me safe and warm," she said, "and he was filled with light."

I asked her what she meant, but she just repeated her description.

I knew then that we'd been sent an angel to help us that rainy night in San Antonio.

~Kathleen Rice Kardon

77

On a Cold Winter Night

Since you are my rock and my fortress,
for the sake of your name lead and guide me.
~Psalm 31:2-4

I finished my last evening shift of the week and could hardly wait to get home, take off my nursing shoes, and relax. I said good-night to the rest of the girls and headed out the door.

It was so cold I could see the ice crystals in the air. As I approached my car, I saw one of my coworkers standing by the bus stop. I thought it would only take a couple of extra minutes to give her a ride home, and besides, it was too cold to be standing outside on the coldest night in January. I didn't know where she lived, but I was confident I would be able to find my way home from her house.

We chatted about our evening of work as I drove and before we knew it, we arrived at her house. As she headed up the steps to her door she turned around. "Do you know how to get to your house from here?"

I assured her I would be okay. "How hard can it be? I'll just backtrack the way I came."

I started driving. Nothing looked familiar, but at first that didn't bother me since I'd never been to this neighborhood before. I kept driving, and soon I sensed that something was wrong. I recognized nothing, not the neighborhoods, not even the street names. I told myself to stay calm. I was sure I would find a familiar street and I'd soon be home snuggled in my bed.

I drove. I was beyond neighborhoods. I was beyond streets. I was even beyond streetlights. I no longer knew if I was heading away from town or back toward town. I crossed over two bridges that I didn't remember crossing earlier. Even though I was the only person in the car, I was embarrassed. How could I be so stupid? My husband would be worried about me and wondering where I was. I looked down at my watch. It was now 2:30 a.m. I'd left work at 11:30 p.m.

I truly was in the middle of nowhere. How could I get myself in such a mess?

I stopped the car and turned off the ignition. I thought I'd better take stock of my situation. It was one of the coldest nights we'd had. My gas gauge was slowly going down. What should I do? I could keep driving, but with no sense of where I was going?

I could stop my car and conserve what gas I had left and wait to be found. I would be able to start it throughout the night to warm myself with the gas that was remaining.

In total defeat I put my head down on the steering wheel and asked for help. My heartfelt prayer came from the deepest part of me. "Please God, help me get out of this mess." I was going through a difficult time at that stage of my life and had lost a lot of my faith. As I look back on it, I realize that I was praying not only for my "physical being" that was lost, but also my lost "emotional being."

I lifted my head. I saw a shadow down the road in front of me. It hadn't been there before. I turned my headlights on. It was a car. It was not running but just sitting there in total darkness. I drove a little closer. There was a silhouette of a person sitting in this car!

What was a car doing in the middle of nowhere at 2:30 in the morning? Was this the answer to my prayer?

Hesitantly, I got out of my car and knocked on the window of the other car. An elderly man slowly rolled his window down. He did not say a word.

I said, "I'm lost and don't know how to get back into town."

In silence, he rolled his window up, turned the ignition on, and started driving.

I ran back to my car, praying to God that I was following someone trustworthy and I drove behind him.

I followed that car… in faith.

Finally I recognized a familiar street. As I turned to head home, I lost sight of my guardian angel. I knew in my heart this was a miracle. As I pulled into my driveway the warning light for my gas tank turned on.

This was such an amazing experience for me, and so very personal, that for many years I did not tell anyone what happened. It gave me hope, it gave me strength, and it confirmed for me that miracles do happen. After this experience, I prayed more often and believed that God was truly in my life. I only needed to "ask." When I finally told my story to someone, she wisely pointed out that perhaps I was the answer to that old man's prayer as well. Why was he just sitting there in the middle of the night, in the middle of nowhere, with his engine off? Maybe he was saying a prayer also, asking God to give an old man a purpose in life. It truly made me think… life is a circle… and perhaps we helped each other.

~Debra Manford

78

Pork Chop Angel

Praise be to the God and Father of our Lord Jesus Christ,
who has blessed us in the heavenly realms
with every spiritual blessing in Christ.
~Ephesians 1:3

I never make pork chops without remembering her face and her kindness. I met her in a gas station on I-75, in 1968. I was young, in a terrible marriage, and I was very pregnant. All I wanted was to reach my sister's house on Christmas Day. My husband and I had left in the early morning. With bad tires and one tank of gas, he assured me we would get to my sister's house. We'd left with no food and no money. I just wanted to feel normal, to laugh with my sister. And I wanted my stomach to feel full again.

The tire blew out somewhere between hope and despair, and my husband managed to flag down a passing motorist, who took him to a gas station to repair the tire. I had plenty of time sitting alongside the interstate to muse over all the events and decisions that had brought me to that moment in my life. I regretted the marriage, but I was also clueless as to how to help myself, and now I was so hungry I thought I would die. It had been twenty hours since I had eaten, and my unborn child was kicking in protest.

Finally, my husband returned with the kind stranger, who drove us to the gas station as the wrecker pulled our car behind. The generous man paid for the tire, the gas… everything, but I was still hungry and ashamed to ask anyone for food.

About that time, a car pulled into the gas station and a beautiful lady stepped out. She was holding an electric stewpot. We exchanged smiles, and I almost fainted at the delicious smell coming from her pot. We spoke a few words, as she moved closer to me.

"Honey, you look like you could use a good meal," she said, her voice soft and coaxing.

"Well, actually, I am very hungry," I admitted, eyeing her kettle.

"You look like you are eating for two." She smiled as she considered my belly.

"As a matter of fact, I feel as though it's been more like starving for two," I chuckled, although I was actually quite serious.

"Here." She opened her pot. "Have a pork chop."

The smell was overpowering.

"Well…" I hesitated.

She insisted and put the luscious food right under my nose.

"Thank you!" I almost cried, reaching into the pot.

When my teeth sunk into the tender, spicy meat, I knew that I had died and gone to heaven! And this sweet lady had to be an angel.

She stood there, clucking her disapproval at a world that would allow a young, pregnant woman to go hungry. She was relentless in her compassion, placing her strong arm around my shoulders as I ate, and I sobbed my gratitude. I ate four pork chops, and they melted in my mouth, sending their warm nourishment into my bloodstream and feeding my baby.

She was an angel of mercy who guessed that the burly young man who could charm someone out of a new tire and money was not all he seemed. She could see I was miserable, that I was homesick, and that my baby and I needed help.

"Remember," she said. "God didn't put us on this earth to be miserable. If there is anything you can do to better yourself, do it. God will take you through. He will go before you, and He will be your rear guard."

She pressed a twenty into my hand, then climbed back into her car and headed in the opposite direction.

Later, I asked the mechanic who she was.

"Who?" he asked.

"You know," I said, "the beautiful lady I was with."

"I don't know what you're talking about," he said, with a growl. "I haven't seen any other lady today."

"She was right there with me. I ate nearly all her pork chops!"

I thought he was an idiot.

"Nope. No lady like that. And if there were pork chops, I'd have smelled 'em!"

I was stunned. Had I eaten four pork chops? It couldn't be that I imagined it. My stomach felt full, and I could still smell the heavenly aroma.

I asked my husband if he remembered her.

"No. Are you out of your mind? You were standing alone, all the while. I was sick of hearing you whine about how hungry you were."

I felt the twenty in my hand, and I hid it.

I felt the food giving me strength. I had not imagined it. She was real.

There are always those who might say it was a dream. Perhaps my hope fed my hunger.

And perhaps God, in his mercy, sent an angel to meet my needs and make me feel His love.

Months later, when I finally escaped from my ex-husband, I became the first person in my family to get a divorce. I was treated like a fallen woman by some, but with each slur I thought of the compassionate African-American woman who shared a loving meal with a pregnant white girl, in a gas station in the segregated South.

She was right. God did go before me.

And He has been with me ever since.

~Jaye Lewis

79

Hurricane Ike

Out of difficulties grow miracles.
~Jean de La Bruyère

When Hurricane Ike blasted into the Texas coast in September of 2008, my life changed forever. Ike's twelve-foot surge ran through our house like a raging river, destroying most of our possessions and our home.

My mother's words rang through my head repeatedly. "Everything happens for a reason and for the best." But what could be positive about a natural disaster destroying our home?

While we were sifting through our belongings, an overwhelming sadness consumed me. Why didn't I take my high school yearbooks, my writing journals or my childhood jewelry box when we evacuated? These pieces of history were now a part of the huge trash heap in front of our home. I tried to focus on the belongings that were saved rather than lost, but I secretly grieved for these mementos.

For years I'd believed that angels are among us. I had a collection of angels made of various materials. These symbols of help were placed throughout my home to remind me of the angels' presence. Ike could not triumph over these angels. Each figurine had floated from room to room and landed gently unbroken. Upon finding each angel coated with a layer of mud, but otherwise unscathed, my faith strengthened.

When the representative from our insurance company finally contacted me, I was distraught to learn that this was her first disaster.

"A newbie," I thought sadly. "God, could you at least send someone who has had some experience?" While working at the house while waiting for the insurance representative to arrive, I noticed an older gentleman visiting with my neighbor. Soon he meandered up to our house. He introduced himself as the State Farm insurance representative and mentioned that his wife, who was part of his team, was on her way down the street.

"I was told that a young lady fairly new at claims would be helping us," I said with a puzzled look.

As if in answer to my prayers, he grinned and said, "Well, she was sent elsewhere, and you are stuck with my wife and me. We've been in the business for too many years to count, so we'll get you through this without much pain."

I wanted to hug him, and I did before the meeting was over. We were blessed with these two insurance reps, who gave me the comfort of loving grandparents at a time when I desperately needed consoling. I was beginning to believe everything does happen for the best.

At times though, my optimism was overshadowed. What were we going to do long term? Where were we going to live? How could we replace all of our possessions? The magnitude of these questions overwhelmed me. After living with my mother-in-law for a month, we knew we had to find a rental property closer to our home. After several calls to realtors and apartments, we realized we had waited too long—there were no homes available. All the rental homes had been taken and our dog and cat were not welcome at the apartments.

In the midst of my panic, something told me to call Katie, my friend and the Girl Scout leader of my daughter's troop. After the storm first hit, Katie had called to tell me her parents had a second home located in Seabrook, which had not flooded, and to let her know if we needed a place to stay temporarily.

I called Katie. "Would your parents consider renting their home to us long term?"

Later that day, Katie called to tell me her mother, Mary, had prayed that her home be spared in the hurricane, and if spared, she'd do whatever God intended with the home. When Katie called and asked if we could rent it, her mom felt that it was God's intention for us to live there.

The best part was that the home was completely furnished, and we had the most wonderful landlords renters could ask for.

I've observed grace in others' lives when a traumatic event takes place, for instance when there is a death in a family. For a short period of time, grace surrounds those closest to the deceased, and though they grieve, they often have a feeling of calm and faith permeating their lives. For the first few months after the hurricane struck, I felt this grace in my life. I felt that everything would work out even in the midst of turmoil.

Whenever I have recurring thoughts like "Why did this happen to us?" I remember the angels who appeared disguised as insurance reps, and the miracle we experienced in finding our rental home. When I look at one of the angels from my collection, which remained intact despite the fury of Ike, I know why this happened. These blessings, large and small, will be with me forever as a reminder that everything happens for a reason and for the best.

~Dawn J. Storey

A Book of Miracles

Everyday Miracles

*Remember the wonders he has done,
his miracles,
and the judgments he pronounced.*

~1 Chronicles 16:13

80

Everyday Miracles

Where there is great love, there are always miracles.
~Willa Cather

The sun rises.

An exhausted woman weeps with joy as her screaming newborn is laid across her breast.

A father beams as his baby girl takes her first steps.

Parents cry with gratefulness when the doctor pronounces their son in full remission.

A pony raises itself on wobbly newborn legs.

A spider fashions its artsy web bejeweled in drops of dew.

An artist creates.

Clouds fill until they rain their much-needed showers onto the earth.

Flowers stretch and yawn and reach their faces upward in praise to God.

By carrying away small stones, a man manages to move a mountain.

In the midst of dreaming, a grieving soul embraces a long lost loved one.

A parent who lost a child feels joy again, and a first day without tears.

A white hand clasps a black hand and we hear, "I understand."

A wrinkled hand holds a smooth little hand. "Let me help you."

A small child fills an empty space in an elderly neighbor's day.

An unbeliever tells a believer, "You know, what you said makes sense to me."

An old man smiles and looks to the corner of his room where a band of angels has come to take him home!

The sun sets.

Everyday miracles! Don't let them pass by you unnoticed.

~Beverly F. Walker

81

The Parable of the Purse

And then she finds it,
she calls her friends and neighbors together and says,
"Rejoice with me, I have found my lost coin."
~Luke 15:9

I t shimmered in the distance, a beacon for weary travelers. Kathy and I were grateful to have made it out of the urban jungle unscathed and drove slowly towards the oasis beckoning to us in the haze... Dunkin' Donuts.

Minutes later we were covered in white powder, thankful we had both opted to wear light colors that day. With heads spinning, high on sugar, we ordered coffees to go. They had a special on the super-sized plastic mug, free refills for a year, and after a bit of maneuvering it was forever fixed to my dashboard. Head filled with thoughts of that next donut stop, wondering if the coffee would taste better because it was free, I steered my silver Ford Festiva back onto the interstate, heading west towards Indiana, to our friend's house, our final destination of the day.

The next two hours went quickly, until full bladders and an empty gas tank made it necessary to stop once again. "I'll get this one," I said, eager to show off my newly minted credit card. Reaching around into the back seat I grabbed for my purse... but it wasn't there. I knew my light brown leather satchel could easily slip under a seat, so I got out and rummaged around. I wasn't worried, yet. We hadn't stopped anywhere, so no one could have taken it. And I'd paid for my plastic coffee mug so I knew I'd had it then.

But after unearthing candy wrappers, old newspapers and half a New York City subway map, I remembered. With all the fuss getting my new coffee mug centered on the dashboard, I had left my purse on the roof of the car, in the Dunkin' Donuts parking lot, in New York City's backyard.

I don't know why I was surprised when it wasn't still there.

Then I panicked, sure that my credit cards had already been maxed out. But something told me to call the Dunkin' Donuts just in case.

"Oh thank goodness," the clerk said when I called. "We were going through your wallet, trying to find a way to get in touch with you. Someone found your purse lying in the parking lot and turned it in."

Refusing any kind of reward, the shop owner express-mailed it to our friend's home. It arrived the next morning, with only postage money missing.

A few years later, on a snowy Minnesota winter night in the middle of downtown Minneapolis, my car's low-gas light was blinking red and I knew I had to stop or risk walking home. I'd switched purses by this time, to something smaller with a strap so I could always keep it with me. I filled up, made sure my purse was securely around my neck and drove home.

But when I got out of the car my purse wasn't there. Déjà vu. A single leather strap wove itself in and out of my dark green scarf, like a vine around a tree, but there was no purse attached to the other end.

I searched repeatedly under, around and between the seats until my fingers were frozen and the knees of my jeans soaked through from kneeling in the slush. Had I lost my purse again?

Knowing my good fortune might not repeat itself, I called the credit card company and my bank to freeze my accounts.

But I needn't have bothered. The next morning I got a call. "Is this Heidi Grosch? We found your purse lying in a snow bank."

It seems I had closed my car door with my purse hanging outside. It had dragged along through the snow until the strap broke. Again, everything was there and the finder refused to accept any payment.

I will always be grateful to those Good Samaritans for the reminder that miracles don't always have to be bigger than life. They can be the little things that hit you unexpectedly and have a happy ending.

I'm trying to recognize the small miracles of daily life, and… to keep track of my purse.

~Heidi H. Grosch

82

The Power of a Penny

Surely you have granted him eternal blessings
and made him glad with the joy of your presence.
~Psalm 21:5

Instead of making last-minute decisions for the upcoming Christmas holiday, my family and I were making last-minute decisions for a memorial service. Upon hearing the news of my mom's death on December 21st, my husband and I attempted to get a flight home to British Columbia. Due to the upcoming holiday, winter storms, and cancelled flights, scheduling was a nightmare. Eventually we managed to get a flight that left on Christmas Eve.

As I packed, I reminisced about a phone call I'd recently gotten from Mom. She wanted to tell me about a Christmas card she received the year before, from a favorite aunt who had since died. Taped inside the card was a single penny with a poem about pennies from heaven. The verse suggested that when an angel in heaven misses you, they toss a penny down to cheer you. So, it reminded us, don't pass by a penny when you're sad.

What a sad Christmas this would be, I thought, as I cried and packed. As other travelers reveled with joy, we arrived at the Kelowna, B.C. airport at 1:30 a.m. Christmas morning with heavy hearts. When my husband Bill and I and our two children walked down the ramp into the arrival area, my Aunt Karen, Mom's sister, waited for us with open arms. After our initial greetings and hugs my five-year-old son Carter said, "Look Mommy, a penny!"

For a little boy, finding a penny is very exciting and fun. For me, seeing that penny in the wake of the poem Mom had shared with me, made me feel like she was there at the end of the ramp just as she had been every other time I'd come home. She couldn't be there in body but she was there in spirit, proven by that penny.

With Carter at my side, I shared the poem and our own encounter with a penny at Mom's memorial service. During the weeks that followed, I was approached by many people who told me that when they had been thinking about Mom, they'd looked down and found a penny on the ground. I was touched by their shared stories and couldn't believe the coincidence.

Accepting that I had to return home to Ontario was difficult, and getting a flight home amidst the continued cancellations and rescheduling proved the same. Finally, on January 13th, we checked our bags and received our boarding passes. I pointed out to the kids that we were sitting in lucky row number 7. After a couple of hours of delays we finally boarded the plane. The kids and I anxiously watched for our lucky row and as we slid into our seats, we looked down at the first seat and saw not just one, but three pennies.

The spirit of my mom had blessed me with a penny at my homecoming on Christmas morning, and her spirit bid me farewell on my return flight to Ontario.

While a penny doesn't have much value as currency, it's worth its weight in gold. It has the power to heal.

~Leesa Culp

83

Twenties from Heaven

To this John replied,
"A man can receive only what is given him from heaven."
~John 3:27

When I was growing up, there were two movies that made an impression on my young mind. The first was *Pennies from Heaven* and the other was *The Money Tree*.

If only I could find the seeds, I too could plant a tree that grew money, or so I believed. My fantasy was shattered once my dad told me that money does not grow on trees. "That's just fantasy thinking," he said. However, I still remained hopeful that dreams and miracles do happen to those who believe.

My father and I had just come home from church one Sunday morning. Ever since our mom passed away, Dad was the official Sunday morning pancake maker. It was a tradition. Sunday morning papers were scattered around us as we enjoyed our breakfast together.

This day, I got all the ingredients down from the cupboard, but when I went to get the eggs, there were none.

"I guess we will have to make a trip to the grocery store," Dad said.

He took some coins from the jar where we kept extra change.

"Dad, are we broke?" I asked.

"No, just a little short."

I had seen Dad put his last $10 into the collection basket at church that morning. He was always generous and willing to help others in need. However, his payday was still five days away.

"What are we going to live on the rest of the week?" I asked.

"Don't worry, we'll make it somehow," he reassured me.

That is when those two movies popped into my head again. "Wouldn't it be wonderful if pennies did come from heaven?"

The wind was blowing hard as we walked from the parking lot into the store. Once we made it to the entrance, Dad stopped outside the sliding glass doors.

Two twenty-dollar bills clung to one door.

"Look at this," he said.

"Wow, this is even better than pennies!" I exclaimed.

We both wondered out loud how, with all the wind, those two bills just lay there against the doors as if waiting for us.

"I guess our prayers were answered," Dad said.

No truer words have ever been spoken.

Dreams and miracles still do happen to those who believe.

~Terri Ann Meehan

The Milk Jug

May you be blessed by the Lord the Maker of heaven and earth.
~Psalm 115:15

I t was 1978 and we were newlyweds. Jon was a full-time student with a part-time job, and I was unable to work in the U.S. because of incomplete immigration status. At one point, our food budget was all of seven dollars per week! Still, we'd committed ourselves to tithing and we faithfully put our ten percent in the weekly church offering, as little as it was.

We bought milk in gallon plastic jugs because we could get money back for the jug, and the gallon lasted a week.

One week we were particularly strapped for cash and skipped our usual milk purchase. We didn't really think about it too much until payday rolled around again and we could afford more milk. But the gallon wasn't empty. Then we did the math. As we added up the days we'd used that milk, and the glassfuls consumed per day, versus the volume of a gallon, we realized the numbers just didn't add up. Somehow that gallon jug had yielded a lot more than one gallon. Furthermore, it had stayed fresh long beyond its expiration date.

On the day Jon received another paycheck, there was still a small dribble of milk in the bottom of the jug, and only then was it sour.

God provided for us, just like He did the widow's oil.

~Terrie Todd

Special Delivery

Do not be like them,
for your Father knows what you need before you ask him.
~Matthew 6:8

As the wife of a pastor and the mother of six small children, I understood firsthand that many times money was not always in abundance. We knew that being in the ministry would challenge us to walk by faith and although we didn't always like having our faith put to the test, we loved seeing the hand of God at work.

I needed a pair of sneakers but we did not have the money. I knew from past experience that the Lord could and would supply me with all that I needed. I remember kneeling by the edge of my bed bringing my petition before the very throne of grace! When I had finished praying, I gave it no second thought for I had cast my care on Him and I knew in His timing, He would answer.

Little did I realize how quickly the answer would come and how I would be a witness to God's creativity in providing for my need. It was a beautiful summer day and I went to bask in the sunshine by sitting on my front steps while watching my children play in the yard.

No sooner had I sat down then an unfamiliar dog came into the yard and made his way toward me. Normally I would have been frightened, but for some reason I wasn't. I noticed he was carrying something in his mouth. To my great surprise, it was a sneaker! I thought it very odd but I took the sneaker, which he apparently wanted me to have. I remember thinking, "Too bad there's only one!" It was not only a high quality leather sneaker, but it happened to be my size! Since there was only one, I took it and threw it in the trash.

The next day, again while sitting on my front steps, the mysterious dog came back carrying the other sneaker! I gently took it from its grasp, and ran into the house to rummage through the trash from the day before to rescue its mate. The rescued "mate" needed some TLC. I cleaned it thoroughly and stood there staring at the two sneakers. They were so incredibly nice that I felt compelled to locate their owner so that I could give them back. I went from house to house showing my neighbors the sneakers and asking them if they had lost them. Time and time again, the answer was "no."

I realized then that the sneakers belonged to me… that my heavenly Father had heard my plea and had answered my need by way of a special delivery!

~Lynn McGrath

86

Pop Goes the Miracle

The demand of the human understanding for causation requires
but the one old and only answer, God.
~Henry Martyn Dexter

Arriving early and sitting in the lobby for my appointment, I became quite thirsty. There was no water fountain in sight. However, I did see a pop vending machine nearby. Unfortunately, I couldn't find the necessary coins in my purse, not even a dollar.

A nice-looking young man sat down beside me. I introduced myself. "Hello, my name is Mary Edwards. What's your name?"

"My name is Michael."

"Michael, do you have change for a ten?"

"No, I'm sorry," he replied. "But what do you need?"

"Seventy-five cents for the pop machine."

He reached into his pocket and handed me the money. "Let me give it to you."

"Thanks so much, Michael. God is going to give you back more than you gave me."

Grateful for my newfound friend, I took the money and headed toward the vending machine. I was happy to see Vernors Ginger Soda, the only pop I drink. I put my coins in the slot and made my selection. Out popped a Vernors with a dollar bill wrapped around it, secured by a rubber band!

I'm so glad I had several wide-eyed witnesses nearby or I would have thought I was hallucinating!

I walked over to Michael and gave him the dollar bill. "Michael, tell these people what I said to you when you gave me seventy-five cents."

"She told me that God was going to give me back more than I gave her."

~Minister Mary Edwards

87

A Very Special Rose

Children are the bridge to heaven.
~Persian proverb

As the six of us crowded into the examination room, the ultrasound revealed Angie and Larry's third blessing was a girl. Six-year-old big brother Joshua and two-year-old sister Mckenna giggled with glee and excitement.

As the parents, two siblings-to-be and we grandparents departed the OB office, our daughter Angie said, "Joshua, you wanted another sister. Do you have a name you would like to give her?"

Without hesitating he answered, "Rose."

Stunned, Angie and I glanced at one another.

Angie inquired, "Joshua, what a beautiful name. How do you know the name Rose? Is there a Rose in your kindergarten class?"

"No."

"Is one of your teachers or an aide named Rose?"

"No."

"Joshua do you know anyone with that name?"

"No."

Gently Angie asked, "Well Joshua, how do you know the name Rose?"

Slightly perturbed Joshua stated, "I just know it."

This time Angie and I looked at one another in astonishment, fighting back tears.

Two years earlier, Angie's sister Gretchen, who was nearing

completion of her three-year residency in pediatrics, died with her husband in a boating accident on Lake Ponchartrain, north of New Orleans. Throughout her adult life Gretchen had planned to name her first daughter Rose. Joshua had never heard that his aunt, who died when he was only four, planned to use that name.

We knew no six-year-old boy thinks up the name Rose.

We knew his parents didn't even have a rose bush in their yard.

We all knew that Gretchen is an angel watching over her siblings, their families, and us.

~Sandra Life

88

My Angel, Carlo

If you seek an angel with an open heart... you shall always find one.
~Author Unknown

On a sunny November morning in Milano, Italy, my friend Rick and I headed to the Duomo, the centre of the city, to take some photos. We stopped at a little café, and as Rick stood in line to order, I opened my purse.

"Rick, I don't have my wallet!" I cried. "It's not in my purse. I don't know where it is!"

My wallet held my passport, credit cards, driver's license, insurance, and almost 500 euros in cash. I had always felt safe in Italy and never had any issues with pickpockets, so I was certain my wallet must have fallen from my purse when I'd taken out my camera.

"I'm not going to worry," I calmly told Rick, as we walked back to the Duomo. "All my life I've believed in angels. I trust a nice person picked up my wallet and it will be returned to me."

I am not sure whether Rick shared my belief; I think he was just thankful I remained so calm.

Arriving at the Duomo, the *carabinieri* (police) were out in full force. Rick approached one of the officers and explained my situation. The policeman gave us directions to the Lost and Found and we followed the route he suggested.

But fifteen minutes later, we realized we were lost, so we retraced our steps to the Duomo. I decided to head to the Tourist Office, highly optimistic that another traveler had picked up my wallet.

My optimism waned when we were told that no one had handed in a wallet. With new directions, we headed off again to the Lost and Found where their reply was the same. Two dead-ends.

At that point, I questioned whether I would ever find my wallet; the chances were getting pretty slim. Because I had lost my passport, I needed to fill out a report at the police station. While walking there, I had a philosophical conversation with Rick as to the meaning of it all. It felt quite surreal walking in a foreign city knowing you had no ID and no money. I was okay with losing my passport and ID, as I knew those items were replaceable. I was upset, though, about the little red envelope containing 200 euros that I had tucked in my wallet. My friend Renee gave it to me to spend on something special in Italy. I knew that even if I got my wallet back, the cash would probably be gone, along with the opportunity to spend her generous gift.

Outside the police station, a man in a booth directed people where they needed to go. He instructed us to turn left. As Rick headed off, I paused, debating whether I should phone and cancel my credit cards.

"Theresa, are you coming to fill out the report?" Rick yelled.

An older gentleman, standing near the booth heard Rick and asked, "Have you lost something?"

Rick walked over. "Yes, she's lost a wallet."

The gentleman looked at me and asked my name.

"Theresa," I replied.

"Theresa, there is your wallet," he said, pointing to the man in the booth.

I approached and there, lying open on the desk, was my wallet! I saw my ID and even the red envelope, torn open with no money inside.

"Rick, my wallet was found and turned in!" I shouted.

The gentleman confirmed that he was the one who'd found it. When I looked into his kind eyes, I knew he wouldn't have taken my money. I expressed my thanks and how grateful I was.

I entered the booth to pick up my things and my intuition told me to look to the left. There in the corner of the desk was a stack of 50-euro bills.

The man in the booth asked if I had everything.

I calmly said, "Yes, all my ID is here and that is my money," I said, pointing to the pile of cash.

He agreed and I counted the money. All 500 euros were there!

Rick was talking with Carlo, the kind gentleman who'd found my wallet. Carlo was saying goodbye, so I quickly gave Rick a 50-euro bill to give to him as a token of my gratitude.

Carlo refused to take the money.

I grabbed my things and rushed out to stop Carlo from leaving. Pleading with him I said, "Please Carlo, is there anything I can buy you to thank you for finding my wallet?"

He thought for a moment and then in a typical Italian response he said, "Okay, un caffè."

Perfect!

We crossed the street and I ordered espressos. We sat down and Carlo told his side of the story.

When he found my wallet on the Duomo floor, he opened it to realize a Canadian tourist had lost all her ID. He phoned his lawyer friend to find out what to do and she told him to go to the police station and fill out a report. He walked to the station and met the man in the booth, who took the wallet without writing down any information. Carlo left the booth but felt uncomfortable about what had happened so he phoned his friend back. She insisted that he return to the station and fill out a police report. At the booth, Carlo saw the wallet ripped open with all the money to one side and wondered what was going on. At that precise moment, he saw me standing there and heard Rick call out.

Rick and I sat in awe. We couldn't believe all the coincidences and the magic of it all.

Looking into Rick's eyes, I expressed what I knew was true. "Rick, meet my angel Carlo."

~Theresa Chan

Terry

Earth hath no sorrow that heaven cannot heal.
~Thomas Moore

I hastily hopped into the nearest checkout line at the discount store, my single purchase in hand. Glancing at the two women in front of me, I halted in my tracks.

"Jan. Charlotte," I stammered. "I can't believe I chose this line at this moment."

"It was no coincidence," Jan said with a half-smile. "There are no coincidences," she repeated, her eyes brimming with tears.

There are no coincidences. Everything happens for a reason. That's what Terry always said. Terry, my best friend, Jan's sister, Charlotte's daughter. It was still incomprehensible to me that just two days earlier we had sat at her bedside as she lay dying of a massive heart attack.

As the three of us hugged at the checkout line, the cashier fiddled with the rubber strip at the end of the conveyor belt. With a flat object, he pried a coin from beneath it.

"What's a dime doing here?" he questioned. "I've never seen that before. How did it get there?" He placed the coin on the checkout stand. "Anybody need a dime?"

After a final hug and a plan to meet at the funeral, Jan and Charlotte left. I rummaged in my purse for my wallet, paid for my item, and headed to the exit. I was surprised to see Jan and Charlotte waiting for me there.

"LeAnn," Terry's mom began, "have you heard of pennies from heaven?"

"Yes," I eagerly replied. "I've just read 3,000 stories for *Chicken Soup for the Soul: A Book of Miracles* and among them were dozens of stories from people who found pennies. They saw them as a sign from above, often sent by someone who is now an angel in heaven."

"Well," Jan said, "in our family it's dimes."

Now *my* eyes brimmed with tears.

Jan went on to tell me about when her disabled son had serious major surgery years before. They had found a dime under his hospital bed before he went into the operating room. They saw that as a sign from heaven that he would be okay.

"And believe it or not," Jan continued, "on the morning after Terry died, we went to the ICU to tell her goodbye, and when we left, under the bed, we found a dime."

"I saw it too," Charlotte confirmed.

I rubbed chills from my arms.

"That's my girl," Charlotte said, her voice amazingly strong for a grieving mother. "She's sending us a sign from heaven."

To my surprise, my heavy grieving heart felt lighter as I walked through the parking lot to my car. When I got in, I was actually giggling. I felt close to Terry again. So excited was I, that I couldn't wait to get home to tell my husband, so I called my daughter who manages our retail store in town. As I concluded the dime story, Christie was duly impressed. "That's awesome, Mom. It's amazing! It really is a sign from God."

I went on, blubbering about how much joy the incident had brought me. As I said goodbye and was about to hang up, Christie said, "Mom, wait. Wait. I just thought of something. This morning I looked down on the floor in front of the cash register and thought, 'What is a dime doing here?' I hadn't had any cash purchases yet today and I had looked at that spot a dozen times as I got bags from under the counter."

So together we blubbered some more about Terry being an angel, sending us signs.

Three days later I had the honor of giving the eulogy at my best friend's funeral.

After telling funny stories of our travels and antics, and serious ones of our girlfriend-talks on death, dying, and going to heaven, I told the dime stories Jan, Charlotte, Christie and I had shared. I alerted the standing-room-only crowd filling the church sanctuary and lobby to be on the lookout. "Knowing Terry, she's at God's right hand, sending more signs and we ain't seen nothin' yet," I teased.

It happened to be Good Friday. I concluded by saying that it was no coincidence that Terry was resurrected into heaven the same week as our Savior.

After the service, before I could even leave my pew, a woman came up to me.

"LeAnn, I'm Mary. I took Terry's old job when she was promoted years ago. Today I walked into the admin building where she worked until her passing, and on the carpet inside the door, there was a dime."

At the reception immediately following the service, a young woman, the best friend of Terry's daughter, approached me. "When I put my baby in the car seat this morning, I thought, 'How did a dime get in here?'"

Terry's longtime childhood friend came to me at the food table. "Yesterday on my kitchen counter, I found a dime, just lying there. I asked my husband how it got there and he said, 'It wasn't there a minute ago.'"

Terry's sister-in-law Kathy caught me at the coffeepot and told me she had found a dime that day.

Terry's brother Dennis from Idaho sauntered over. "See this tie tack? I haven't worn it in twenty years, but for some reason I put it on today."

I didn't have my glasses on and I squinted. "What is it?"

"It's a dime."

That next week, we all tried to get on with our lives, whatever that means. I called Terry's husband Tom every day and we shared our tears and continued disbelief.

One evening he came over for supper and as he walked in the door he said, "Do I have a story!"

Tom recalled how his son had raked their beautiful backyard garden when he was home for the funeral, no doubt as a vent for his grief. He had arranged for a family friend to haul the lawn waste away that next week. Tom helped the young man hold the two tarps on the windy afternoon, then went indoors as the friend loaded his pickup truck nearly full of refuse.

A short time later there was a knock at the door. Tom was surprised to see the young man there again. "I have something for you," he said. "I found it in the bottom of those mounds of waste."

And he handed Tom a dime.

Tom's eyes overflowed as he told that story, and then he and I and my husband Mark laughed and cried some more and made a toast to Terry.

A week later, I rushed onboard an airplane, off to my next speaking event, my heart alternating between joy for Terry and sadness for those she left behind.

I plopped into my aisle seat and took a deep breath. I vowed I was going to rush less and be calm more, like Terry. I smiled as I thought of her.

Then I looked across the aisle, on the floor under a seat, and saw a penny. Chuckling I looked heavenward and said out loud, "We don't do pennies, girlfriend."

A few minutes later, still amused, and recalling all those pennies from heaven stories I'd read, I crossed the aisle. I reached under the seat and picked up the penny.

And three inches from it lay a dime.

Terry and God are still at it. And we ain't seen nothin' yet.

~LeAnn Thieman

A Book of Miracles

Divine Appointment

Well done good and faithful servant!

~Matthew 25:21

Skid Row

And you will be called priests of the Lord,
you will be named ministers of our God.
~Isaiah 61:6

Determined to stock up on as much diverse life experience as possible before settling down, I spent my first year teaching in a remote Arizona school. It was an intense and exciting year, but I was restless to seek out new experiences. At the end of the academic year, I packed my bags to head for Los Angeles to work in a skid row soup kitchen.

My good friend and wise teacher, Angela, hugged me goodbye, and said, "If you ever run into my friend Jim, tell him I said hello. I haven't seen him since high school, and I heard he ended up on skid row."

We both smiled, imagining the immensity of the big city, and the winning-the-lottery odds of running into Jim. Nevertheless, I assured her that I would keep her request in mind.

A busy year followed, filled with new friendships, profound insight and good healthy manual labor. Days were often exhausting, preparing and serving meals for soup lines that sometimes wound around the block and swelled to nearly 1,000 hungry guests. Among them were men who visited the kitchen daily during winter, then hit the rails in spring in search of migrant work. There were young hopefuls, confident they were about to make it big in Hollywood, but for now, were "just visiting the kitchen temporarily" to help subsidize dwindling savings. There were the elderly, the lonely, the confused and the abused, each with unique and moving stories.

As my first year at the kitchen drew to a close, I decided it was time to head back to the Midwest to be among my family to sort out my options before venturing to new places. It was during my last week at the kitchen that I was busy one morning mechanically chopping vegetables for the day's meal. I was lost in thought, or perhaps just tuned out, in an attempt to bury my ambivalence about leaving. In the midst of my preoccupation, a man who was probably younger than he looked walked unsteadily into the kitchen, which was normally off-limits to anyone but staff. I was too distracted to pay much attention, until he insisted on talking.

"What's your name?" he asked.

"Bernadette," I answered absent-mindedly.

"Like the saint, huh?" he countered.

I offered a weak smile. "Yep, like the saint," I mumbled, and kept chopping.

"Where you from?" he pressed on.

"Arizona. I was a teacher there," I said, and named the school for him.

"Hey, that's where I'm from, and that's where I went to school," he answered, as I looked up in time to see his face light up.

By then, I was back in the present moment. "Really," I said, only half believing.

He rattled off a few names I didn't recognize.

"You know Angela?" I asked casually, adding her last name.

"Of course!" he blurted out. "We went to school together. She was my girlfriend in high school."

The inevitable question was next. "What's your name?"

"It's Jim," he said softly.

The day's soup and my commitment to it no longer seemed so important.

"Would you like to write her a note?" I offered. "I'll send it to her."

He nodded, and I hastily placed the lid back on the trashcan to improvise a desk. I grabbed an old vegetable crate and stood it on end for a stool. Jim sat down with the paper and pencil I had handed him, and I left him alone with his thoughts. I went back to my vegetables, but couldn't help stopping long enough to glance at him. There was no question our conversation had cleared both of our minds. He brushed tears from his eyes as he carefully wrote his letter.

I sent the letter off to Angela the next day. By the time she answered his letter, in care of the soup kitchen, I had moved on.

I heard from Angela myself later that summer. She wrote that Jim had jumped the first train he could find, and headed back to Arizona. He immediately looked Angela up when he arrived. She had never married, so they took up where they'd left off in high school, years before.

Jim stopped drinking, and his fine skills as an electrician resurfaced. He found a small house to rent and a job. Our meeting was a reality most people would have argued couldn't have happened. But God made sure it did.

~Bernadette Agronsky

Spirit in the Classroom

There is nothing on earth worth being known, but God and our own souls.
~Gamaliel Bailey

"Those things never really happen," said Michael, sitting in the front row of my eighth-grade classroom. I had just read a story from *Chicken Soup for the Soul* about a teenager who dropped his books while walking home from school one day. He was planning to commit suicide. However, because another boy stopped to help him pick up his books, his mind was changed and he went on to be successful in high school and beyond.

My students had listened quietly while I was reading. I was surprised to hear Michael's voice filled with so much doubt.

I defended the story, saying, *"Chicken Soup for the Soul* is a book series telling only true stories that happen to ordinary people. Actually, I have a personal story of a similar event that could be in a *Chicken Soup for the Soul* book."

I don't know why I said that; I didn't want to tell my personal story. It was so unbelievable that most non-Christians would think I was crazy.

However, the class begged to hear about my experience. Even Michael seemed interested. Looking at the clock, I decided that there was just enough time before the bell rang. Starting slowly, choosing the words to my religious story very carefully, I shared:

"I attended a church youth group on Wednesday nights when I was in high school. One night while I was sitting on the floor in the audience listening to the youth pastor, I heard a voice in my head. It kept saying, 'Go take the microphone. I have something for you to say.' I argued with the voice in my head, looking around to see if anyone else was hearing things.

"The voice reassured me, 'Go up on stage. Tell the man that you need the microphone. I will give you the words.' I argued some more, seriously beginning to worry that I had lost my mind.

"However, I found myself on the small stage, interrupting the pastor who was just about to dismiss the group to play games. He gave me the microphone and I stood facing the audience of about sixty teenagers, my peers.

"I don't know where the words came from but I heard myself saying, 'Someone here tonight is planning to commit suicide. The Lord has asked me to come up here and tell you not to do it. He has a plan for you and loves you. Tell someone how you feel.'

"I sat down fast and was in shock at what I had done. Now, the story could end here, with my friends looking at me oddly, but it doesn't. A couple of months later, my mom bumped into a woman from the church, an acquaintance of hers. They exchanged pleasant-ries and then the woman told my mom a story about her daughter. She had been planning to commit suicide but didn't. She arrived home one night after youth group and told her mom what she was thinking about doing and what I had said that night."

Looking around, I noticed that my students were very quiet as they listened to me reminisce. I smiled. "I have shared this story with only a few people. It still gives me goose bumps to think about it."

As I took a deep breath and wondered if I had said too much in a public school, the classroom radio popped on, loudly playing the song "Spirit in the Sky." No one was near the radio.

The whole class sat in awed silence for several moments. Everyone looked around a bit dazed, listening to the Spirit in the sky... and our classroom.

~Kristy Duggan

92

A Gift to Each Other

Where thou art — that — is Home.

~Emily Dickinson

I was born with a wandering spirit. After college, I joined a theatre company and traveled all over North America and Europe. I was far away and broke most of the time, but no matter where I wandered, I made it home to Colorado for Christmas. This was a fairly significant feat, and yet I had managed to do it every year without fail. It sometimes involved days and nights of driving through blizzards, gallons of espresso, twelve-hour plane rides, lost baggage, and customs officials who always seemed to pick me for scrutiny.

Our holiday traditions were pretty average — tree, presents, way too much food, Christmas Eve service at church, watching the movie *White Christmas* with my sister. Nothing extraordinary happened, but living so far away made it essential to be there. I needed to stay current in my siblings' lives. I wanted to know my nieces and nephews and have them know me. If I wasn't there for Christmas I feared I would just fade out of the family.

My fiancé Calvin and I traveled back to Colorado for our wedding, which was the "opening ceremony" of a huge Fourth of July family reunion. I wasn't a girl who imagined my wedding as the pivotal point of human history anyway, so a simple affair was just my style. But even small and simple broke the bank for us. We headed back to work in Europe knowing there would be a slim chance of another trip home anytime soon. Christmas would likely be a cozy twosome.

"This is okay," I told myself. "We're our own family now. It will be romantic." Plus, our tour ended in Switzerland, so that's where we'd be stuck for Christmas. Definitely worse places to be!

But as the tour drew to a close, my morale crumbled. Watching our teammates excitedly depart, talking about cherubic nieces and nephews, trees, stockings, and family traditions, left me feeling less than lucky about my own situation. Yes, I was a newlywed and the world was supposed to be rosy, but in truth, spending our first six months of marriage in a van with a team of kooky performers and sleeping on pull-out couches in people's dens had placed a strain on the marital bonding process. Our harmony was a little off-key, to put it mildly. Three solid weeks of undiluted togetherness was looking about as awkward as the sixth grade dance and even less appealing. A little padding of friends and family would have been so much less stressful.

The lack of company wasn't the only check in my negative column, either. We had no home. Like I said, we traveled in a van and were housed as part of our performance contracts. Being on break meant that we'd have to find a place to stay. Someplace free. And who wants a couple of bickering vagabonds hanging around at Christmas? Even if someone did take pity and invite us into their "stable," I was really stretching to dig up any gratitude for someone's pull-out couch.

Then there was the shortage of trappings and trimmings. Our performing-artist-lifestyle left us without discretionary funds, so gifts were pretty much out. And to top it all off, Calvin got sick with an infected wisdom tooth. He was delirious with pain. So much for romance.

First things first. Although Calvin and I were alternately ticked off and bewildered by one another, I did still have regular moments of fondness toward him. I didn't enjoy seeing him in pain. Especially because it made him all whiny and meant I had to do all the driving. We needed to get that tooth taken care of. We prayed.

"Lord, we haven't been very nice to each other lately and we know that bothers You. We're going to try and improve, but in the meantime Calvin's in a lot of pain and it's Christmas and all, and we were hoping that maybe You could toss us a miracle or something. A little sprinkle of healing power. Please."

It was something like that. Not a very spiritual sounding prayer, just desperate. We stopped on our way out of town at the home of our area representative, Jean-François, to drop off a calendar for our next tour.

He took one look at Calvin and declared with widened eyes "zut alors!" This can mean many things, but in this case it was an expression of alarm.

He made a phone call. He spoke way too fast for me to follow his French, but it sounded very emphatic and convincing and twenty minutes later the source of distress was being extracted from Calvin's jaw by Jean-François' friend, who also happened to be a dental surgeon and who also decided he didn't want to be paid since it was two days before Christmas. God is so cool, and His people can be really cool sometimes too. On this day He was also really speedy, which was such a nice bonus.

While Calvin was being repaired, I wandered the streets of Lausanne soaking up Christmas Spirit from all the colors and lights and using my tiny store of Swiss francs to buy a few chocolate coins, a nice writing pen, a recording of Calvin's favorite artist, and a few other tidbits. I could wrap each one separately and tie little bows and we could have a miniature Christmas. It would be a peace offering—my promise of a fresh start. Our harmony had already improved with the pressure of touring off our shoulders. A little privacy might be tolerable after all.

With that thought came the reminder that we needed a place to stay. We actually had an offer but I had put off phoning them. Timothy and Pierette were the elderly uncle and aunt of a colleague. They lived in a remote mountain village a couple of hours from Geneva, and we had met them earlier that tour. Timothy was an egg farmer and Pierette ran the general store in the village. They mentioned that they had a little apartment in their basement and that we were welcome to stay anytime, including the holidays.

Why hadn't I called them? I had a picture in my mind of a spider-infested stairway leading to a dank room with a bare flashlight hanging down, a chamber pot in one corner and a hot plate with questionable wiring in the other. I was thinking WWII, French Resistance. This would be the space between two walls where they hid Jewish neighbors and secret radios. Of course this was neutral Switzerland, so none of that actually happened here, but my imagination always tended toward the dramatic. There would be an old wooden door with a broken latch. Chickens would be pecking outside the door and snow would blow in through the cracks. We'd sleep on separate army cots under threadbare blankets and we'd have scrambled eggs for Christmas dinner. Truthfully, I was kind of reveling in the whole sad and wretched picture and imagining the screenplay.

I was brought back to reality when Calvin arrived, all swollen-cheeked. "Tho, dith joo make dath phwone cawwl?"

Darn. We really had no alternatives, but I was sure the experience itself wouldn't be as fun or glamorous as the eventual movie version. I prayed again. "God, I miss my family. So far, marriage is not really what I expected, and I feel like Heidi going to stay on some mountainside in a scary basement with some old people I don't really know. I want to make the best of this. I know it's really not all about me. I know I should ask You to help me grow up and be selfless like You, but I also want to pray that we have a really nice, fun holiday together."

I made the call, got directions, and turned the van up the winding mountain road. As we pulled into the little town we had to wait for a herd of cows making its way down the main street. With Calvin mumbling the directions through wads of cotton we arrived at Pierette's general store.

I knocked hesitantly. The door flew open and Timothy and Pierette greeted us like their own grandchildren back from a war, or a refugee camp, or from just having received a Nobel Prize. We were ushered directly into the parlor where a fire was crackling and a tree was twinkling. There were cookies right out of the oven, and hot chocolate with lots of whipped cream.

Over steaming cups they asked us all about our tour, all about our wedding, all about our families. We learned all about egg farming and life in a tiny Swiss village. We laughed, and smiled and ate cookies. God had answered our prayer. He knew what our marriage needed, and He prepared this place for us long in advance. This was the most calm, nurturing place in the world to spend Christmas, or any other day for that matter. Of course I hadn't seen the little apartment in the basement yet, but Pierette said we were welcome to join them upstairs as much as we liked, so maybe we wouldn't have to hang out with the spiders.

The phone rang, disrupting our relaxed conversation. We heard a "zut alors!" in the conversation. Timothy returned to us with a frown.

The village was in an uproar. The pastor was sick. He had a fever and had lost his voice. There would be no Christmas Eve program. This was a considerable crisis, tantamount to the plague or a foreign army marching over the Alps. Timothy and Pierette exchanged distressed glances and Pierette immediately began clearing away the dishes. Whenever a solution is unclear, it's always helpful to tidy up in Switzerland.

Calvin raised an eyebrow at me, and I answered with a grin and a nod. This was a no-brainer! We jumped up and offered to save the day.

We'd been doing nothing but Christmas programs for weeks. We had a vast repertoire to choose from. Relief spread over our hosts' faces.

We began gathering props, running lines, and planning all the music we could do with only the two of us. With a quick change of clothes we set off. We chose a play about two lonely people who meet in an airport on Christmas Eve. As the characters hesitantly begin to converse, they share their stories, their loneliness, and a reminder of God's gift to us in the birth of Jesus. My character, a believer, realizes that they were put there for that reason—put there to answer one another's need. They read the Christmas story from the book of Matthew, and share an impromptu celebration.

Calvin's character, with spiritual eyes opening for the first time, declares, "You'll have to lead me. I've never had a real Christmas before."

We were in the zone. We were a perfect team that night, and I remembered why I had chosen to spend the rest of my life with this man. Performing this play on Christmas Eve, for these people, was perfect. As I spoke my lines, the truth of them penetrated my own heart—we answered each other's need. We were put here for that reason. The paradox of God's sovereignty struck me. Somehow, in the complexity of God's love and provision, He cares about my smallest details and desires. And yet, at the same time, it's all about Calvin, and it's all about the man in the front row with tears streaming down his cheeks, and it's about Pierette and her general store, and the dental surgeon, and all of my teammates at home with their families. We are God's gift to each other. Like a master composer, He brings all the instruments together, each with a different tone, each playing a different part, and He makes it turn out so beautifully.

After the program we were invited to the evening meal, full of cheese and chocolate and all the yummiest Swiss things. Not a single scrambled egg. Later, we grabbed our suitcases and at last made it down the staircase to the place that would be home for the next three weeks.

The staircase was steep, and the basement was indeed dark and creepy. We opened the apartment door and were greeted by twinkling lights, a small decorated tree in the corner, and evergreen boughs, all adorning a newly remodeled, sparkling clean studio. There was modern plumbing and a kitchenette with perfect wiring. There was a tantalizing fruit basket on the table and a big, soft bed covered with the whitest and fluffiest down comforter I'd ever seen. Calvin spontaneously lifted me over the threshold.

"Merry Christmas," I sighed. He set me down, wrapping his arms around me. I wrapped back. We were God's gift to each other.

~Kristi Hemingway

93

A Higher Purpose

I was a stranger and you invited me in.
~Matthew 25:35

After two days of presenting seminars in New England, I made a mad dash to the airport. Finding myself with a little time to spare, I sat in the main terminal for a few minutes of relaxation. Although this tiny airport appeared to be fairly new, it was unusually empty for 4:30 p.m. on a weekday. From my vantage point, I counted four people.

I sat idly for a few minutes, and then the woman who checked me in at the counter approached me by name and said, "I told you earlier that your seat was confirmed, but the flight before this one has been canceled. I can't guarantee that you'll get on, but it looks good so far."

As the only standby passenger for this flight, I waited patiently. About a dozen confirmed passengers at the gate started to board the small plane. When I asked about my standby status, the woman hand-counting the tickets delivered the disappointing news. "All nineteen seats are full, sir."

Being a "doubting Thomas" of the first degree, I waited at the gate until the plane was actually rolling down the runway before I gave up and returned to the main terminal. For some reason, I wasn't terribly upset about missing the plane. I frequently tell my seminar participants, "Things happen for a reason. The universe is trying to tell us something." I thought, "Okay, it's time to trust my own advice. Why am I here tonight?"

I sat down at one of the four wooden tables outside the airport's dining area and took an apple from my briefcase. Each bite made a conspicuous crunching sound. I felt uneasy, as if I were being watched. Glancing around, I noticed two pieces of unattended luggage on the floor about a foot away, leaning against the next table. As I considered reporting this to security, I noticed a young man dressed in a dark blue suit, tie and turban, using the microwave nearby. He walked slowly over to his table, carefully cradling a large cup, and slumped into his chair. As he ate, he looked over at me several times and smiled politely. I smiled back.

When I stood up to discard the remains of my apple, the young man got up too, following right on my heels with his trash. We exchanged the typical small talk of strangers thrown together by circumstance for a brief moment in time.

My new acquaintance said, "I'm in town for an interview. I plan to become a doctor, and I've applied to the residency program at the hospital here. It looks favorable."

"What kind of doctor?" I asked.

"I don't know," he answered sheepishly.

"If you don't know what kind of doctor you want to be, how do you hope to become what you want?" I inquired.

"Are you a philosopher or something?" he asked, raising a dubious eyebrow.

"No. I'm a professional speaker and I give seminars," I answered. "Would you like a seminar on goal setting?"

Without hesitating, he replied, "Yes, actually… I'd like someone to speak to me." Thrusting his hand toward mine, he introduced himself.

As he motioned for me to sit next to him, I moved my luggage to his table, and we continued talking. In this unexpected arena, we discussed our goals and dreams. It wasn't a seminar, but within minutes it turned into a deep sharing session. The young man told me how lonely he was since moving from India only weeks before. He said, "I felt that I had to leave my homeland in order to find myself."

It was clear he was troubled. He confided feelings that he said he rarely told anyone. He had broken off his engagement to a young woman in India, shortly before their arranged wedding. He also revealed that, as a young boy, he had been sexually abused by one of the family servants. The horrors of that event still haunted him. I marveled at this man's ability to share such confidences with a stranger.

"The man is locked up now," he said sadly. After pausing for a few moments to stare at the floor, he continued, "I wonder if blaming the servant was justified." It was obvious that this young man was struggling with many troublesome issues in his life.

Then the young man's dark, despondent eyes met mine as he added, "I wish my problems would just disappear."

It seemed to me that the banished servant wasn't the only imprisoned soul.

As he shared his buried thoughts, I could see how much he had to offer the world.

He stared at me with intense eyes. "I don't know why I am even telling my secrets to a total stranger."

Hoping to reassure him, I said, "God has placed us together tonight so we could help each other. Someday it will be your turn to listen and to help someone else, to soothe his troubled soul."

The young man had a promising career ahead of him. I pointed out all the positives in an attempt to make him feel better about himself. It seemed my words were of some benefit. He smiled and thanked me for listening.

When his flight was called, we both stood up. As we shook hands, his fingers hesitated to let go. He seemed to be holding on in order to absorb some of my strength. In those two short hours, we had created a bond, a bridge between two diverse cultures and generations. We exchanged a brotherly hug, and he parted.

I meandered over to the departure area window to catch a glimpse of him. I wanted to wave as he boarded his plane. As I watched his plane on the tarmac, I looked up in disbelief at the familiar, almost supernatural, reflection in the dingy glass. My new friend was standing right behind me! Astonished, I turned around.

With a somber face he said, "I have just one more thing to tell you."

"What is it?" I asked, eagerly.

"Thank you for being here tonight... and for listening to me." He stopped suddenly to take a deep breath. Then he said, tearfully, "I was planning to... kill myself tonight." Stopping to take my hand, he added, "But now... I feel like there's hope."

We shook hands and then embraced for the last time. Words were insignificant. I felt a tear on my cheek as I waved to him and watched him board his flight.

That night, I felt a new connection to God, like I had just been given a signal. I felt renewed with a sense of a higher purpose.

~Tom Lagana

94

Miracle Meeting

Therefore, what God has joined together, let man not separate.
~Matthew 19:6

Growing up with a last name like Miracle made for a lot of puns. When I was born, my parents could honestly say without boasting that I was a Miracle child. On the playground in elementary school I heard, "Hey Miracle Whip!" In junior high school, "It's a Miracle!" echoed through the halls as I carried a toppling stack of books. It wasn't until I reached high school and college that I really found consolation in my name.

I didn't believe I would ever marry, even though that is what I wanted. I would laugh and tell my best friend, "At least I have a good last name because it is never going to change."

Years after my pessimistic marriage prediction, I started my career as a fifth-grade teacher. One day I was walking innocently down the hall, minding my own business after taking my students to the bus. Beth, one of my fellow teachers, emerged from her classroom into the empty hallway.

"There is someone you should meet," she said. Her eyes danced and her lips curled into a smile.

"Oh no," I thought to myself. "Not another blind date." A thousand alarm systems shrilled in my head, and I imagined myself making a U-turn and sprinting, Olympian style, to the nearest exit. I was a single newcomer in town and everyone seemed interested in plotting out my love life. As afraid as I was of never getting married, I was becoming more and more afraid of blind dates.

I politely said, "No thanks, I'm already seeing someone," which was true.

Despite my refusal, Beth, without pausing for breath, continued to tell me about Jesse, the nice man she had met at church. Jesse's mother, Sharon, had taught at our school, but died tragically in an automobile accident long before I could ever meet her. Other teachers and past students fondly remembered her kindness, and each year a senior at the high school was awarded a scholarship in her memory. I was sure this devoted woman had raised a nice son; I just didn't like blind dates. Dating in general could be troublesome, and I certainly didn't want to intentionally invite trouble into my life.

Persistence became Beth's mantra. Each time during the school year when she asked if I would like to meet Jesse, I adamantly refused. I explained that I was dating someone and I was comfortable with that.

Then that relationship went south, literally.

That summer the man I had been dating left the country on a mission trip, mailing a letter from the airport revealing his decision to end our courtship. Tearing into his letter with great expectation only brought stinging hot humiliation to my cheeks.

It felt like my love life had died a death so dark it was far beyond resuscitation. My faith told me God was with me, but my doubt made me wonder where He was in my love life. I decided my youthful declarations might be true; it looked like it really would be a miracle if this Miracle ever married.

School started again and I moved to a new apartment. It wasn't my first choice. Plans for another apartment fell through, and by word of mouth, a friend found this one for me near the school.

Those days were filled with definite highs. I loved learning and laughing with my wide-eyed students. When they said, "Miss Miracle, you're the best teacher ever," it softened the hard edges of life. But I was still lonely and wanted to meet someone special—someone with whom I could have a future.

Day after day I graded papers and looked out my new back patio window into the carefully maintained square. A variety of vibrant pots filled with looping vines and late summer flowers clung to neighborly-looking balcony rails. The common area was shared by twelve apartment buildings. I could have lived in any of them. Initially I hadn't considered how choosing this particular building, overlooking this peaceful plot, would be such a good plan for my life.

Months went by. The summer pots disappeared from the square, replaced by snow and ice that clung to the balcony rails instead.

One wintry February morning, I was scraping my car windshield and talking to one of my new neighbors who lived downstairs in my building. He was tall, friendly, my age, and it hadn't taken long for me to notice his movie star smile. When our paths had crossed in the stairwell, we would say hello and engage in brief conversations. If the truth be known, I was developing a crush, and we had never even been formally introduced.

That particular February morning, this handsome neighbor was concerned for the other tenants' safety, as the sidewalks were slick with a thick sheet of ice. He warned each person who walked by of hazardous spots, and I saw how kind he was. We talked as we de-iced our cars and he asked me where I taught.

"Second Street School," I answered, as my scraper flicked shavings of ice that melted on the warming car hood.

His whole face lit up with interest, igniting his perfect smile. "My mother taught there," he told me with pride.

"Really?" I said enthusiastically. "Would I know her?"

"No." In a quiet voice that sounded far away and tinged with sadness he said, "She died in a car accident."

This tall friendly man began describing his mother's beautiful qualities and telling me about the scholarship that family, students, and friends had started. But his words were muffled, as if making their way down a long tunnel to my brain. My breath caught in the frigid air. My neighbor, who introduced himself as Jesse, was the man I had refused to meet for more than a year. And yet there he was, standing before me.

Much has happened in the nine years since that memorable discovery. My students and I raised money for the Sharon Lewis Scholarship Fund by recycling aluminum cans. My gloomy guess at how life would turn out was wrong. My last name changed after all, and I taught at the school until two days before our handsome baby boy was born.

Now on wintry icy mornings I snuggle close to my husband Jesse in our warm little home and I feel like I'm still a Miracle.

~Janeen Lewis

A Shower of Roses

But my mouth would encourage you;
comfort from my lips would bring you relief.
~Job 16:5

Excited to see the spectacular fall foliage, my brother Gene flew into New Hampshire from Iowa for a visit. After getting settled, we started out first thing in the morning on the feast of St. Thérèse, October 1st, to take in the picturesque beauty of our state. I have a special fondness for St. Thérèse, who promised followers a showering of mystical roses of assistance in times of trouble. As the long day of leaf viewing went on, I grew very weak and tired from my multiple sclerosis. Gene took the car keys, called it a day and told me to relax as he drove.

We were on a busy highway about an hour from home when a dark sedan sped by us. I heard my brother gasp as I opened my eyes to look out of the front window. With its brake lights still beaming, the speeding car soared into flight, rolling three or four times in the air before landing in the woods.

My brother pulled over to the side of the road and ran toward the overturned car. It was getting dark and hard to see. He yelled back to me, "There is no one in the car." I got my cell phone and called 911.

Gene walked through the tall grass and woods, constantly retracing his steps, looking for someone. He found car debris everywhere, but no victims.

A few more people stopped by the roadside to assist him. For fifteen minutes they painstakingly searched. Then, in the stillness, Gene heard labored breathing. They found a young man seventy-five feet from the car.

My brother came back to our car. "Diana, I need you. He's still alive. You're a nurse."

I relayed that the driver had been found to 911 on the cell phone. Gene helped me out of the car, down the ditch through the tall weeds, and into the woods. A young man lay motionless before us. Gene helped me sit next to the man's head, took my crutches and placed them beside the victim's body.

The small man had prolonged gasping respirations and periods of no breaths… symptoms of severe head trauma and near death.

Gene took a flashlight from the car and shown it on the man. He looked barely out of his teens.

I vowed he would not die alone.

I brushed his dark brown hair and looked into his brown eyes that were opened and dull. His neck veins bulged, his pulse was rapid and surprisingly strong.

Then his breathing nearly stopped.

"Take a breath, honey," I said out loud. I grasped his hand in mine. His skin was still warm. I rubbed his cheek and noted the stubby dark growth. "Come on honey, breathe." He took a labored breath.

My back was to the highway so I was oblivious to the commotion going on. My brother told me that police cars had arrived. Within seconds, I heard a reassuring voice promise that the ambulance was pulling up.

With my face next to the young man's, I talked soothingly, stroked his cheek, and checked his pulse. Still strong. My hair brushed his unblemished face. I couldn't take my eyes off his.

"Take a breath, honey." He did. Blood oozed from his mouth and nose. I cleared his airway, stroked his arm and squeezed his hand in mine. I noticed his blood on my body.

Then silence.

"He's stopped breathing," I called out. His pupils were fixed and dilated. I heard the trooper assure me that the ambulance was here. Paramedics ran down the slope.

As they took over, I kept one finger on the boy's pulse and my other hand grasping his. His pulse grew weaker. His hand cooled.

I prayed, "God if this man cannot be saved, then welcome him with open arms."

When the EMTs positioned him for CPR, the young man's massive head injuries were obvious.

My brother helped me up and brought me to the ambulance. Someone emerged from the back, gowned from head to toe in plastic and rubber gloves, to clean the young man's sticky blood off me. I was shaking. They asked if I needed oxygen, if I was okay. I told them I had MS and always shook. "I'm fine."

It was cold and we were told to wait in our car and fill out paperwork.

When the state trooper took our report, he said the EMTs had gotten a faint rhythm with CPR. This unknown victim would be transported to the nearest emergency room in critical condition. But it did not look good.

I asked the trooper to tell the boy's family that, once found, he was never alone, that he was never conscious or in pain. That he was prayed for. As a mother, this information would be very important to me.

Most of the ride home was silent. The entire episode was surreal. My brother alternated between anger and distress because he'd felt so helpless. But there were other feelings, too… a profound love and deep compassion for the boy, someone we didn't even know.

That night the state trooper called to thank my brother and me for calling 911 and for finding and staying with the young man. He had relayed my message to the family just before the boy was pronounced dead.

Gene's last days with us were spent in the White Mountains enjoying spectacular views. There was a peace and quiet understanding between my brother and me. We knew that separately we would have accomplished little at that horrific accident. But together, we assisted a person into his next life. This might have been of comfort to the family. But we would never know.

A year later, October 1st, on the feast day of Saint Thérèse, I visited my very special Sister in the cloistered monastery of the Precious Blood. She listened intently to our story of the young man and the accident. She sat back, looked at me intently and said the young man's name.

I was shocked. She had heard this story before.

"Wait here; don't leave," she said.

Within minutes, she brought from the chapel the young man's grandparents who a year ago entrusted St. Thérèse with his care. They'd been seeking the handicapped woman and her brother who didn't leave their grandson's side. Today they were in the chapel to thank St. Thérèse for sending someone with faith to be with him in his time of need.

I imagined mystical rose petals falling softly around us.

~Diana M. Amadeo

96

A Charmed Charm Bracelet

But now, Lord, what do I look for?
My hope is in you.
~Psalm 39:7

When I was sixteen, my mom and dad purchased a charm bracelet for me at the very best jewelry store in Syracuse, New York. I was thrilled. The bracelet was fourteen-karat gold and each charm they chose had a significant meaning for me and me alone. There was a golden cheerleader, a small shoe with a tiny diamond in it, and a lovely gold and peridot engraved circle that celebrated my August birthday. I loved that bracelet and I wore it for every special occasion.

It became even more special to me after Mom died. Even though I was blessed with the world's best father, I missed her terribly but my charm bracelet made me feel continuously connected to her.

After I graduated from nursing school, I took a job at one of the local hospitals on an orthopedic floor. We were instructed to wear very little jewelry, so the only thing I ever wore was my bracelet; it was on my wrist every single day of my life. It was a part of her, and I felt empty and sad if it wasn't touching me. My patients commented on the beauty of the bracelet and I was only too happy to tell them the story behind it.

The hospital was located in a hilly area of town, and the nurses' parking lots were at the bottom of the hill. One snowy January morning, I parked my car and started the long trek up to the hospital. I was bundled like an Eskimo in the bitter cold. The wind and snow made the usual climb even more difficult, and by the time I entered the lobby, I was practically frozen. I left my mittens on for a while to warm my hands.

After morning report, I began the narcotic count and readied myself for passing the day's medications. It was then I noticed that my bracelet was gone!

Devastated, I ran to the locker room and searched frantically for it. I looked in my mittens and hat and shook the scarf silly in hopes the bracelet would appear. But it was nowhere to be found. I felt sick.

I had lost the best memory of my mother.

I could barely concentrate on work, but somehow made it through to the 10:30 morning break. I quickly put my snow gear on and headed down the snowy hill to the parking lot, hoping it had fallen off my wrist and was lying next to my car.

When I got to the gigantic parking lot, I was even more upset. The entire lot had been plowed. Mountains of snow were piled against the fences.

My precious bracelet was lost forever. I walked back to the hospital crying like a child.

One of the nuns, Sister Anne, noticed my tear-stained face and tried to comfort me. I explained my heartbreaking loss. She promised to pray for me, then suggested I say special prayers to St. Anthony, the patron saint of all things lost. I began praying immediately.

By April, I had resigned myself to the fact that the bracelet was gone forever. The original jewelry store was no longer there and no other store in the area carried that special piece. By this time, St. Anthony and I were practically on a first-name basis. Several times a day, I sent him short requests for his intercession in finding my hopelessly lost bracelet. I assumed he was busy with more important services.

One Tuesday morning, another nurse found me in a patient's room.

"The janitor wants to see you."

I was way too busy so I asked her to tell him I'd connect with him later. I spotted Mike at lunchtime.

He began to explain that this winter had been one of the snowiest ever. The mounds of snow were still melting. I didn't understand what this small talk had to do with me.

"While I was shoveling snow yesterday, I noticed something shiny. For some odd reason, I picked it up and put it in my pocket. Later, I happened to show it to Sister Anne. She suggested I show it to you."

There, dangling from his hand was my bracelet! It was a bit mangled, but it had survived the winter and found its way back to me.

My eyes filled with tears. I could barely whisper, "Thank you," as I hugged him.

The bracelet was repaired to look as good as new. I don't wear it every day now for fear of losing it again, but when I do place it on my wrist, I am very aware of the miracle, thanks to the intercession of my mother and St. Anthony.

~Marianne LaValle-Vincent

97

Miracle in the Highlands

He trusts in the Lord; let the Lord rescue him.
Let him deliver him, since he delights in him.
~Psalm 22:8

All my relatives are from Northern Ireland but my cousin's husband-to-be was Scottish so they chose to be married in Braemar, a quaint storybook parish that has been home to kings, noblemen and luminaries of the art world for centuries. I was happy to attend the wedding and tour the village, surrounded by the legendary and dramatic Scottish highlands, full of thatch-roofed cottages, emerald green pastures, deep forests, rocky cliffs and outcroppings, abundant wildlife, and arched stone bridges over icy cold, babbling brooks.

I was eager to explore the highlands but the duties of the wedding and family consumed most of my time. The wedding was held in a quaint ancient, stone church full of warmth and yellow light. I had some time to myself the next day so I walked to a bicycle shop in the village, rented a mountain bike and cut out for the highlands. I called my mother from a phone booth to tell her I would be gone for the day. She said, "If you see any white heather, pull a few sprigs for me. It's good luck. Purple heather is lucky, too, but white heather is very lucky."

It took me an hour to get into the hills but the Scottish Highlands were everything I ever dreamed they'd be. I stopped by a river flowing past a whitewashed cottage and saw fish jumping in and out of the water, rabbits and gray squirrels cavorting on the bank, and a stag resting in the shade on the other bank. The air was also replete with bluebirds, butterflies and a variety of other insects. It was like I had stepped into Bambi. I thus named one of the rabbits Thumper.

I continued my journey by riding uphill along the riverbank until I reached a bridge. I crossed it and found verdant pastures dappled with sunlight. I strayed into a field and got chased by a herd of cows, which was quite frightening until I realized they were more afraid of me than I was of them, and they were only following me because they thought I had food. When I stopped, they would all stop and stare at me. When I stepped toward them, they would all step back. They could have easily crushed me into a fine powder but they were afraid of me. It was very surreal for a city boy.

Farther down the road, I saw a hedgehog, as well as enormous slugs, birds I couldn't identify, a wild goat, and a red fox. The hedgehog rolled itself into a ball when I came near it. I sat down and waited for it to open up and walk again. It finally did and I got so caught up in watching it, I didn't notice the dense fog rolling in. The day went from clear to stormy within half an hour, proving a line familiar to anyone from Great Britain, "If you don't like the weather, just wait fifteen minutes."

Without the sun, the temperature dropped about twenty degrees. The clouds were growing darker and threatening. In my hasty departure, I had failed to pack a coat, long pants, a blanket, or water. I said goodbye to the hedgehog and began riding in what I thought was the direction home. However, all the dirt roads looked the same, and I couldn't simply follow my same path back because I had come over hill and dale to reach where I was. The terrain was a natural roller coaster. The clouds had obliterated the sun so I could not use it as a guide. I rode for an hour before admitting to myself that I was hopelessly lost. I thought, "I know I rode west, then north. If I only had a compass."

But I didn't have a compass. I didn't have anything. It was the perfect formula for disaster… no proper clothing, no food or water, no compass, no people anywhere to ask for help (I hadn't seen another living soul for hours), and to top it off, a violent storm was moving in. I took refuge in an abandoned barn until the rain let up, rubbing my arms to keep from freezing entirely. Not wanting to spend the night in icy cold hay, however, I pressed on.

The day grew darker still and the initial stages of hypothermia were beginning to set in when I passed a small hill covered with purple heather. At the very top of the hill, there was a small patch of white heather, the only white heather I had seen all day. I thought, "Well, at least if they find my body up here, I'll be holding in my cold, dead hands the white heather that my beloved mother had asked me to pick for her."

I laid down the bike and climbed to the top of the hill. I began to break off a branch of the heather when I saw something shining beneath it. I pushed the heather aside and saw… a compass. I almost jumped out of my shoes when I saw it. It was exactly what I had asked for.

Except for that compass, there was no other sign of the presence of another human being, not even a footprint. It was a cheap, plastic compass, but it worked just fine.

The direction it pointed me in was the opposite of the way I was planning to go. When I peddled into town I learned that the clouds that had been gathering produced one of the worst storms the area had seen in ages. It is quite possible I could have frozen to death had I not found the compass. But then I thought, why shouldn't a miracle happen here? This is God's country, one of the most spectacular pieces of land He ever created.

Soaking wet and freezing, I arrived home and gave my mother the white heather. Later that evening, as I sat with my family by the fireplace, safe and warm from the howling wind and rain buffeting our small cottage, I recounted my harrowing tale.

I thanked my mother for asking me to find the white heather… and God for providing the compass hidden beneath it.

~Mark Rickerby

98

Phil and Louie

Just as the Son of Man did not come to be served, but to serve.
~Matthew 20:28

"Please, Phil, would you look up my son in Vietnam?"

Yup, that was my mom, talking to a complete stranger following a service in our country church in Cottonwood, Minnesota. In one of her letters to me in Vietnam, she told me about the Palermo Brothers, Phil and Louie. They had made five trips to Southeast Asia in the past three years, beginning in 1969, and were headed back there again. Sponsored by World Vision, they were commissioned to minister to military personnel, refugees, prisoners of war, and patients in hospitals, anyone who needed their spirits lifted.

I could just see Mom anxiously waiting for an answer to her question. Didn't she realize there were tens of thousands of Marines in Vietnam?

"Well, ma'am, why don't you write to your son and tell him to look for us? It's possible that we may go to his base," Phil responded. He kept a small book in which he wrote notes from family members in the States to share with sons or daughters in the military. Mom watched as he wrote, "Terry Gniffke, Cottonwood, Minnesota."

Letters from Mom provided more information as she encouraged me. "Be on the lookout for two short Italian guys singing with a guitar and accordion."

I was more than skeptical about connecting with them in Vietnam or anywhere else.

Several months later as I approached the chapel service at Bien Hoa airbase, I thought I heard the sounds of a guitar, an accordion, and people singing gospel music. I was late to the service because the bomb crew and I were assembling bombs and rockets for use by Marine Corps fighter aircraft, providing close air support against the siege of the provincial capital, An Loc.

In the front of the chapel, bouncing along with their instruments, were two short Italian guys singing in familiar Minnesotan dialect. It was just like a piece of home. As a tough eighteen-year-old Marine, I hung out at the back of the chapel, observing the program. Then Phil began talking about a personal relationship with God and how I could have peace in this war-torn place.

Something happened inside my heart and mind as he shared from God's Word.

I could hardly wait to speak to them after the service. When I approached Phil and Louie, I couldn't hold back the tears. "I'm Terry Gniffke from Cottonwood, Minnesota. My mom asked me to look for you over here. She's been praying for years that I would put God first in my life. Would you pray with me?"

That night I committed my life to the Prince of Peace. My mom's prayers for me were answered, and my life transformed forever.

Thirteen years later, far from the war in Vietnam, I was living in southern California, working as an air conditioning salesman. I received a referral to a couple who lived close to my home. When we met, in addition to talking about air conditioning, the three of us began sharing our life stories. The first thing we discovered was that we all had previously lived in Minnesota. When the conversation turned to more serious topics, I began to explain how I had come to faith in God.

"I was a Marine in Vietnam, and one night I went to a chapel service and there were these two little Italian guys...."

Before I could say another word, the woman burst into tears.

Sniffling and wiping her eyes, she blurted out, "Those men were my dad and uncle."

Now all three of us were wiping the tears away. The woman, Phyllis, was Phil Palermo's daughter. She and her husband, Jim, had recently moved from Minnesota to California.

A coincidence? No, a divine appointment. A reminder of a mother's persevering prayers for her son so far away from home.

"Where are Phil and Louie Palermo now?" I questioned.

"They were singing evangelists, traveling to fifty-five countries around the world during sixty years of ministry. They worked for Youth for Christ for thirty-seven years and even participated in Billy Graham crusades."

She continued, "Louie and his wife still live in Minnesota, but Dad and Mom live just a few minutes away. I know they'd love to see you again." Phyllis smiled.

Shortly after that appointment, Phil and I met and then had several more opportunities to share what God had done in our lives during subsequent years.

Fast forward eighteen years. At Phil Palermo's memorial service I told our story to hundreds of friends and relatives. I closed with these words: "If it weren't for Phil and Louie Palermo I would not be standing here today, knowing that I will see them again in heaven."

~Terry Gniffke as told to Darlene Palermo

99

I Will Make Darkness Light

And I will bring the blind by a way that they know not;
I will lead them in paths that they have not known:
I will make darkness light...
These things I will do unto them,
and not forsake them.
~Isaiah 42:16

Even though I am partially sighted and night blind, I knew the bus driver had not let me off in front of the high school for my night class. "Oh no, it's pitch black and I'm lost!" I exclaimed in frustration. "What'll I do now?"

My pulse quickened. Breathing slowly, I tried not to panic.

I prayed while my stomach whirled. "Lord, I've got myself into a mess and I'm scared. You know where I am, and I don't. Please help me find my way."

How could I listen to God's answer while my heart raced with anxiety? I made an effort to calm down.

When I grew quiet, in my turmoil the impression came strongly. "Go to where you can see lights."

I squinted, and where there had been none, I could see a light shining like a beacon in the distance. I felt peaceful. I sensed God guiding me.

As I ventured toward the light, my white cane tapped only cement. Some unseen Power was helping me stay in the middle of the sidewalk.

I eventually came to what appeared to be a parking lot and found my way to the front of a building. Seconds after going through the doors, a familiar voice called out to me, "Pam, what are you doing here in my church, so far away from your home?"

Oh, Susan!" I choked out my unbelievable relief to my sister-in-law. "I got lost on my way to a class. The bus dropped me at the wrong stop. I'm so glad to see you!" Then breathlessly, I told her my story.

Susan hugged me. "I just happened to be here for a Bible study at the exact moment you needed to be found. We both know that was no coincidence."

I smiled and nodded my agreement.

While Susan drove me to the high school for my class, I described where I had been walking. As we passed that place, Susan exclaimed, "There are ten-foot deep trenches on both sides of the path you were on!"

I sat in stunned silence. God had delivered me from imminent danger and led me on paths I did not know.

~Pam Bostwick

100

Christmas Grace

You are excellent of men
and your lips have been anointed with grace,
since God has blessed you forever.
~Psalm 45:2

Snow continued its determined onslaught outside the assisted living facility windows. By late evening, I grew anxious about how the roads would be when I headed home. It was the week before Christmas. I should have been on my way home by now. The evening receptionist who was scheduled to relieve me had phoned to say she'd been unable to get her car started. Why was I the unlucky one stuck behind a receptionist's desk when I should have been home sipping hot cocoa and decorating the Christmas tree?

The telephone shrilled. Answering a little grouchily, I heard a man's voice. "Is this Avis rental car?"

I tried to remain calm. "No, I'm afraid our phone number here at the assisted living facility is one digit different than Avis. Let me give you that number so you don't have to look it up again." Sighing, I quickly glanced at the familiar number of the car rental company on the pad of paper in front of me. I finished giving the gentleman the number, wishing him a Merry Christmas. Just as I was about to hang up, I heard his voice in midair.

"Wait a minute please!"

"Yes?"

"I know this must sound insane, but I have to ask: do you believe in miracles?"

I sat straighter in my chair, startled at such a question from a total stranger.

"Definitely; why do you ask?"

"I'll try to make a long story short. My parents recently passed away in a car accident. I have no one left in the world but a grandmother somewhere in Virginia who I haven't seen since I was little. An uncle placed my grandmother in an assisted living facility when he grew too ill to care for her any longer. He's gone on to heaven as well. I have to ask—do you happen to have a Grace Sheperd at your facility?"

My heart beat faster as I recognized the familiar name. I pictured the gentleman holding his breath on the other end while I listened to the pinging sound of the icy precipitation pelting the window to my right.

"Are you still there?" he asked finally.

"Yes, I'm here. I wish I could give you the information you're after. I'm afraid there's a privacy policy that prohibits me from answering. The director of the facility will be in her office on Monday morning, however."

"I understand your responsibility in protecting the residents." The young man sounded so sad. "Thank you for your time, and Merry Christmas!"

"Wait!"

"Yes?"

"Virginia is a beautiful state to visit at Christmas time! Let me give you our address in case you happen to be traveling through our area any time soon!"

"Bless you!"

Christmas Eve I arrived at work earlier than usual. Christmas lights twinkled on the decorated trees up and down the hallways. Carols drifted from beneath a resident's closed door as I delivered the morning papers.

I was passing Grace Sheperd's room when I suddenly froze in

place. Grace sat in her usual rocking chair, her Bible open in her lap. Seated on the stool directly in front of her was a handsome young man with curly dark hair. His hand gently clasped Grace's as she read *The Christmas Story*.

Suddenly Grace spotted me. "Paul, here's the woman who helped you find me! Mary, please come and meet my grandson, Paul!"

I hurried inside as tears clouded my vision. The young man slowly rose to his feet, taking my hands in his.

"How can I ever thank you for leading me to my grandmother?" Shaking my head, I attempted to talk around the enormous lump in my throat.

"We both know it was a Christmas miracle!"

"Yes it was… Merry Christmas!"

"Merry Christmas, Paul. Merry Christmas, Grace!"

Making my way back to the reception area, I sent a silent prayer heavenward.

"Father, now I know why I was meant to stay late the other night. Thank you for the miracle of Christmas and for your abiding grace…. Paul's Grace too!"

I couldn't help smiling. It was going to be a glorious Christmas!

~Mary Z. Smith

Family Resemblance

Trust in the Lord with all your heart,
and lean not on your own understanding.
~Psalm 3:5

Mrs. Martina Himes, a woman I'd never met before, took one look at me and uttered seven words that changed my life forever. Not more than ten minutes after I arrived at my girlfriend's party, she gave me the once-over and then announced, "Girl, you look just like Sandra Penn!"

I'd been searching for my birthmother for more than twenty years. All I ever knew about her was that her last name was Penn. After a brief conversation with this enchanting woman, I knew in my heart that this was no coincidence. Mrs. Himes began to cry as we agreed that God had brought us together for something awesome. We could feel it.

Although she'd spent most of her adolescent years hanging out with this Sandra Penn, she hadn't laid eyes on her in fifteen years. She hadn't even thought that much about her, until now.

Our search for Sandra Penn began. Mrs. Himes's sister was the one who'd last been in touch with her. All she had to do was find Sandra's phone number and call her.

Two weeks later, she did. And that was it. Seventeen days after meeting Mrs. Himes, my lifelong needle-in-a-haystack search for my birthmother was over, because the "needle" called me on my cell phone.

We were reunited two Saturdays later, exactly one week after my thirty-fourth birthday. The minute I laid eyes on Sandra, my birthmother, I understood what all of Mrs. Himes' fuss was about. I really did look just like her. I'd been obsessed with family resemblance ever since I could remember. For all of the wonderful gifts that Mom and Dad (my adoptive parents) gave to me, resemblance was not among them. I didn't have Daddy's eyes or Momma's smile or any other unique physical trait that belonged to them. When my birth family came rushing through my door all at once that day—my mother, my brother, my sister and my little niece—there was family resemblance as far as the eye could see! Not only do I look like my mother, I'm the spitting image of my younger sister too. My brother looks like a combination of us all and my niece looks like my sister and like me.

God had, indeed, brought us together for something awesome. We could feel it.

~Pam Durant Aubry

Meet Our Contributors

Bernadette Agronsky holds a BA from Xavier University, New Orleans, Louisiana and an MEd. from Lesley University, Cambridge, Massachusetts. She works in a library and also offers journaling workshops. She believes writing is an effective means of sorting out life's truths. She can be reached at bagronsky712@gmail.com.

Diana M. Amadeo has been married to Len for thirty-four years. They have three children and three grandchildren. Besides writing books, articles and stories, Diana enjoys her Beagle, indulges in travel and reaps the harvest of her greenhouse. This is her seventh publication in the *Chicken Soup for the Soul* series. Contact her at DA.author@comcast.net.

Monica A. Andermann is a writer who lives on Long Island with her husband/proofreader Bill, and their cat, Charley. Her work has been widely published both online and in print, including several credits in *Chicken Soup for the Soul* and *A Cup of Comfort* collections.

Kim D. Armstrong has been a registered nurse for thirty years. She has published two books of stories about the miraculous healing of patients who were given a death sentence. Kim lives in western Pennsylvania with her husband, teenage daughter and son. E-mail her at kimdarlenearmstrong@embarqmail.com or check out her website: www.kimarmstrong.net.

Pam Durant Aubry is a freelance writer, mommy and former plus-sized model. She is a graduate of Temple University and has a Bachelor of Arts degree in journalism. Pam is also a Microsoft Certified Trainer and teaches classes at a computer training school. She is working on her first novel. E-mail her at pameladurant@comcast.net.

Mita Banerjee loves being a writer, teacher, mother, wife and friend. She is passionate about saving the environment, and spends much of her time firing that enthusiasm in the children of her neighborhood. She lives by the simple motto of doing (at least) one good deed a day. Contact her via e-mail at mitabaner@gmail.com.

Steve Barr creates his cartoons in a tiny cabin in the mountains of North Carolina. His art has appeared in a wide variety of newspapers and magazines, and he is also the author and illustrator of the *1-2-3 Draw* series of art instruction books. You can e-mail him at stevebarr@windstream.net.

Keisha Bass has written articles for two online publications, The Christian Pulse and sober24.com. She has also been published in *Vista* by Wesleyan Publishing House and *Living Magazine*. She enjoys singing, dancing, and playing sports. She is currently working to complete her first Christian fiction novel. Please e-mail her at keishabass@att.net.

Cynthia Bilyk is currently working on her bachelors in psychology. She recently quit her job and became a stay-at-home mom. She enjoys reading, the outdoors, and volunteer work. Please e-mail her at ufodonkey@gmail.com.

Pam Bostwick's many articles appear in Christian magazines, newspapers and anthologies, including several in *Chicken Soup for the*

Soul. Although visually and hearing impaired, she enjoys her country home, loves the beach, plays guitar and is a volunteer counselor. She has seven children and eleven grandchildren and is happily remarried. E-mail her at pamloves7@verizon.net.

Connie Sturm Cameron is a speaker and the author of the book, *God's Gentle Nudges*. She's been published dozens of times, including many *Chicken Soup for the Soul* books. Married thirty-one years, Connie and Chuck have three children and three grandchildren. Contact her at: www.conniecameron.com or via e-mail at connie_cameron@sbcglobal.net.

Theresa Chan is an entrepreneur, world traveler and published author from Toronto, Ontario. This is her second story appearing in the *Chicken Soup for the Soul* series, the first appearing in *Chicken Soup for the Bride's Soul*. Her story is a tribute to all the angels in her life. Contact her via e-mail at tccsheba@yahoo.ca.

Jane McBride Choate received her Bachelor of Science from Brigham Young University with honors. She spent the next thirty-five years being a full-time mother. Now she delights in being a grandmother to four beautiful grandchildren. When she is not playing with her grandchildren, she spends her time reading and writing.

Jeri Chrysong resides in Huntington Beach, California, where you will often find her walking her Pug Mabel. Jeri loves being a grandma to Lucas and Clay. She enjoys Hawai'i and photography. Her writing's current focus is her weight loss journey into wellness. Visit Jeri's weight loss blog at http://jchrysong.wordpress.com.

Joan Clayton is a retired teacher. Joan was the "Woman of the Year" in 2003 in her town and has been twice in *Who's Who Among America's Teachers*. Joan is the religion columnist for her town's local newspaper Visit her website at www.joanclayton.com.

Bobbie Clemons-Demuth is originally from Washington but is currently "living life to the fullest" with her husband Tom in the Bay Area of California. Together they love to travel and explore many of the surrounding areas such as Lake Tahoe, Napa Valley and Santa Cruz.

Denise Colton-D'Agostino lives in Florida where she works for the Sheriff's Department. She has volunteered for the Sexual Abuse Victim Services for over twenty-three years. She has two daughters, Shalane and Christina, who were adopted from Romania in 1991. Denise and Barbara Canale became friends during the adoption process.

This is a true story that happened to **Paula J. Coté** as she was praying for her nine-year-old granddaughter.

Lisa Cox is the widowed mom of an amazing teenage daughter, Breeanna. She is working on a degree in Information Technology. She works for a preschool in Spottsville, Kentucky. Lisa enjoys reading, writing, crocheting and would love to learn to knit. Please e-mail her Breezmom37@yahoo.com.

Jennifer Crites is a Honolulu-based writer and photographer whose words and images exploring travel, contemporary lifestyles and cultures, food, education, nature and science have been published in magazines and books worldwide. Enjoy more of Jennifer's work at www.jennifercritesphotography.com.

Leesa Culp resides outside of Niagara Falls, Ontario along with her husband and two children. Leesa enjoys writing, running, hockey and spending time with her family. She is currently working on her first non-fiction book about a Western Canadian hockey team. She can be reached via e-mail at leesadculp@yahoo.ca.

Barbara Davey received her bachelor's and master's degrees from Seton Hall University where she majored in English and education. She spent nearly twenty-five years as a vice president of marketing and public relations at a teaching hospital. She enjoys freelance writing, teaching journaling, and frequenting ethnic restaurants with her husband, Reinhold Becker. Reach her at BarbaraADavey@aol.com.

Wendy Delaney has a teaching degree from the University of Wisconsin. She has taught in public and private schools in Wisconsin and Chicago where she now resides. Wendy enjoys traveling, golfing, biking and being a Hoya mom for her daughter Margaret at Georgetown. She is hoping to have her first children's book published soon.

Deborah Derosier is the mother of four and Memaw of two. She enjoys fishing, scrapbooking and writing poetry.

Kristy Duggan has taught at the middle school level over fourteen years. Kristy enjoys photography, scrapbooking, and spending time with her children. Her mother and grandmother are both published writers.

Minister Mary Edwards is an author, editor and publisher. She is the founder of a Christian writer's guild in Detroit, Michigan, www.thecalledandreadywriters.org. She was a previous contributor to *Chicken Soup for the African American Soul*. Please e-mail her at edwardsmd@sbcglobal.net.

Diane Ganzer has written professionally for the past five years. She lives in Minnesota with her husband, children and pets. Her website is www.dianeganzer.com.

Gene Giggleman received his Doctor of Veterinary Medicine degree from Texas A&M University in 1981. He is a full-time college administrator, teaches human anatomy and has a small animal veterinary practice. He enjoys reading, riding motorcycles and bicycles, fishing, gardening, being outdoors, and spending time with his grandchildren.

Terry Gniffke is active in his church, CEO of Caliber Media Group, Inc. and co-founder of Websites for Heroes. Terry and his wife have three grown children. Darlene Palermo's father and uncle were itinerant evangelists who travelled the world for sixty years. Their stories are her heritage.

Cindy Golchuk lives near Las Vegas, Nevada, with her husband, her not-so-angelic grandson, Zack, and two dogs who rule the house with iron paws. In her spare time she enjoys reading, walking with friends, rewriting her three manuscripts geared toward a female readership and polishing her three book series for tweens.

Rosemary Goodwin was born in the lovely country town, Bury St. Edmunds in Suffolk County, England. You can see her hometown on her website www.Rosemary-Goodwin.com. After moving to the U.S. with her military husband, Rosemary lived in New England and currently lives in a historic town in Eastern Pennsylvania.

Judy Lee Green is an award-winning writer and speaker whose spirit and roots reach deep into the Appalachian Mountains. Tennessee-bred and cornbread-fed, she has been published hundreds of times and received dozens of awards for her work. Her family is the source for many of her stories. She lives in Tennessee. Reach her at JudyLeeGreen@bellsouth.net.

Heidi H. Grosch (www.heidigrosch.com) is an international writer and educator who daily celebrates the miracle of learning. She works in the Norwegian school system, writes for the *Norwegian American Weekly* (www.norway.com) and is developing a new website focused on English as a global language (www.childrensliteraturenetwork. org).

Elaine Hanson lives in Fort Collins, Colorado near Vaughn and his family. After telling the story in a Bible class, she was delighted when Linda L. Osmundson wanted to write it for a *Chicken Soup for the Soul* book. Linda's stories have appeared in eight *Chicken Soup for the Soul* books as well as over sixty other publications.

Donna Hartley is an international speaker, owner of Hartley International, former Miss Hawaii, and author of *Fire Up Your Life!* Donna survived a DC-10 plane crash, and overcame melanoma and open heart surgery. She adopted a daughter late in life who brings her Firepower! E-mail her at hartley@donnahartley.com.

Mandy Hastings is the pen name of Jennie Ivey, who lives in Tennessee. She is a newspaper columnist and the author of three books. She has published numerous fiction and non-fiction pieces, including stories in several *Chicken Soup for the Soul* books. Contact her at jivey@frontiernet.net.

Jonny Hawkins has been cartooning professionally for twenty-four years. His work has been in over 600 publications and in hundreds of books. He creates several cartoon-a-day calendars including Medical Cartoon-a-Day, Fishing, Teachers, etc. He lives in Sherwood, Michigan with his wife Carissa, and their three young children. Contact him at jonnyhawkins2nz@yahoo.com.

Teresa Anne Hayden is a writer who lives in Cayce, Kentucky, with her husband Mike. They have three children and six grandchildren. Her work has appeared in *Catholic Digest*, the *Rural Kentuckian* and *The Western Kentucky Catholic* where her column, "Pray About It," spanned a decade.

David Heeren has written numerous books, including a series of five basketball books based on the Tendex statistical system he invented. His latest book, *In His Steps Again*, is an update of the 21st century Charles Sheldon classic written in 1896. Please e-mail him at enoch7@comcast.net.

Kristi Hemingway loves her life in Denver, Colorado, where she works as a teacher, writer and actress. Her perfect day includes gardening, biking, French food, dancing and snuggling with her husband and two children. She has recently completed a snarky spiritual memoir and her first novel. E-mail her at klhemingway@comcast.net.

A writer with extensive credits in television and theatre, **Doug Heyes, Jr.** received his BA in Psychology from UCLA. An avid athlete and outdoorsman, he regularly participates in triathlons, century rides and other endurance challenges. He is also an EMT and ski patroller in Southern California. Contact him at thelivingproof@earthlink.net.

Jeanne Hill is an author, inspirational speaker and a contributing editor to *Guideposts* magazine. Her award-winning short stories and articles are often chosen for anthologies. She has authored monthly columns in magazines and published two inspirational books: *Daily Breath* (Word Books) and *Secrets of Prayer Joy* (Judson Press).

Morgan Hill is a former TV/radio account executive, broadcaster and actress. She has a Master of Science in Special Education. Teaching in Los Angeles, she hopes insights from her own background will inspire her inner-city high school students towards getting their first job and making positive plans after graduation. E-mail her at mhwriter5@gmail.com.

Warren F. Holland received his Bachelor of Arts from Washington & Lee University in 1990 and his Master of International Business Studies from the University of South Carolina in 1993. He is currently employed by Bank of America Merrill Lynch and lives in Charlotte, NC with his wife and three children.

Kristen Hope received her Master of Arts in English from State University of New York College at Brockport. She currently resides in South Florida with her daughter, and teaches high school and college English. She enjoys reading, writing, and swimming, and is currently writing a young adult novel. Please e-mail her athopekristen@hotmail.com.

Ellen Javernick is a second grade teacher in Loveland, Colorado. When she's not teaching or writing, she enjoys spending time with her ten grandchildren. Her most recent picture books are *The Birthday Pet* and *What If Everybody Did That?*

BJ Jensen, song signing artist, author, speaker and dramatist has been the Director of Love In Motion Signing Choir since 1990 (www.signingchoir.com). She is married to Dr. Doug Jensen, her favorite cheerleader and encourager. They enjoy living in San Diego, California near their three wonderful granddaughters. E-mail her at jensen2@san.rr.com.

Pat Kane who resides in Joplin, Missouri with her husband Walter and their two Yorkies, is a published author who enjoys writing stories and novels for children and inspirational stories of real-life events. She's a member of The Society of Children's Book Writers & Illustrators and The Missouri Writers Guild. E-mail her at pat-curtis@sbcglobal.net.

Kathleen Rice Kardon retired from teaching English to middle school students in 2009. She is a local playwright, actor, and part of a writers' group that meets monthly to write poetry, fiction, and non-fiction. Kathi loves spending time with her children, grandchildren and her Bulldog, Angus. She can be reached at kathkard@satx.rr.com.

Heidi Krumenauer has published more than 1,200 newspaper and magazine articles, has authored nine books, and has contributed to more than a dozen book projects. Her professional career, though, is in upper management with an insurance company. Heidi and her husband raise their two sons in Southern Wisconsin.

Lynn Worley Kuntz is an award-winning writer whose credits include five books for children, magazine and newspaper articles for a variety of publications, and essays and stories in a number of anthologies. She has co-written five films for children and one feature family film. Contact her via e-mail at saralynnk@hotmail.com.

Tom Lagana is a professional speaker, author, volunteer, and engineer. He is co-author of *Chicken Soup for the Prisoner's Soul*, *Chicken Soup for the Volunteer's Soul*, *Serving Time, Serving Others*, and *Serving Productive Time*. Contact him at P.O. Box 7816, Wilmington, DE 19803, Tom@ TomLagana.com, or via his website at www.TomLagana.com.

Marianne LaValle-Vincent is the Executive Director of an adult home in Auburn, New York. She has published three full-length poetry collections and hundreds of short stories. She resides in Syracuse, NY with her daughter Jess and her extended family which includes three grandchildren.

Janeen Lewis is a freelance writer living in central Kentucky with her husband and two children. She has previously been published in several newspapers, magazines and three *Chicken Soup for the Soul* anthologies. Please e-mail her at jlewis0402@netzero.net.

Jaye Lewis is an award-winning inspirational writer who sees life from a unique perspective, celebrating the miracles in the everyday. Jaye enjoys being a part of the Chicken Soup for the Soul family. She lives and writes in the mountains of Virginia. Visit Jaye's website at www.entertainingangels.org.

Sandra Life is devoted to her remaining five children (and their spouses), one of whom she gave birth and four from Korea who she and Richard adopted. Today the "lights of her life" are ten grandchildren, including one adopted. Sandra remains an active volunteer in church and community.

Debra Manford is a fifty-five-year-old woman with three grown children and many grandchildren. She is currently working full-time with mentally challenged adults. Debra loves her job, loves her life, and truly believes the best is yet to come! Contact her via e-mail at free_2bee@hotmail.com.

Tina Wagner Mattern is a Portland, Oregon writer who has been blessed with every kind of miracle possible and is ever so grateful. This will be the third story published in *Chicken Soup for the Soul*. Contact her via e-mail at freddiestina@gmail.com.

Monica Matzner is the mother of two precious boys, Colby (age 5) and Blake (age 3). Her free time is usually spent at the boys' sporting events, including baseball where she is the team mom. Monica has a Masters Degree in IT and works as a computer programmer and web designer.

Lynn McGrath has been in ministry with her loving husband, Pastor Donald McGrath, for over twenty years. She adores her six children; Sarah, Crystal, Josh, Jesse, Bethany and Annie. Lynn loves laughing, camping, reading, singing and seeing the Lord at work in people's lives. She plans on living for Jesus.

Kimberly McLagan is a wife, mother of four, writer and Christian speaker with a compelling testimony of how to survive the trenches of infertility. A former corporate executive, consultant, and college instructor of management and marketing, her new book supports women experiencing barrenness with prayers and direction. www. infertilityprayerresource.com.

Terri Ann Meehan grew up in Ohio where most of her stories take place. Since moving to England in 1991, Teri enjoys writing about family, friends, and the memories they shared. She has been published in several books and magazines, including various *Chicken Soup for the Soul* titles.

David S. Milotta, a retired pastor, has had several supernatural experiences which led him into investigating the paranormal. His upcoming book, *White Crows — God's Special Messengers*, details these events. Married and living in Hawaii, he enjoys windsurfing, stand-up paddle surfing, and raises Great Danes. Contact him via e-mail at milottad001@hawaii.rr.com.

Martha Moore taught English for many years. She is an award-winning author of three young adult and middle-grade novels: *Under the Mermaid Angel*, *Angels on the Roof*, and *Matchit*. She believes that childhood experiences are important. Some are miracles in themselves. Others become miracles when we share them.

Pat Tiernan Morris is married with three children. The story "Mustard Seed Angel" is a message of faith inspired by her late daughter Tera and friends they met along the journey. www.mycmsite.com/patmorris. Lisa Dolensky, the author of the story, is a mom to three miracles, pre-K teacher and ghostwriter who has a site at www.wingblots.com.

Yolanda Mortimer was born in Toronto and currently lives in Wildwood, MO with her husband Doug and her Golden Retriever, Baron. She has three grown sons; Steve, Dan and Bob. She has been active in choirs all her life and has always enjoyed writing. This is the first time she has been published.

Lava Mueller lives in Vermont. She enjoys hiking with her daughter, playing games with her son, and going on dates to really good restaurants with her husband. Lava wakes each morning at 3:00 a.m. to meditate and give thanks for the amazing grace that fills her life. She can be reached via e-mail at lavamueller@yahoo.com.

Brittany Newell, an avid opera singer, has recently written her first novel. Previous short stories/essays have been published in *Chicken Soup for the Soul*, *Dylan Times*, and *The Ark Newspaper*. In 2008 her play received an honorable mention in Young Playwrights Festival National Playwriting Competition. Brittany, 16, is a junior in high school.

Herchel E. Newman, has been writing seriously for ten years, but has been a seasoned storyteller all his adult life. He is a skilled photographer, enjoys motorcycle riding with his club and as a family man, he and his wife enjoy mentoring young married couples. Please e-mail him at ZoomN500@juno.com.

Mary Treacy O'Keefe, has an MA in Theology, is a Spiritual Director, radio show host, author, speaker and President of Well Within, a nonprofit wellness center in St. Paul. For information on her books and presentations, please visit www.marytreacyokeefe.com or e-mail her at mary.treacy.okeefe@gmail.com.

Romona Olton received her Bachelor of Science in Chemistry, with honors, and Master of Philosophy in Chemistry from the University of the West Indies St. Augustine in 2005. She teaches science at a secondary school in West Trinidad. Romona enjoys kayaking, hiking and working with children. Please e-mail her at: romona_olton@hotmail.com.

Sharon Patterson, retired educator, career military wife, and leader in women's ministry has written works of inspirational encouragement for over thirty years. Sharon's most recent publications are two books, *A Soldier's Strength from the Psalms* and *Healing for the Holes in Our Souls*.

Donna Paulson lives on the island of Martha's Vineyard with her four children, dog and cat. She works at a local Counsel On Aging, and enjoys writing, reading a good novel, going to church, laughing with friends and family, and looking for sea glass. You can e-mail her at dpaulson31@verizon.net.

Gisele Reis instilled in her children a belief in the miraculous and the joy of life. She grew up in Belgium during WWII, where she served in the Resistance along with her siblings and parents. Giselle allowed Marie-Therese Miller to write about Mariette's miraculous cure in hopes that it would inspire others. Please visit Marie-Therese Miller's website: www.marie-theresemiller.com.

Kelly Stewart Rich received her Bachelor of Science in Education and Master of Science in Education from the College of the Southwest. She is a lifelong resident of Hobbs, New Mexico, where she and her husband raise their four children. Kelly can be reached via e-mail at krich@valornet.com.

Mark Rickerby is a freelance writer living in California. His work has been featured previously in *Chicken Soup to Inspire the Body & Soul* and *Chicken Soup for the Soul: Older & Wiser*. Please visit www. MarkRickerby.com for information about his published works and current projects. He can be reached via e-mail at markjrickerby@yahoo.com.

Courtney Rusk received her BA, with honors, and master of adult education from Northwestern State University. She teaches twelfth grade English in Pineville, LA, where she lives with her husband and two children. Courtney has a passion for reading, teaching, and spending time with her family. Please e-mail her at courtleerusk@yahoo.com.

Michelle Sedas is author of *Welcome The Rain* and *Live Inspired* and co-author of *The Power of 10%*. She is host of the Inspired Living Café and Cofounder of Running Moms Rock. Michelle graduated from Texas A&M University and lives in Texas with her husband and children. Visit Michelle via her website at www.michellesedas.com.

Veronica Shine's professional writing career began after successful careers in fashion, travel and showbiz. She is an avid traveler and resides in Spain and the U.S. Her published works are featured in magazines, websites and as a contributor to two books. She can be contacted via e-mail at mediterraneandreams@msn.com.

David Michael Smith believes in miracles including three special ones; his wife Geri, and two children, Rebekah and Matthew. He's a Marketing Specialist for the DE Department of Agriculture by day and writer by night. He's been widely published in the past including *Chicken Soup for the Soul*. Please e-mail David at davidandgeri@hotmail.com.

Laurel A. Smith resides in New Hampshire. She is the author of *The Quest for Quinnie* and *Pinboy*. She and her sons are writing a Revolutionary War novel based on their own family's experience. Laurel has three additional manuscripts in the works. Contact her via e-mail at dwedcola@nhvt.net.

Mary Z. Smith resides in Richmond, Virginia with her husband Barry of thirty-three years. They enjoy visits from their grown children and grandchildren. When Mary isn't writing for her favorite publications like *Chicken Soup for the Soul*, *Guideposts* and *Angels on Earth*, she can be found walking her Rat Terrier Frankie or gardening.

Marisa A. Snyder earned her BS in 1992. She taught in several capacities and coordinated religious programs. She is blessed with two sons and a fiancé. Marisa has Stargardt's disease, prompting her boutique which features "Seeing with Style" necklaces. She writes poetry, inspirational stories and tween novels. Contact her at marisasboutique@yahoo.com.

Johnna Stein is happily married and the mother to two spunky teenagers. She loves teaching reading to dyslexic kids. She's an avid reader and writer, and her stories have appeared in *Chicken Soup for the Soul*,

Guide, Susie Magazine and *Discipleship Journal*. Her first middle-grade humorous novel is nearly ready to find a home.

Dawn J. Storey is a mother, writer, and systems analyst for a major corporation. Although technical writing is her focus on the job, she enjoys writing inspirational stories with the hopes of uplifting readers. Dawn's writing reflects the feeling side of life.

Marcia Swearingen is a non-fiction freelance writer whose column, Transparent Thoughts, appears regularly at www.madetomatter.org. Her stories have also appeared in *Guideposts*, other *Chicken Soup for the Soul* and *A Cup of Comfort* books, and numerous local publications. She and Jim have been married thirty-nine years and have a married daughter. E-mail her at mswearingen@comcast.net.

Amy Tate, a member of SCBWI and American Christian Fiction Writers, has written for children's magazines, regional publications, and *Chicken Soup for the Soul: NASCAR*. A resident of Boones Mill, VA, Amy currently writes middle-grade novels. She enjoys blogging (thevirginiascribe.blogspot.com) and spending time with her family.

Donna Teti has been published in both *Guideposts* magazine and Cecil Murphey's *Christmas Miracles*. She is also a 2008 winner of the Guideposts Writers Workshop Contest. Through her inspirational writings, Donna hopes to bring comfort to those who are grieving. Her website is donnateti.com and her e-mail is donnateti@verizon.net.

R.J. Thesman writes from the heartland of Kansas where she also teaches ESL classes. She enjoys gardening, cooking and reading as well as editing and writing. Rebecca lives in Olathe, KS with her son and an elderly cat.

Terrie Todd writes from Portage la Prairie, Manitoba, Canada where she is an administrative assistant at City Hall. She and her husband

Jon are the parents of three adult children and have two adorable grandsons. You can reach her via e-mail at jltodd@mts.net.

Kristen Torres-Toro received her BA in English in 2007 from Toccoa Falls College and woke up three weeks later in the Amazon jungle. She is a missionary with Adventures In Missions and hopes to one day publish a novel. Please e-mail her at kristentorrestoro@gmail.com.

Connie Vagg is a California native, retired secretary, has two daughters, and granny to four. Her annual Christmas tradition is making personalized gingerbread houses, and she is fondly referred to by family and friends as "The Gingerbread Lady." Connie's first story was published in *Chicken Soup for the Soul: Living Catholic Faith*. Contact her at cvagg@netzero.net.

Mary Vaughn earned her education from raising five kids and a husband. She was driven by strong faith and love for family and friends. For her, every day was a chance to do the Lord's work. Sally O'Brien's stories have appeared in several publications. Contact Sally at sobrien95@msn.com.

Beverly F. Walker lives in Greenbrier, Tennessee with her retired husband. She enjoys writing, photography, and scrapbooking pictures of her grandchildren. She has stories in many *Chicken Soup for the Soul* books, and in *Angel Cats: Divine Messengers of Comfort*.

Emily Weaver is a freelance writer living in Springfield, Missouri. Her work can be found in multiple *Chicken Soup for the Soul* editions. She has three children, and enjoys spending time with her husband, gardening and traveling.

Shannon Woodward writes and edits from Marysville, Washington, where she lives with her husband (a Calvary Chapel pastor) and their two children. She is a columnist for Christian Women Online, a contributor to several anthologies, and the author of three non-fiction books. Visit Shannon at www.shannonwoodward.com or www.windscraps.blogspot.com.

Elisa Yager is a mom of two outstanding teenagers, two cats, Ms. Elmer the bunny, and four goldfish. When she is not writing she's dreaming of publishing success. Elisa works full-time in the field of Human Resources. You can reach her at Proud2blefty@yahoo.com. Elisa welcomes your feedback!

Meet Our Authors

Jack Canfield is the co-creator of the *Chicken Soup for the Soul* series, which *Time* magazine has called "the publishing phenomenon of the decade." Jack is also the co-author of many other bestselling books.

Jack is the CEO of the Canfield Training Group in Santa Barbara, California, and founder of the Foundation for Self-Esteem in Culver City, California. He has conducted intensive personal and professional development seminars on the principles of success for more than a million people in twenty-three countries, has spoken to hundreds of thousands of people at more than 1,000 corporations, universities, professional conferences and conventions, and has been seen by millions more on national television shows.

Jack has received many awards and honors, including three honorary doctorates and a Guinness World Records Certificate for having seven books from the *Chicken Soup for the Soul* series appearing on the New York Times bestseller list on May 24, 1998.

You can reach Jack at www.jackcanfield.com.

Mark Victor Hansen is the co-founder of Chicken Soup for the Soul, along with Jack Canfield. He is a sought-after keynote speaker, bestselling author, and marketing maven. Mark's powerful messages of possibility, opportunity, and action have created powerful change in thousands of organizations and millions of individuals worldwide.

Mark is a prolific writer with many bestselling books in addition to the *Chicken Soup for the Soul* series. Mark has had a profound influence in the field of human potential through his library of audios, videos, and articles in the areas of big thinking, sales achievement, wealth building, publishing success, and personal and professional development. He is also the founder of the MEGA Seminar Series.

Mark has received numerous awards that honor his entrepreneurial spirit, philanthropic heart, and business acumen. He is a lifetime member of the Horatio Alger Association of Distinguished Americans.

You can reach Mark at www.markvictorhansen.com.

LeAnn Thieman is a nationally acclaimed professional speaker, author, and nurse who was "accidentally" caught up in the Vietnam Orphan Airlift in 1975. Her book, *This Must Be My Brother*, details her daring adventure helping to rescue 300 babies as Saigon was falling to the Communists. LeAnn and her incredible story have been featured in *Newsweek Magazine's Voices of the Century* issue, Fox News, CNN, PBS, BBC, PAX-TV's *It's A Miracle*, and countless radio and TV programs.

Today, as a renowned motivational speaker, LeAnn inspires audiences to balance their lives, truly live their priorities and make a difference in the world.

After her story was featured in *Chicken Soup for the Mother's Soul*, LeAnn became one of Chicken Soup's most prolific writers. That, and her devotion to thirty years of nursing, made her the ideal co-author of *Chicken Soup for the Nurse's Soul*. She went on to co-author *Chicken Soup for the Caregiver's Soul*, *Chicken Soup for the Father and Daughter Soul*, *Chicken Soup for the Grandma's Soul*, *Chicken Soup for the Mother and Son Soul*, *Chicken Soup for the Christian Woman's Soul*, *Chicken Soup for the Christian Soul 2*, *Chicken Soup for the Nurse's Soul, Second Dose*, *Chicken Soup for the Adopted Soul* and *Chicken Soup for the Soul: Living Catholic Faith*.

LeAnn is one of about ten percent of speakers worldwide to have earned the Certified Speaking Professional Designation award and in 2008 she was inducted into the Speakers Hall of Fame.

She and Mark, her husband of forty years, reside in Colorado.

For more information about LeAnn's books and tapes or to schedule her for a presentation, please contact her at:

LeAnn Thieman, CSP, CPAE
6600 Thompson Drive
Fort Collins, CO 80526
1-970-223-1574
www.LeAnnThieman.com
e-mail LeAnn@LeAnnThieman.com

Thank You

O ur first thanks must always go to our contributors. We know you pour your hearts and souls into the stories you share with us, and ultimately the world. We appreciate your willingness to open your lives to Chicken Soup for the Soul readers. Your stories of miracles will truly bless so many people—we know because we get countless letters telling us how our books have changed their lives.

We can only publish a small percentage of the stories that are submitted, but we read every single one, and even the ones that do not appear in the book have an influence on us and on the final manuscript. We strongly encourage you to continue submitting to future *Chicken Soup for the Soul* books.

A special thanks to friends and fellow writers whose input and final edits made the book its best: Karen Kishpaugh, Kerrie Flanagan, Peter Springberg, Ellen Javernick, Sally Engeman, Berniece Duello, and Judy Danielson.

We thank D'ette Corona, our Assistant Publisher, who seamlessly manages a dozen projects at a time while keeping all of us positive, focused and on schedule. Our gratitude goes to Barbara LoMonaco, Chicken Soup for the Soul's Webmaster and Editor; Chicken Soup for the Soul Editor Kristiana Glavin, for her assistance with the final manuscript and proofreading; and Leigh Holmes, who keeps our office running smoothly.

We owe a very special thanks to our Creative Director and book producer, Brian Taylor at Pneuma Books, for his brilliance on our covers and interiors.

The ultimate thank you goes to Amy Newmark, Publisher of Chicken Soup for the Soul whose vision, expertise and diligence create each book and make it excellent.

Finally, none of this would be possible without the business and creative leadership of our CEO, Bill Rouhana, and our president, Bob Jacobs.

Thanks as always to Amy Williams, who manages LeAnn's speaking business while she writes... and writes.

A special thanks to LeAnn's mother, Berniece Duello whose role modeling provided the foundation for LeAnn's faith and abilities.

And to God for His divine guidance and abundant blessings.

Chicken Soup for the Soul

Improving Your Life Every Day

Real people sharing real stories—for seventeen years. Now, Chicken Soup for the Soul has gone beyond the bookstore to become a world leader in life improvement. Through books, movies, DVDs, online resources and other partnerships, we bring hope, courage, inspiration and love to hundreds of millions of people around the world. Chicken Soup for the Soul's writers and readers belong to a one-of-a-kind global community, sharing advice, support, guidance, comfort, and knowledge.

Chicken Soup for the Soul stories have been translated into more than forty languages and can be found in more than one hundred countries. Every day, millions of people experience a Chicken Soup for the Soul story in a book, magazine, newspaper or online. As we share our life experiences through these stories, we offer hope, comfort and inspiration to one another. The stories travel from person to person, and from country to country, helping to improve lives everywhere.

Share with Us

We all have had Chicken Soup for the Soul moments in our lives. If you would like to share your story or poem with millions of people around the world, go to chickensoup.com and click on "Submit Your Story." You may be able to help another reader, and become a published author at the same time. Some of our past contributors have launched writing and speaking careers from the publication of their stories in our books!

Our submission volume has been increasing steadily—the quality and quantity of your submissions has been fabulous. We only accept story submissions via our website. They are no longer accepted via mail or fax.

To contact us regarding other matters, please send us an e-mail through webmaster@chickensoupforthesoul.com, or fax or write us at:

Chicken Soup for the Soul
P.O. Box 700
Cos Cob, CT 06807-0700
Fax: 203-861-7194

One more note from your friends at Chicken Soup for the Soul: Occasionally, we receive an unsolicited book manuscript from one of our readers, and we would like to respectfully inform you that we do not accept unsolicited manuscripts and we must discard the ones that appear.

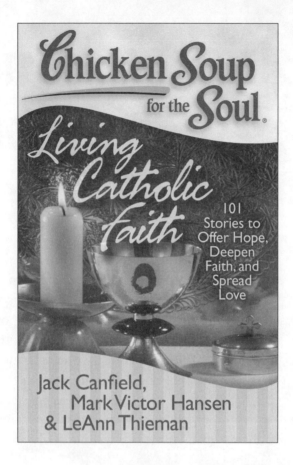

Chicken Soup for the Soul
Living Catholic Faith

101 Stories to Offer Hope, Deepen Faith, and Spread Love

Jack Canfield,
Mark Victor Hansen
& LeAnn Thieman

This beautiful book is relevant to all Catholics, from the once-a-year attendee at Christmas Mass, to the devout church volunteer and daily worshipper. With 101 poignant and spirit-filled stories, this book covers the gamut, from fun stories about growing up Catholic to serious stories about sacraments and miracles. Whether a cradle Catholic, a convert, simply curious or struggling, these stories describe what it means to be a Catholic and provide happiness, hope, and healing.

978-1-935096-23-8

More Inspirational

Chicken Soup for the Soul
for the Soul.
Stories of Faith
Our 101 BEST STORIES

Inspirational
Stories of
Hope, Devotion, Faith,
and Miracles

Jack Canfield
& Mark Victor Hansen
edited by Amy Newmark

Everyone needs some faith and hope! This book is just the ticket, with a collection of 101 of the best stories from Chicken Soup for the Soul's past on faith, hope, miracles, and devotion. These true stories, written by regular people, tell of prayers answered miraculously, amazing coincidences, rediscovered faith, and the serenity that comes from believing in a greater power, appealing to Christians and those of other faiths—anyone who seeks inspiration.

978-1-935096-14-6

Stories of Faith & Hope

Chicken Soup for the Soul

www.chickensoup.com